EDUCATE.IE

SHAKESPEARE

SERIES

OTHELLO

educate.ie

Dedication

I would like to dedicate this book to all my wonderful friends, especially Catherine Kelly, Sinéad Kelly, Frank Madigan, John Winters and Janet Syms, with love and thanks for their support and friendship over the years.

Acknowledgements

I would like to thank everyone at Educate.ie for all that they have contributed to this edition of Othello, especially Peter Malone and Síofra Ni Thuairisg. Thanks to Janette Condon for her invaluable advice. Thanks to Peadar Staunton of the Design Gang for illustrating and designing this edition so beautifully. Finally, thanks to my supportive colleagues and inspiring students, past and present, at Yeats College Waterford.

– Mary Barron

EDUCATE.IE
SHAKESPEARE
SERIES

- THE TRAGEDY OF -

OTHELLO

THE MOOR OF VENICE

INTRODUCTION & NOTES BY
MARY BARRON

educate.ie

PUBLISHED BY:
Educate.ie
Walsh Educational Books Ltd
Castleisland, Co. Kerry, Ireland
www.educate.ie

ASSOCIATE EDITOR:
Janette Condon

PRODUCTION EDITOR:
Kieran O'Donoghue

DESIGN/ILLUSTRATIONS:
The Design Gang, Tralee

PRINTED AND BOUND BY:
Walsh Colour Print, Castleisland

PHOTOGRAPHS –
Main theatre production photographs by Karl Hugh (courtesy of Utah Shakespeare Festival, USA). See page 288 for full list of actors and productions.
   Other photographs/images courtesy of Shakespeare Globe Theatre, BigStock, Istock, Stockbyte/Getty.

The author and publisher have made every effort to trace all copyright holders. If any have been overlooked we would be happy to make the necessary arrangements at the first opportunity.

ISBN: 978-1-908507-89-1

CONTENTS

PREFACE

This edition of Shakespeare's Othello has been designed with you, the student, in mind. The text is packed with notes, summaries, character studies and sample essays – in short, everything you need for exam success.

While it is true to say that every word in Othello is significant, all of the play's most important quotations have been underlined. This is to draw your attention to those that are most meaningful and will also help you to decide which quotations you need to memorise. When you are doing that, you should try to choose quotations from a range of characters and themes. Choose multifunctional ones when possible. A quotation such as 'It is the green-eyed monster which doth mock / The meat it feeds on' could be used for character questions on Othello or Iago, for stylistic questions on imagery, or for thematic questions, such as the theme of jealousy, for example.

For ease of reference, each act is colour-coded, and the notes include an explanation or modern translation of each scene, as well as a longer analysis of each act. These notes are presented in a concise, focused way, so you can learn them confident in the knowledge that you can use all the material therein in the exam.

Many scenes have been translated into modern English. Although Shakespeare's language is very eloquent, it is also interesting to see how these words might be spoken today. These scenes are useful for revision and will help you to get to know the text really well, though of course they are not meant to replace the poetry of Shakespeare's own dialogue.

There are detailed character studies here, too. You will have formed your own impressions of the characters by the time you have finished studying the text. Considering your opinions and these notes together will help to give you a well-rounded view of the characters in the play.

All of the important themes in Othello are explained thoroughly in the notes. As well as that, there is a comprehensive section on how to answer exam questions, and there are many helpful sample essays for you to emulate in your own writing. Othello is a provocative and compelling play, written by a playwright with an astounding insight into human nature, so enjoy the play, and form your own opinions of it. Your own opinions and insight are the most important things to develop as you study the play, as your own personal response to Othello is crucial in the Leaving Certificate exam.

Mary Bannen

INTRODUCTION

*O*THELLO, WRITTEN between 1602 and 1604, is one of the four great tragedies of Shakespeare; the others are *Hamlet, King Lear* and *Macbeth*. Most of Shakespeare's plays were loosely inspired by existing stories, plays or historical events, but he put a lot of his own thoughts, philosophy and, of course, eloquent language into each and every one. Two of the sources for *Othello* are *Un Capitano Muro (A Moorish Captain)* by an Italian writer, Cinthio, and A *Geographical History of Africa* by Leo Africanus. Cinthio's novella has a broadly similar plot to *Othello*, but Shakespeare changed many details and created several additional characters. Africanus's book (which is not factual, but heavily biased) mentions the jealousy of African men, and how they would rather kill their wives, and themselves, than suffer the indignity of infidelity.

Othello is famous for being a play about jealousy. However, it is about much more than this. It is a play about being an outsider, about feeling that you're different from everyone else. It is a play about love, and the sad truth that some people lash out when they are in pain and hurt the person they love the most. 'Yet each man kills the thing he loves, / By each let this be heard, / Some do it with a bitter look, / Some with a flattering word, / The coward does it with a kiss, / The brave man with a sword!' (Oscar Wilde, 'The Ballad of Reading Gaol'). *Othello* is a play about manipulation and evil. It is a devastating exploration of what it means to be human. And, yes, it is also about jealousy, and what an excruciatingly illogical and overpowering emotion it can be.

Othello is one of Shakespeare's most difficult plays to watch. Shakespeare presents us with characters, such as Desdemona, whom we really care about. Once our emotions are invested in the characters, Iago's machinations become almost unbearable. However, the reason for the audience's discomfort is not just the constant dramatic irony, but the realism. The events presented in *Othello* are exaggerated versions of situations most of us will have to confront at some point in our lives, such as how we cope with our own underlying insecurities, how we deal with people who seek to manipulate us for their own ends and how we deal with emotions – jealousy, hate, love – that can overwhelm us if we let them.

Othello's status as an outsider is central to the play. He is a Moor (African) and is the only black man in this society. He stands out physically, because of his colour, and the other characters are either repelled by his difference (Brabantio) or attracted to it (Desdemona). Most people, especially teenagers, know the feeling of being, or just feeling, different, and this in itself makes the play easy to relate to. The 2001 film *O* is a modern adaptation of *Othello* set in an elite American school, where Odin (Othello) is the only African-American student, attending on a basketball scholarship. The success of the film shows how relevant this theme of being an outsider continues to be. More recently, the 2004 film *Stage Beauty* also uses the story of *Othello* as a backdrop.

Othello is a spectacular piece of writing. The language in this play is eloquent and rich in imagery. The antagonist's great skill is his rhetoric. Words are his weapons, and he uses them to devastating effect. The tension and suspense is relentless, the characterisation superb. This is a play which fascinates and appals us in equal measure, but it also truly engages us. Enjoy it.

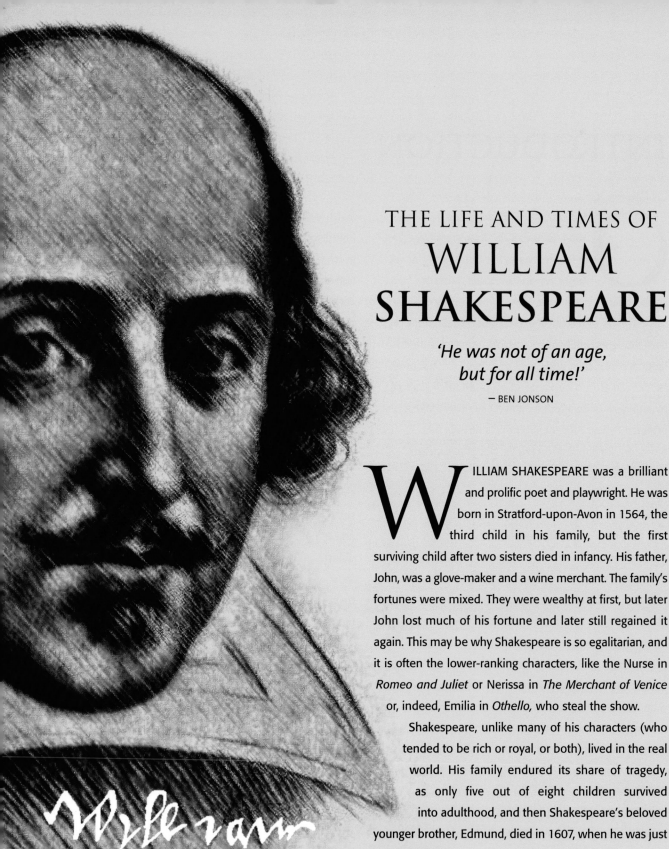

THE LIFE AND TIMES OF
WILLIAM SHAKESPEARE

*'He was not of an age,
but for all time!'*

— BEN JONSON

WILLIAM SHAKESPEARE was a brilliant and prolific poet and playwright. He was born in Stratford-upon-Avon in 1564, the third child in his family, but the first surviving child after two sisters died in infancy. His father, John, was a glove-maker and a wine merchant. The family's fortunes were mixed. They were wealthy at first, but later John lost much of his fortune and later still regained it again. This may be why Shakespeare is so egalitarian, and it is often the lower-ranking characters, like the Nurse in *Romeo and Juliet* or Nerissa in *The Merchant of Venice* or, indeed, Emilia in *Othello,* who steal the show.

Shakespeare, unlike many of his characters (who tended to be rich or royal, or both), lived in the real world. His family endured its share of tragedy, as only five out of eight children survived into adulthood, and then Shakespeare's beloved younger brother, Edmund, died in 1607, when he was just twenty-seven.

We presume that Shakespeare went to grammar school in Stratford, but he did not attend either Oxford or Cambridge, so he was obviously self-taught, which makes his achievements all the more astonishing. Books were not easily accessible in those days, but it is clear that Shakespeare was incredibly well read and that he went to a lot of effort to educate himself. It is obvious from the breadth and depth of his works that he had a voracious curiosity about the world around him.

An interesting point to ponder is whether the Shakespeare family was Catholic or Protestant. All of Shakespeare's plays show that he was a man with a devout belief in God and goodness, but in a particularly Catholic way. While the two faiths are quite similar, one way in which Catholicism is differentiated is in its veneration of Mary, the mother of God. In Shakespeare's *Othello,* the heroine, Desdemona, is often reminiscent of the Virgin Mary, as is Cordelia in *King Lear*.

Religion was a major issue in Shakespeare's day. The Reformation of the 1520s and 1530s saw England change from a medieval Catholic society into a modern Protestant one. It was not an easy transformation: people were forced on pain of death to convert to Protestantism. Then, when King Henry VIII's daughter Mary came to the throne in 1553, she forced her subjects to revert to Catholicism. When Elizabeth I came to power in 1558, she immediately decreed that England be Protestant once more! So, while the Shakespeare family would certainly have been seen to be practising the correct religion, Michael Wood, in his fascinating book, *In Search of Shakespeare*, suggests that in their hearts the family may have been more Catholic than Protestant.

Shakespeare married at the early age of eighteen. It is often presumed that, like Romeo and Juliet, everyone in Shakespeare's era married in their teens. In fact, the average marriage age was in the mid-twenties, and the age of consent for a man was twenty-one. Shakespeare, however, married for one of the most obvious of reasons: his bride, Anne Hathaway, was pregnant. She was twenty-six, eight years his senior, so there was quite a significant age gap between them – something that was particularly scandalous at that time. The couple's first daughter, Susanna, was born in 1583, followed by twins, Hamnet and Judith, two years later. Tragically, Hamnet died aged eleven, and this had a profound effect on Shakespeare's writing. It became deeper and darker after his terrible loss.

Given that the couple had just three children and that Shakespeare spent most of his adult life in London, many biographers surmise that the marriage of William and Anne was not a happy one. Much has been made of the fact that in his will, Shakespeare bequeathed Anne his 'second-best bed' and nothing more! This sounds rather unchivalrous, but in fact it was common practice to leave everything to your children rather than your spouse. And the second-best bed would have been the marital bed; the best one would have been kept for guests. Still, while the evidence, as always, is scant, many would agree that the couple did separate, in deed if not in word. There have been many hypotheses put forward about Shakespeare's relationships with other women (and there have also been unsubstantiated rumours of dalliances with men), but in the end we simply do not know. What we do know is that Shakespeare definitely experienced great passion. His many sonnets often concern themselves with that most universal of themes: love.

There were some black people living in London in Shakespeare's day, but not many. Slave ships docking in England en route to America was the main reason for black people being there. Some were left in England as exotic servants or prostitutes. Elizabeth I had black musicians in her court, but in 1596, she ordered that 'those kinde of people should be sente forth of the land', showing the complicated attitude to multiculturalism that in many respects still exists today.

What is significant to the study of *Othello* is that several of Shakespeare's sonnets suggest that he may have had a relationship with a black woman. In Sonnet 127, he writes *In the old age black was not counted fair / Or if it were, it bore not beauty's name; / But now is black beauty's successive heir, / And beauty slandered with a bastard shame*, and in Sonnet 130 he describes his mistress as being black: *If snow be white, why then her breasts are dun* [brown]*; / If hairs be wires, black wires grow on her head*.

Despite the fact that so much of Shakespeare's writing is still extant, we tend to feel we know very little about him, especially in comparison with more modern writers. He is sometimes viewed as an unreliable charlatan, who bluffed his way through an amazing dramatic career (many volumes have been devoted to the study of lacunae – gaps or missing parts – in his works). However, some scholars are convinced that he was a man to whom honour meant everything. What we do know is that Shakespeare was an astute observer of the human condition. His plays indicate that he was a detached spectator, someone on the periphery of society, well placed to judge those around him. He saw the misfortune and cruelty of life – this was an age when unfortunate criminals might be hanged on the street – but rather than losing his humanity, he became a compassionate recorder of what it means to be human. Shakespeare recognised that not many people are truly evil, and few are completely good. Morality is not always black and white. There is often a huge grey area between good and evil, and it is on this that *Othello* and his other great tragedies, *Hamlet*, *King Lear* and *Macbeth*, focus, while also presenting us with characters (such as Desdemona) who are truly good and others (such as Iago) who are truly evil.

After leaving Stratford-upon-Avon in his early twenties, the life Shakespeare lived must have been colourful. He was drawn to the theatre – most biographers believe that he would have found settled family life no substitute for the dramatic world – and he began his career as an actor. Acting troupes regularly visited Stratford, and one may have recruited him there, or he may have followed it to London. His experience as an actor helped him forge a real connection with the audience; he knew what made them laugh and what made them cry. Writing was a natural progression, and he learned how to create brilliant stories to capture his audiences' attention.

Shakespeare began to make a name for himself as a poet and, with certain powerful personalities such as the Earl of Southampton numbered among his admirers, he quickly grew in stature. Shakespeare's success as a poet gave his name a certain cachet, and drew audiences to the point where his troupe of actors, the Lord Chamberlain's Men, later the King's Men, was easily the most successful of the day. London's theatres had to shut for some years because of the plague, and when they reopened in 1593, there was a void to be filled. Shakespeare was just the playwright to fill it. Timing and circumstances played as much a part as talent, as they often do.

Shakespeare deals with many themes in his plays and poetry: love, hatred, kingship, ambition, mercy, greed, violence, war, filial duty and revenge. All these themes are universal, and so they are always relevant. He portrays his characters in all their human frailty; his heroes are not infallible, and that is why they engage our sympathy.

Shakespeare's plays are sorted into tragedies, comedies and histories. The tragedies are full of torment and suffering, whereas the comedies are full of humour

and happy endings. Yet every tragedy has at least some comic elements (such as the Musicians scene in *Othello*), and every comedy has a little tragedy. All of Shakespeare's heroes have 'fatal flaws', human weaknesses that contribute to their downfall. This makes the characters so very believable, and their tragedy all the more poignant.

Shakespeare regularly presented plays for Queen Elizabeth I's enjoyment. She was not easy to please and would often send specific instructions on the kind of play she wished to see. This would sometimes call for last-minute rewrites and a lot of improvising! Elizabeth ruled England, without ever marrying, for over forty years. For a woman to hold the highest position in the kingdom was an amazing accomplishment at a time when women had no social power and were considered mere possessions of men. Sometimes, to prove that she was just as strong as any man, Elizabeth acted in ways that later bothered her conscience, such as when she had her own cousin, Mary, Queen of Scots, executed for treason.

Shakespeare was clearly trying to please the queen when he wrote strong female characters such as Portia, who saves the day in *The Merchant of Venice*, even though she is obliged to disguise herself as a man. This is all the more remarkable when you remember that, during this period, women weren't actually allowed on stage, so their parts were played by men.

Shakespeare was ahead of his times in his treatment of female characters. While many of his contemporaries polarised women into angels or whores, Shakespeare's female characters are realistic human beings, in all their frailty. No doubt, the reign of such a strong woman as Elizabeth I influenced Shakespeare's view of women.

Elizabeth left no heirs. When she died in 1603, England's 'Golden Age', a period during which theatre and the arts flourished, ended with her.

Shakespeare wrote many of his greatest works – *King Lear*, *Othello*, *Hamlet* and *Macbeth* – between 1600 and 1605. They made him famous in his own lifetime and he was able to retire to Stratford-upon-Avon a wealthy man. He continued writing almost to the end of his life, but the passion and ferocity of the great quartet of tragedies was notably absent from his later plays. While his writing continued to be as elegant and insightful as ever, Shakespeare mellowed in his later years, and as a result, his later works tend to be more gentle and philosophical.

It is not just as a writer that Shakespeare excels, but also as a man with the deepest level of human understanding. Shakespeare understood people. He understood the human condition, our triumphs and our failings, the fact that we are capable of the ridiculous, but also the sublime. His insight was an innate gift, the kind of transcendent knowing that we find in a van Gogh painting or a Beethoven concerto. Certainly many of the playwright's lines have passed down through the years as gems of wisdom, such as the expression 'be true to yourself' which comes from *Hamlet: **to thine own self be true. / And it must follow, as the night the day, / Thou can'st not then be false to any man;*** and 'wearing your heart on your sleeve' and the ***green-eyed monster***, which come from *Othello*.

Much has been written about William Shakespeare, and if you want to find out more about his life, Bill Bryson's entertaining book, *Shakespeare: The World as Stage*, is well worth a read, as is *In Search of Shakespeare* by Michael Woods, which is very insightful and beautifully illustrated. The film, *Elizabeth* (1998), starring Cate Blanchett, gives a great insight into Elizabeth I's life and reign. *O* (2001) and *Stage Beauty* (2004) are also well worth watching for more insight into *Othello* specifically.

ELIZABETHAN THEATRE

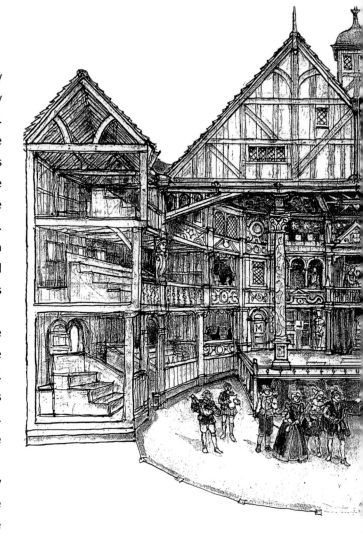

THE LAYOUT of the Elizabethan stage was very simple. There were few props, no scenery and the actors were on view the entire time. The stage, which projected out into the theatre, had a rectangular shape. The theatre itself was a large semicircle. The pit immediately around the stage was not covered with a roof. This was where the groundlings (poorer members of the audience) stood. Around the perimeter were tiered rows of seats, which were covered against the elements, for the merchant and noble classes. In the centre, directly facing the stage, was the royal box for the monarch and her retinue.

Shakespeare's company put on its productions at the Globe Theatre (built in 1599) until 1608, when it leased the Blackfriar's Theatre, which had the advantage of a full roof. The Lord Chamberlain's Men, which later became the King's Men, included some of the most famous actors of the day. Acting was a hard existence for most, though. Actors were badly paid and often ill-treated by their audience.

The Elizabethans who came to the theatre were a very different audience from any we might find today. We are saturated with media in the twenty-first century. We have cinema, television, radio, iPads, computers, iPods, and as many books, magazines and newspapers as we could want. Imagine a time when none of these were available; when, if you were very wealthy, you might be lucky enough to own a few books. Most people, however, were illiterate, and they worked long hours with very little respite or entertainment. Even a long church service lasting several hours was a welcome break in those dreary times. Indeed, touring companies brought 'Passion Plays' around the country, where they would act out scenes from the life of Christ on the village green. We would probably find these plays quite heavy going, but in those days people would eagerly queue for hours to see them.

When Shakespeare's audience members came to the theatre, they wanted to be entertained with stories. They wanted to hear about the lives of the wealthy and the titled, to learn of exotic countries which they knew they would never see. They expected drama, intrigue and suspense. A tragedy had to be really tragic; a comedy had to make them laugh heartily. If the audience did not like the play, the actors were pelted with eggs and rotten fruit in protest. Often, people would start throwing missiles during the briefest lull in a play, so Shakespeare and other playwrights had to make sure to hold their interest. The audience were incredibly hardened in some respects – they would often have seen dead bodies hanging from

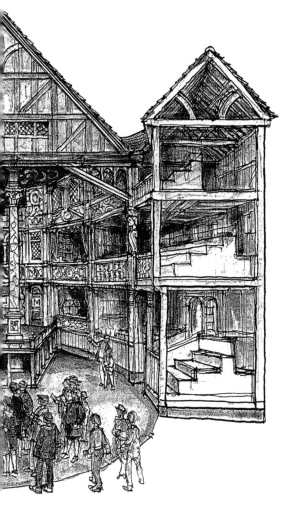

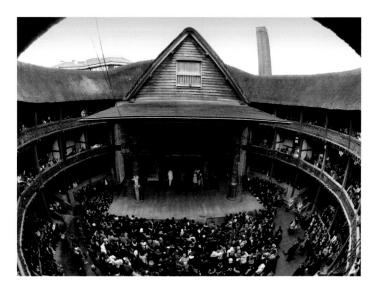

LEFT: *An artist's impression of London's Globe Theatre in Shakespeare's day, showing a cross-section of the building*

BELOW: *The Globe Theatre, reconstructed in 1997 and dedicated to the exploration of Shakespeare's work*

the gallows or people being tortured in the most inhumane ways. But, on the other hand, they were quite innocent. They believed in ghosts and witches, for example, and were terrified of them. Shakespeare used such fears to grab their attention.

Plays in the Elizabethan era were principally for entertainment, but they could also be vehicles for social or political criticism, just as they often are today. *King Lear* highlights the plight of the poor and the excesses of the rich. *The Merchant of Venice* seems anti-Semitic today, but in its time it was seen as pro-Christian. In *Macbeth*, Shakespeare criticises those who would do anything for power, and there were many such people in his day. *Othello*

is probably one of the first texts ever to explore racism.

As you read through *Othello* in class and see it performed on stage or in film, always think of the original audience for whom it was written. Think about how they might have felt about *Othello*. Imagine their hatred of Iago, and how the omnipresent dramatic irony would have caused them to interact vigorously with the action, constantly shouting advice and warnings. This will help you to understand the brilliance of Shakespeare's drama and give you a unique insight into the play.

You might also like to note that the 1998 film *Shakespeare in Love,* while almost entirely fictional, gives a great portrayal of Shakespeare's life in the theatre.

SHAKESPEARE'S ENGLISH

YOU MAY find the language used in Shakespeare's plays difficult at first, but as you grow more familiar with the play, you will find that it becomes easier to understand. Language is always in a state of flux – always growing and changing. Ten years ago, for example, you might have said, 'I'll look that up on the internet,' but now you might just say, 'I'll Google it.' Or someone might say, 'I have to do the Hoovering,' when what they really mean to do is vacuum the carpet. 'Hoover' is a brand of vacuum cleaner, but, like Google, Hoovers were so widespread that the word became a common noun and a verb. Another example of how language is constantly changing is that the *Oxford English Dictionary* added the expression 'D'oh!' to the lexicon in 2002. Because *The Simpsons* is so popular, Homer's catchphrase has become known, and used, the world over.

You can tell a lot about a society from its language. The English spoken in Ireland is known as Hiberno-English, and it has a particular character and poetry. An Irish person might say, 'I'm after doing that already,' an expression that makes no sense to an English person (for whom 'after' means 'behind' or 'later than'), but we know what it means because it comes from the Irish *'tar éis'*. Ireland has traditionally been a very religious country, too, and our greetings make this apparent. We say *'Dia duit'* for hello, and the response is *'Dia is Muire duit.'* These characteristics give the works of writers like John B. Keane and Patrick Kavanagh a particular eloquence, of which Irish people are naturally proud. English was never formally taught in Ireland until it eventually replaced Irish as our main language, and this accounts for the relative informality of Irish speech. 'I had a right mare of a day,' we might say, to describe a particularly hard day, or a person from the country might be described as a 'culchie'.

If you consider that *Othello* was written over 400 years ago, it is no wonder that the language is so different from the language we use today. What is not so different, however, are people themselves. We use language as a tool for communication. It expresses our practical needs, but also our deeper emotions and desires. Language is our most eloquent form of expression.

The Elizabethans had an incredibly colourful language. Some words are almost onomatopoeic. To 'beslubber' someone, for example, meant to say something bad about them. Even if we are not familiar with the word, 'beslubber' still sounds like an awful thing to do! They also had lots of words for partying and making merry, like 'carousing' and 'capering'. Some words and phrases considered rude then would not be considered at all offensive today. A 'worsted-stocking knave' was a terrible insult. It meant that your stockings (men wore white knitted stockings under puffy shorts) were sagging, and someone could take deep offence at such a remark. On the other hand, 'shit' is considered impolite now, but in Shakespeare's day it was a perfectly acceptable verb.

With Shakespeare, it can be the thous and thees that put us off, as those terms are no longer in common usage. Also, there is a tendency to drop 'e's, as in 'quench'd', 'shriek'd' or 'drugg'd', so the word looks unfamiliar on the page. However, you soon get used to it, and to the characters' tendency to greet each other formally, with 'Noble sir' and 'Good signor'.

The word order in sentences is often reversed in Shakespearean English, but this is not very complicated. ***You best know the place.*** *You know the place best.* Or *to speak the truth / Shall nothing wrong him. I can't hurt him if I tell the truth.* Here are some of the more commonly used words and phrases, and their modern equivalents:

Thou	You
Thee	You
Hath	Has
How now?	How is everything going?
Wherein	In which or when
Wouldst?	Would you?
Didst?	Did/do you?
Is't?	Is it?
O'	Of
Th'	The
I'	In

The trick to understanding the language is to just take it sentence by sentence. For example:

If it were now to die

If I died right now

'Twere now to be most happy; for I fear

I would be completely happy, because I'm afraid

My soul hath her content so absolute

My soul feels such complete joy now

That not another comfort like to this

That there could be no greater happiness

Succeeds in unknown fate

That the unknown future can hold for me

There are also numerous cultural references, which might not be immediately obvious to us, but we can understand in the context of the time. Therefore 'to horse' means to start a journey, whereas we might say, 'Let's get on the road.'

There are many times in *Othello* where the English used is really not so different from the English we use today. For example:

And little of this great world can I speak
More than pertains to feats of broil and battle,
And therefore little shall I grace my cause
In speaking for myself. Yet, by your gracious
> **patience,**
I will a round unvarnish'd tale deliver
Of my whole course of love, what drugs, what
> **charms,**
What conjuration and what mighty magic –
For such proceeding I am charged withal –
I won his daughter.

And I can say little about this great world
Other than what pertains to feats of battle,
And therefore I probably won't help my cause
In speaking for myself. Yet, if you will be patient,
I will tell you a simple, unvarnished tale
Of the course of my love, with what drugs, what
> *charms,*
What enchantments and what magic –
For this is what I am charged with –
I won his daughter.

In conclusion, Shakespeare's language is certainly different from ours, but it is also eloquent, poignant and historically interesting, teaching us so much about the way of life four centuries ago, as well as telling us stories that are simply timeless.

TRAGEDY AS A GENRE

IN GREEK, the word tragedy – *tragōidia* – means 'goat song'. In the ancient dramatic festivals of classical Greece, a goat would have been part of the prize. 'Tragedy' is a word that is used daily in popular speech to mean that something terribly sad has occurred. The genre of tragedy is very different, however, in that you cannot simply call a play with sad events a tragedy; it must also adhere to the conventions of the genre. Put simply, this means that there are certain rules that a tragedian must follow, and this is what Shakespeare did in his plays. These are the conventions of the genre of tragedy:

• A tragic hero generally passes from good fortune to bad fortune. (King Lear goes from being a beloved king with great wealth and power to being homeless and destitute.)

• A tragic hero generally possesses a *hamartia* or fatal flaw, which causes his downfall. He brings disaster upon himself. In Lear's case, it is his rashness and his lack of self-knowledge, while in *Romeo and Juliet,* it is Romeo's temper.

• When a tragic hero's actions produce results opposite to those he had anticipated (for example, when Lear's daughters do not respond to the love test as he thought they would), they are said to be 'ironic'.

• When the audience knows what is going to happen to a character before he or she does, it is called 'dramatic irony'. For example, in *King Lear,* Edmund tricks Gloucester and Edgar, while we know the truth.

• Essentially, all tragedies portray suffering and cause a catharsis in their audience: a purging of negative emotions (or a good cry, which actually causes the expulsion from the body of negative chemicals which make you feel sad).

• The 'fickleness of fortune', fate, predestination, etc. all play a role in the hero's downfall. In the end, certain things in life cannot be avoided, no matter how hard we try. In *Othello*, particularly, luck and coincidence play a major role in the plot.

The Shakespearean hero is nearly always a man of exceptional character, a man of exaggerated consciousness and overflowing emotions. He feels everything to an extreme pitch. But despite his excellent characteristics, events and fate – and his own fallibility – combine to create a force he cannot defeat. Nonetheless, the action of the play relies on the audience's empathy with the hero and their hope that he will in fact overcome the terrible obstacles he faces.

King Lear, Othello and Hamlet are great tragic heroes, while Macbeth is an anti-hero. Othello initially seems more in control than either Lear or Hamlet, but whereas all three experience a reversal of fortune, neither Lear nor Hamlet descend to the level of Othello.

– THE TRAGEDY OF –

OTHELLO

THE MOOR OF VENICE

BY WILLIAM SHAKESPEARE

DRAMATIS PERSONAE (CHARACTERS)

Othello	*the Moor*
Brabantio	*father to Desdemona*
Cassio	*an honourable lieutenant*
Iago	*a villain, ensign or standard-bearer, and third in command to Othello*
Roderigo	*a gulled[1] gentleman*
Duke of Venice	
Senators	
Montano	*Governor of Cyprus*
Gentlemen of Cyprus	
Lodovico **Gratiano**	*noble Venetians, kinsmen to Brabantio*
Sailors	
Clown, in Othello's retinue	
Desdemona	*wife to Othello*
Emilia	*wife to Iago*
Bianca	*a courtesan*
	Sailors, Messengers, Herald, Officers, Musicians, and Attendants

---

[1] *Deceived*

OTHELLO

ACT 1

VENICE. A STREET

Enter Roderigo and Iago

Roderigo	Tush, never tell me! I take it much unkindly
	That thou, Iago, who hast had my purse
	As if the strings were thine, shouldst know of this.

Iago   'Sblood,[2] but you'll not hear me!
If ever I did dream of such a matter, abhor me.[3]   5

Roderigo   Thou told'st me thou didst hold him[4] in thy hate.

Iago   Despise me
If I do not. Three great ones[5] of the city,
In personal suit to make me his lieutenant,
Off-capp'd to him;[6] and by the faith of man   10
I know my price, I am worth no worse a place.
But he, as loving his own pride and purposes,
Evades them with a bombast[7] circumstance[8]
Horribly stuff'd with epithets of war,[9]
And, in conclusion,   15
Nonsuits[10] my mediators;[11] for 'Certes,' says he,
'I have already chose my officer.'
And what was he?
Forsooth,[12] a great arithmetician,
One Michael Cassio, a Florentine,   20
A fellow almost damn'd in a fair wife,[13]
That never set a squadron in the field
Nor the division of a battle knows
More than a spinster – unless the bookish theoric,[14]
Wherein the togaed consuls[15] can propose   25
As masterly as he. Mere prattle without practice
Is all his soldiership; but he, sir, had th'election,
And I – of whom his eyes had seen the proof
At Rhodes, at Cyprus, and on other grounds
Christened and heathen – must be beeled[16] and calm'd   30
By debitor and creditor. This counter-caster,[17]
He in good time must his lieutenant be,
And I – God bless the mark! – his Moorship's ensign.[18]

Roderigo   By heaven, I rather would have been his hangman.

Iago   Why, there's no remedy. 'Tis the curse of service.   35

The very first words in the play give a negative impression of Iago, who has been taking money from Roderigo for helping him woo Desdemona

2 By Christ's blood
3 Regard me with disgust
4 Othello
5 Important noblemen
6 Took off their caps (deferred to him respectfully)
7 High-sounding but empty   8 Language
9 Full of military references
10 Refuses   11 Supporters
12 An archaic expression to express indignation
13 Who may ruin himself with his choice of wife
14 Theory
15 Officials, who wear togas
16 A sailing reference – the wind must be taken out of his sails
17 Someone who counts counters (i.e. he is a book-keeper)
18 Othello's flag-bearer

Preferment goes by letter and affection,
And not by old gradation, where each second
Stood heir to th' first. Now, sir, be judge yourself,
Whether I in any just term am affined.[19]
To love the Moor.[20]   40

Roderigo   I would not follow him then.

Iago   O sir, content you.
I follow him to serve my turn upon him.
We cannot all be masters, nor all masters
Cannot be truly follow'd. You shall mark   45
Many a duteous and knee-crooking[21] knave
That, doting on his own obsequious bondage,[22]
Wears out his time much like his master's ass
For naught but provender,[23] and when he's old, cashier'd.[24]
Whip me such honest knaves.[25] Others there are   50
Who, trimm'd in forms and visages of duty,[26]
Keep yet their hearts attending on themselves,
And, throwing but shows of service on their lords,
Do well thrive by 'em and when they have lined
        their coats,[27]
Do themselves homage.[28] These fellows have some soul, 55
And such a one do I profess myself – for, sir,
It is as sure as you are Roderigo,
Were I the Moor I would not be Iago.
In following him, I follow but myself.
Heaven is my judge, not I for love and duty,   60
But seeming so for my peculiar end.
For when my outward action doth demonstrate
The native act and figure of my heart
In compliment extern, 'tis not long after
But I will wear my heart upon my sleeve   65
For daws to peck at. I am not what I am.

Roderigo   What a full fortune does the thick-lips owe[29]
If he can carry't thus!

Iago   Call up her father,
Rouse him, make after him, poison his delight,   70
Proclaim him in the streets; incense[30] her kinsmen,
And, though he in a fertile climate dwell,
Plague him with flies. Though that his joy be joy,
Yet throw such changes of vexation[31] on't,

| | As it may lose some colour. | 75 |

Roderigo   Here is her father's house. I'll call aloud.

Iago   Do, with like timorous accent and dire yell
As when, by night and negligence, the fire
Is spied in populous cities.

Iago tells Roderigo to shout to Brabantio using the frighteningly urgent tones normally reserved for news of a fire in a densely populated city

Roderigo   What ho, Brabantio, Signor Brabantio, ho!   80

Iago   Awake, what ho, Brabantio, thieves, thieves, thieves!
Look to your house, your daughter, and your bags.
Thieves, thieves!

Brabantio appears above, at a window

Brabantio   What is the reason of this terrible summons?
What is the matter there?   85

Roderigo   Signor, is all your family within?

Iago   Are your doors lock'd?

Brabantio   Why, wherefore ask you this?

Iago   'Swounds,[32] sir, you're robb'd. For shame, put on
your gown;
Your heart is burst, you have lost half your soul.   90
Even now, now, very now, an old black ram
Is tupping[33] your white ewe. Arise, arise!
Awake the snorting citizens with the bell,
Or else the devil will make a grandsire[34] of you.
Arise, I say.   95

[32] *By Christ's wounds*

[33] *Copulating with*

[34] *Grandfather*

Brabantio   What, have you lost your wits?

Roderigo   Most reverend signor, do you know my voice?

Brabantio   Not I. What are you?

Roderigo   My name is Roderigo.

Brabantio   The worser welcome.   100
I have charged thee not to haunt about my doors.

In honest plainness thou hast heard me say
My daughter is not for thee, and now in madness,
Being full of supper and distempering draughts,[35]
Upon malicious bravery dost thou come   105
To start my quiet.[36]

Roderigo   Sir, sir, sir.

Brabantio   But thou must needs be sure
My spirits and my place have in their power
To make this bitter to thee.   110

Roderigo   Patience, good sir.

Brabantio   What tell'st thou me of robbing? This is Venice.
My house is not a grange.[37]

Roderigo   Most grave Brabantio,
In simple and pure soul I come to you.   115

Iago   'Swounds, sir, you are one of those that will not
serve God if the devil bid you. Because we come to
do you service and you think we are ruffians, you'll
have your daughter covered with a Barbary horse,[38]
you'll have your nephews neigh to you, you'll have   120
coursers[39] for cousins and gennets[40] for germans.[41]

Brabantio   What profane wretch art thou?

Iago   I am one, sir, that comes to tell you your daughter
and the Moor are now making the beast with two backs.[42]

Brabantio   Thou art a villain.   125

Iago   You are a senator.

Brabantio   This thou shalt answer, I know thee, Roderigo.

Roderigo   Sir, I will answer any thing. But I beseech you,
If't be your pleasure and most wise consent –
As partly I find it is – that your fair daughter,   130
At this odd-even[43] and dull watch o'th' night,
Transported with no worse nor better guard
But with a knave of common hire,[44] a gondolier,

[35] Intoxicating liquors

[36] To disturb my rest

[37] Farmhouse

[38] A North African horse

[39] Racehorses [40] Mules [41] Relations

[42] Othello and Desdemona are having sexual relations

[43] Between midnight and one

[44] A common servant

To the gross clasps of a lascivious[45] Moor –

If this be known to you and your allowance,   135

We then have done you bold and saucy[46] wrongs.

But if you know not this, my manners tell me

We have your wrong rebuke. Do not believe

That, from the sense of all civility,

I thus would play and trifle with your reverence.   140

Your daughter, if you have not given her leave,

I say again hath made a gross revolt,[47]

Tying her duty, beauty, wit, and fortunes

In an extravagant and wheeling stranger

Of here and everywhere. Straight satisfy yourself.   145

If she be in her chamber or your house,

Let loose on me the justice of the state

For thus deluding you.

Brabantio   Strike on the tinder, ho!

Give me a taper, call up all my people.   150

This accident is not unlike my dream;

Belief of it oppresses me already.

Light, I say, light!

Exit above

Iago   Farewell, for I must leave you.

It seems not meet nor wholesome to my place   155

To be produced – as, if I stay, I shall –

Against the Moor, for I do know the state,

However this may gall him with some check,[48]

Cannot with safety cast[49] him, for he's embark'd

With such loud reason to the Cyprus wars,   160

Which even now stands in act, that, for their souls,

Another of his fathom[50] they have none

To lead their business, in which regard –

Though I do hate him as I do hell pains –

Yet for necessity of present life   165

I must show out a flag and sign of love,

Which is indeed but sign. That you shall surely find him,

Lead to the Sagittary[51] the raised search,

And there will I be with him. So, farewell.

Exit

Enter, below, Brabantio, and Servants with torches

[45] *Sex-obsessed*

[46] *Outrageous*

[47] *A huge mistake*

[48] *Reprimand*

[49] *Cannot get rid of Othello*

[50] *Expertise*

Due to his military expertise, Othello is invaluable to the state of Venice, but this does not mean he is fully accepted there

[51] *The inn where Othello and Desdemona are staying. It may also refer to Othello himself, as Sagittarius is depicted as a centaur, and Iago has already referred to Othello as a horse*

Brabantio   It is too true an evil. Gone she is,   170
                  And what's to come of my despised time
                  Is naught but bitterness. Now, Roderigo,
                  Where didst thou see her? – O unhappy girl! –
                  With the Moor, say'st thou? – Who would be a father? –
                  How didst thou know 'twas she? – O, she deceives me   175
                  Past thought! – What said she to you? Get more tapers,
                  Raise all my kindred. Are they married, think you?

Roderigo   Truly, I think they are.

Brabantio   O heaven, how got she out? O, treason of the blood!
                  Fathers, from hence trust not your daughters' minds   180
                  By what you see them act. Is there not charms
                  By which the property of youth and maidhood
                  May be abused? Have you not read, Roderigo,
                  Of some such thing?

Roderigo   Yes, sir, I have indeed.   185

Brabantio   Call up my brother. O, would you had had her!
                  Some one way, some another. Do you know
                  Where we may apprehend her and the Moor?

Roderigo   I think I can discover him, if you please
                  To get good guard and go along with me.   190

Brabantio   Pray you lead on. At every house I'll call;
                  I may command at most. Get weapons, ho,
                  And raise some special officers of night.
                  On, good Roderigo. I'll deserve your pains.

                  Exit

THE PLAY BEGINS in dramatic fashion, with news of a scandalous elopement. We are introduced to two characters: Iago and Roderigo. Iago has been taking money from Roderigo for helping him to woo Desdemona, but it transpires that Desdemona has married Othello in secret, and Roderigo is bitter that his suit has been in vain.

Iago has reasons of his own to hate Othello: he has been passed over for promotion in favour of Michael Cassio. Iago is duplicitous, and proud of it. He despises loyalty, and seeks to advance himself whatever the cost to others. Yet Roderigo somehow seems to think that Iago will be loyal to him.

We do not meet Desdemona or Othello, but we learn that Othello is a high-ranking general, whose military expertise is essential to Venice's interests and safety. He is also black, and, on that account, very different to those around him.

Iago and Roderigo shout at Brabantio from the street below in order to wake him up and give him the bad news that his daughter has eloped. Brabantio initially is irritated by Roderigo – he has clearly been a regular and unwelcome visitor to the house. Brabantio repeats that Desdemona is not for him, but then discovers that Roderigo has come with a new, startling agenda. The news the men bring is clearly shocking; so shocking that Brabantio does not at first believe it. But when he discovers that Desdemona's chamber is empty, he realises the truth.

Brabantio is convinced that Othello must have used witchcraft on his daughter in order to seduce her. He wants the torches lit and Venice searched. He even says he would have preferred her to marry Roderigo. Roderigo is clearly Othello's inferior in every way but one – Roderigo is white.

Meanwhile, Iago slips away into the shadows. Like a puppet-master, he has pulled all the strings, and makes his exit before anyone can connect him with any wrongdoing.

KEY **POINTS**

- *Iago hates Othello because he has promoted Cassio ahead of him.*

- *Roderigo is in love with Desdemona.*

- *Desdemona has married Othello without her father's permission.*

- *Brabantio is enraged both by his daughter's disobedience and by her choice of husband.*

- *Othello is a valued military general, but is still an outsider in Venice nonetheless.*

*I take it much unkindly
That thou, Iago, who hast had my purse
As if the strings were thine, shouldst know of this*

– RODERIGO

ANOTHER STREET

Enter Othello, Iago, and Attendants with torches

Iago	Though in the trade of war I have slain men,
	Yet do I hold it very stuff o'th' conscience[1]
	To do no contrived[2] murder. I lack iniquity[3]
	Sometime, to do me service. Nine or ten times
	I had thought to've yerk'd[4] him here, under the ribs. 5
Othello	'Tis better as it is.
Iago	Nay, but he prated,[5]
	And spoke such scurvy[6] and provoking terms
	Against your honour
	That, with the little godliness I have, 10
	I did full hard forbear him. But I pray you, sir,
	Are you fast married? Be assured of this:
	That the magnifico[7] is much beloved,
	And hath in his effect a voice potential
	As double as the Duke's. He will divorce you, 15
	Or put upon you what restraint and grievance
	The law, with all his might to enforce it on,
	Will give him cable.[8]
Othello	Let him do his spite.
	My services which I have done the signory 20
	Shall out-tongue[9] his complaints. 'Tis yet to know –
	Which, when I know that boasting is an honour,
	I shall promulgate[10] – I fetch my life and being
	From men of royal siege, and my demerits
	May speak unbonneted to as proud a fortune 25
	As this that I have reach'd. For know, Iago,
	But that I love the gentle Desdemona,
	I would not my unhoused free condition
	Put into circumscription and confine
	For the seas' worth.[11] But look, what lights come yond? 30
Iago	Those are the raised father and his friends:
	You were best go in.
Othello	Not I. I must be found.
	My parts,[12] my title, and my perfect soul[13]
	Shall manifest me rightly. Is it they? 35

Margin notes:

[1] The whole point of having a conscience
[2] Deliberate/premeditated   [3] Malice
[4] Stabbed
[5] Babbled
[6] Insulting
[7] Brabantio – a 'magnifico' is a very powerful man in society
[8] Rights
[9] Othello's services to the state will outdo Brabantio's complaints
[10] Make widely known

Othello says that he comes from royal blood, and is just as noble as the woman he has married

[11] Othello wouldn't have given up his single life for anything other than love

[12] Talents   [13] Clear conscience

Iago	By Janus,[14] I think no.
	Enter Cassio, and certain Officers with torches
Othello	The servants of the Duke, and my lieutenant!
	The goodness of the night upon you, friends.
	What is the news?
Cassio	The Duke does greet you, general, 40
	And he requires your haste-post-haste[15] appearance,
	Even on the instant.
Othello	What is the matter, think you?
Cassio	Something from Cyprus, as I may divine;
	It is a business of some heat.[16] The galleys[17] 45
	Have sent a dozen sequent[18] messengers
	This very night at one another's heels,
	And many of the consuls,[19] raised and met,
	Are at the Duke's already. You have been hotly[20] call'd for,
	When, being not at your lodging to be found, 50
	The senate sent about three several quests
	To search you out.
Othello	'Tis well I am found by you.
	I will but spend a word here in the house
	And go with you. 55
	Exit
Cassio	Ensign, what makes he here?
Iago	Faith, he tonight hath boarded a land-carack.[21]
	If it prove lawful prize, he's made for ever.
Cassio	I do not understand.
Iago	He's married. 60
Cassio	To who?
	Re-enter Othello
Iago	Marry, to – Come, captain, will you go?

[14] *The God of beginnings and endings, also two-faced, like Iago*

[15] *Immediate*

[16] *Urgency* [17] *Warships*

[18] *Consecutive*

[19] *Senators*

[20] *Urgently*

[21] *Treasure ship (i.e. Desdemona)*

Othello	Have with you.
Cassio	Here comes another troop to seek for you.
Iago	It is Brabantio. General, be advised. 65 He comes to bad intent.

*Enter Brabantio, Roderigo, and Officers with
torches and weapons*

Othello	Holla, stand, there!
Roderigo	Signor, it is the Moor.
Brabantio	Down with him, thief!

They draw on both sides

Iago	You, Roderigo? Come, sir, I am for you. 70
Othello	Keep up your bright swords, for the dew will rust 'em. Good signor, you shall more command with years Than with your weapons.
Brabantio	O thou foul thief, where hast thou stow'd my daughter? Damn'd as thou art, thou hast enchanted her, 75 For I'll refer me to all things of sense, If she in chains of magic were not bound, Whether a maid so tender, fair, and happy, So opposite²² to marriage that she shunned The wealthy curled darlings²³ of our nation, 80 Would ever have, t'incur a general mock, Run from her guardage²⁴ to the sooty bosom Of such a thing as thou – to fear, not to delight. Judge me the world, if 'tis not gross in sense That thou hast practised on her with foul charms, 85 Abused her delicate youth with drugs or minerals That weaken motion.²⁵ I'll have't disputed on. 'Tis probable, and palpable to thinking.²⁶ I therefore apprehend and do attach²⁷ thee For an abuser of the world, a practiser 90 Of arts inhibited and out of warrant.²⁸ Lay hold upon him. If he do resist, Subdue him at his peril.

²² *Opposed*
²³ *Rich and elegant young Venetian men*
²⁴ *Safe home*
²⁵ *The senses*
²⁶ *Easily proved*
²⁷ *Arrest*
²⁸ *Witchcraft/black magic*

Othello	Hold your hands, Both you of my inclining[29] and the rest. Were it my cue to fight, I should have known it Without a prompter. Whither will you that I go To answer this your charge?
Brabantio	To prison, till fit time Of law and course of direct session Call thee to answer.
Othello	What if I do obey? How may the Duke be therewith satisfied, Whose messengers are here about my side Upon some present business of the state To bring me to him?
1st Officer	'Tis true, most worthy signor; The Duke's in council, and your noble self, I am sure, is sent for.
Brabantio	How, the Duke in council? In this time of the night? Bring him away, Mine's not an idle cause. The Duke himself, Or any of my brothers of the state, Cannot but feel this wrong as 'twere their own; For if such actions may have passage free, Bondslaves and pagans shall our statesmen be.

Exit

95

100

105

110

115

[29] *On my side*

MODERN ENGLISH VERSION

ANOTHER STREET

Enter Othello, Iago, and Attendants with torches

Iago   Even though I have killed men on the battlefield, my conscience would never allow me to kill anyone unlawfully. Sometimes I think I'm just too nice. I felt like stabbing him nine or ten times at least.

Othello   I'm glad you didn't.

Iago   But the way he was babbling on, saying such terrible things about you! Only for having a little patience, I would have killed him. But, sir, are you securely married? Brabantio is nearly as powerful as the Duke. He can have you divorced, and has the power to do a lot more besides.

Othello   Let him do his worst. I have served the government well, and their praises will drown out his complaints. I don't go on about this, because it is not good to boast, but I come from a royal family, and I'm just as noble as the woman I've married. And I really love Desdemona. I assure you, I would not have given up my carefree bachelor life for anything other than true love. Who's approaching us bearing torches?

Iago   Maybe it's Brabantio, and his friends. You'd better go inside.

Othello   No: I've nothing to be ashamed of. I am a man of high rank, and I have a clear conscience. Is it him?

Iago   Actually, I don't think it is.

Enter Cassio, and Officers with torches

Othello   It is my lieutenant and the Duke's servants. Good night to you all, what is going on?

Cassio   The Duke needs you urgently, as soon as possible.

Othello   What is going on, do you know?

Cassio   It's something to do with Cyprus – something urgent. The ships have sent a dozen messengers, one after the other. The senators are at the Duke's already. They went to your lodgings looking for you, and when they didn't find you there, the senate sent three search parties out to find you.

Othello   I'm glad you found me. I just have to go inside for a moment, and then I'll be right with you.

              Exit

Cassio   What's going on here, sir?

Iago   Let's just say that tonight Othello has boarded a treasure ship. If it's legal, he's going to be very rich.

Cassio   What do you mean?

Iago   He's married.

Cassio   To whom?

              Re-enter Othello

Iago   Will we go?

Othello   Yes, let's get going.

Cassio   Here comes another search party looking for you.

Iago   It's not a search party, it's Brabantio. General, be careful – he's in a dangerous mood.

              Enter Brabantio, Roderigo, and Officers with torches and weapons

Othello   Hey! Don't come any closer!

Roderigo   Signor, it is the Moor.

Brabantio   You thief! I'll kill you!

              Both sides draw weapons

Iago   I'm going to kill you, Roderigo.

Othello   You're not going to use those swords. They will rust before I will allow that. Brabantio, you command us more with your age and title than you ever could with your weapons.

Brabantio   You thief! What have you done with my daughter? You must have used witchcraft to enchant her – there's no way she'd have left her safe, happy home with me if you hadn't cast a spell on her. She wasn't even interested in marriage, she refused many a nice, young Venetian boy – so why would she have run to a foreigner like you? You used black magic on her, or drugged her. It's the only possible reason for this. I am going to have you arrested and charged with stealing, and with using black magic.

Othello

Everybody, stop. Even those of you who are on my side. I don't need anyone to fight my battles for me. Where do you wish to question me about these charges?

Brabantio

In prison, and then, in due course, in court.

Othello

And if I obey, how would you explain my absence to the Duke, who has sent all these men to find me?

1st Officer

This is true. The Duke has called an emergency council. I'm sure he's expecting you to be there as well.

Brabantio

Why is the Duke in council in the middle of the night? Arrest him. I have valid reason to arrest him, and when the Duke and other senators hear what Othello has done, they will be just as outraged as I was. If this kind of behaviour is tolerated, slaves and heathens will soon be in charge!

> *Good signor, you shall more*
> *command with years*
> *Than with your weapons*
>
> – OTHELLO (ACT I SCENE II)

A COUNCIL-CHAMBER

The Duke and Senators sitting at a table;
Officers attending

Duke	There is no composition[1] in these news That gives them credit.[2]
1st Senator	Indeed, they are disproportion'd.[3] My letters say a hundred and seven galleys.
Duke	And mine, a hundred-forty.
2nd Senator	And mine two hundred. But though they jump not on a just account[4] – As, in these cases, where the aim reports[5] 'Tis oft with difference – yet do they all confirm A Turkish fleet, and bearing up to Cyprus.
Duke	Nay, it is possible enough to judgement: I do not so secure me in the error, But the main article I do approve In fearful sense.[6]
Sailor	*[Within]* What ho, what ho, what ho!
1st Officer	A messenger from the galleys.

Enter a Sailor

Duke	Now, what's the business?
Sailor	The Turkish preparation makes for Rhodes. So was I bid report here to the state By Signor Angelo.
Duke	How say you by this change?
1st Senator	This cannot be, By no assay[7] of reason – 'tis a pageant[8] To keep us in false gaze.[9] When we consider The importance of Cyprus to the Turk, And let ourselves again but understand That, as it more concerns the Turk than Rhodes,

Line numbers: 5, 10, 15, 20, 25

Footnotes:
[1] Consistency
[2] Credibility
[3] Inconsistent
[4] Although the accounts differ
[5] Which is to be expected when estimating
[6] Despite the differing reports, there is good reason to be fearful
[7] Test [8] Trick
[9] To get us to look in the wrong direction

[10] *It can be captured more easily than Rhodes*

[11] *It is not well defended*

[12] *Rhodes is well defended*

It seems unlikely that Turkey would try to attack the well-defended Rhodes, where they would definitely fail, instead of the poorly defended Cyprus, where success is practically guaranteed

[13] *Turks*

[14] *They have joined with another fleet*

[15] *Turn around (they're going back to Cyprus)*

[16] *Informs*

[17] *Immediately*

[18] *Missed*

So may he with more facile question bear it,[10]
For that it stands not in such warlike brace,[11]
But altogether lacks th'abilities   30
That Rhodes is dress'd in[12] – if we make thought of this,
We must not think the Turk is so unskilful
To leave that latest which concerns him first,
Neglecting an attempt of ease and gain
To wake and wage a danger profitless.   35

Duke   Nay, in all confidence, he's not for Rhodes.

1st Officer   Here is more news.

Enter a Messenger

Messenger   The Ottomites,[13] reverend and gracious,
Steering with due course toward the isle of Rhodes,
Have there injointed them with an after fleet.[14]   40

1st Senator   Ay, so I thought. How many, as you guess?

Messenger   Of thirty sail: and now they do restem[15]
Their backward course, bearing with frank appearance
Their purposes toward Cyprus. Signor Montano,
Your trusty and most valiant servitor,   45
With his free duty recommends[16] you thus,
And prays you to believe him.

Duke   'Tis certain then for Cyprus.
Marcus Luccicos, is not he in town?

1st Senator   He's now in Florence.   50

Duke   Write from us to him post-post-haste.[17] Dispatch.

1st Senator   Here comes Brabantio and the valiant Moor.

Enter Brabantio, Othello, Iago, Roderigo, and Officers

Duke   Valiant Othello, we must straight employ you
Against the general enemy Ottoman.
[To Brabantio]
I did not see you. Welcome, gentle signor;   55
We lack'd[18] your counsel and your help tonight.

Brabantio	So did I yours. Good your grace, pardon me;
	Neither my place, nor aught I heard of business,
	Hath raised me from my bed, nor doth the general care
	Take hold on me; for my particular grief	60
	Is of so floodgate and o'erbearing nature
	That it engluts[19] and swallows other sorrows,
	And it is still itself.

| Duke | Why, what's the matter? |

| Brabantio | My daughter! O, my daughter! | 65 |

| Duke/Senators | Dead? |

Brabantio	Ay, to me.
	She is abused, stol'n from me, and corrupted
	By spells and medicines bought of mountebanks.[20]
	For nature so preposterously to err,	70
	Being not deficient, blind, or lame of sense,
	Sans[21] witchcraft could not.

Duke	Whoe'er he be that in this foul proceeding
	Hath thus beguiled your daughter of herself
	And you of her, the bloody book of law	75
	You shall yourself read in the bitter letter
	After your own sense, yea, though our proper son
	Stood in your action.

Brabantio	Humbly I thank your grace.
	Here is the man, this Moor, whom now it seems	80
	Your special mandate for the state affairs
	Hath hither brought.

| Duke/Senators | We are very sorry for't. |

| Duke | *[To Othello]* What, in your own part, can you say to this? |

| Brabantio | Nothing, but this is so. | 85 |

Othello	Most potent, grave, and reverend signors,
	My very noble and approved good masters,
	That I have ta'en away this old man's daughter,
	It is most true, true I have married her.
	The very head and front of my offending	90

[19] Overwhelms

[20] Quack doctors

[21] Without

Brabantio explains that he is not present in connection with the Turkish threat, but because of his personal situation, which is much more important to him

Brabantio claims that the only plausible reason for Desdemona marrying Othello is black magic, or that she was drugged

The Duke is determined to punish the man in question, even if it is his own son (until he discovers it is Othello)

Hath this extent, no more.[22] Rude am I in my speech,[23]
And little bless'd with the soft phrase of peace,
For since these arms of mine had seven years' pith[24]
Till now some nine moons wasted,[25] they have used
Their dearest action in the tented field,[26]   95
And little of this great world can I speak
More than pertains to feats of broils[27] and battle,
And therefore little shall I grace my cause
In speaking for myself. Yet, by your gracious patience,
I will a round unvarnish'd[28] tale deliver   100
Of my whole course of love, what drugs, what charms,
What conjuration[29] and what mighty magic –
For such proceeding I am charged withal –
I won his daughter.

Brabantio   A maiden never bold,   105
Of spirit so still and quiet that her motion
Blush'd at herself[30] – and she in spite of nature,
Of years, of country, credit, everything,
To fall in love with what she fear'd to look on!
It is a judgement maim'd[31] and most imperfect   110
That will confess perfection so could err
Against all rules of nature, and must be driven
To find out practises of cunning hell,
Why this should be. I therefore vouch again
That with some mixtures powerful o'er the blood,   115
Or with some dram[32] conjured to this effect,
He wrought[33] upon her.

Duke   To vouch this is no proof
Without more wider and more overt test[34]
Than these thin habits and poor likelihoods[35]   120
Of modern seeming do prefer against him.

1st Senator   But, Othello, speak:
Did you by indirect and forced courses
Subdue and poison this young maid's affections?
Or came it by request and such fair question   125
As soul to soul affordeth?

Othello   I do beseech you,
Send for the lady to the Sagittary,
And let her speak of me before her father.
If you do find me foul in her report,   130

The trust, the office I do hold of you
Not only take away, but let your sentence
Even fall upon my life.

Duke Fetch Desdemona hither.

Othello Ensign, conduct them. You best know the place. 135

Exit Iago and Attendants

And till she come, as truly as to heaven
I do confess the vices of my blood,[36]
So justly to your grave ears I'll present
How I did thrive in this fair lady's love,
And she in mine. 140

Duke Say it, Othello.

Othello Her father loved me, oft invited me,
Still[37] question'd me the story of my life
From year to year, the battles, sieges, fortunes,
That I have passed.[38] 145
I ran it through even from my boyish days
To th' very moment that he bade me tell it,
Wherein I spoke of most disastrous chances,[39]
Of moving accidents by flood and field,
Of hair-breadth scapes[40] i'th' imminent deadly breach,[41] 150
Of being taken by the insolent foe[42]
And sold to slavery, of my redemption thence,[43]
And portance in my travels' history:
Wherein of antres[44] vast and deserts idle,
Rough quarries, rocks and hills whose heads touch heaven, 155
It was my hint to speak. Such was the process,
And of the cannibals that each other eat,
The Anthropophagi,[45] and men whose heads
Do grow beneath their shoulders. These things to hear
Would Desdemona seriously incline, 160
But still the house-affairs[46] would draw her thence,
Which ever as she could with haste dispatch
She'd come again, and with a greedy ear
Devour up my discourse;[47] which I observing,
Took once a pliant[48] hour, and found good means 165
To draw from her a prayer of earnest heart
That I would all my pilgrimage dilate,[49]

[36] He will be as honest with them as he is with God

[37] Continually

[38] Fought in

[39] Unfortunate disasters

[40] Escapes by a hair's breadth (by the skin of his teeth)
[41] The threat of imminent death
[42] Arrogant enemy
[43] He gained his freedom
[44] Caves

[45] A race of cannibals

[46] Household duties

[47] Listen to every word he said
[48] Favourable

[49] He would tell of all his adventures at length

50 *Little bits at a time*

51 *Continuously*

52 *Bring her to tears*

Whereof by parcels[50] she had something heard,
But not intentively.[51] I did consent,
And often did beguile her of her tears[52]   170
When I did speak of some distressful stroke
That my youth suffer'd. My story being done,
She gave me for my pains a world of sighs:
She swore, in faith 'twas strange, 'twas passing strange,
'Twas pitiful, 'twas wondrous pitiful.   175
She wish'd she had not heard it, yet she wish'd
That heaven had made her such a man. She thanked me,
And bade me, if I had a friend that loved her,
I should but teach him how to tell my story.

53 *Seduce*

54 *Survived*

And that would woo[53] her. Upon this hint I spake.   180
She loved me for the dangers I had pass'd,[54]
And I loved her that she did pity them.
This only is the witchcraft I have used.
Here comes the lady. Let her witness it.

Enter Desdemona, Iago, and Attendants

Duke   I think this tale would win my daughter, too.   185
Good Brabantio,

55 *Try to make the best of the situation*

Take up this mangled matter at the best.[55]
Men do their broken weapons rather use
Than their bare hands.

Brabantio   I pray you hear her speak.   190
If she confess that she was half the wooer,

56 *False accusations*

Destruction on my head if my bad blame[56]
Light on the man! Come hither, gentle mistress.
Do you perceive in all this noble company
Where most you owe obedience?   195

Desdemona   My noble father,
I do perceive here a divided duty.
To you I am bound for life and education.

While Desdemona concedes that she has a duty to both her father and her husband, she states that ultimately her loyalty lies with Othello

My life and education both do learn me
How to respect you. You are the lord of duty,   200
I am hitherto your daughter. But here's my husband,
And so much duty as my mother show'd
To you, preferring you before her father,
So much I challenge that I may profess
Due to the Moor my lord.   205

57 *He is finished with his daughter*

Brabantio   God b'wi'you, I ha' done.[57]

Please it your grace, on to the state affairs:
I had rather to adopt a child than get it.[58]
Come hither, Moor:
I here do give thee that with all my heart   210
Which, but thou hast already, with all my heart
I would keep from thee. For your sake, jewel,
I am glad at soul I have no other child,
For thy escape would teach me tyranny,
To hang clogs on 'em. I have done, my lord.   215

Duke   Let me speak like yourself, and lay a sentence[59]
Which, as a grece[60] or step, may help these lovers
Into your favour.
When remedies are past, the griefs are ended
By seeing the worst, which late on hopes depended.   220
To mourn a mischief that is past and gone
Is the next way to draw new mischief on.[61]
What cannot be preserved when fortune takes,
Patience her injury a mockery makes.
The robb'd that smiles steals something from the thief;[62]   225
He robs himself that spends a bootless grief.

Brabantio   So let the Turk of Cyprus us beguile,
We lose it not so long as we can smile.
He bears the sentence well that nothing bears
But the free comfort which from thence he hears,   230
But he bears both the sentence and the sorrow
That, to pay grief, must of poor patience borrow.
These sentences, to sugar or to gall,
Being strong on both sides, are equivocal.
But words are words. I never yet did hear   235
That the bruised heart was pierced through the ear.
I humbly beseech you proceed to th'affairs of state.

Duke   The Turk with a most mighty preparation makes for
Cyprus. Othello, the fortitude[63] of the place is best
known to you, and though we have there a substitute   240
of most allowed sufficiency,[64] yet opinion, a more
sovereign mistress of effects, throws a more safer
voice on you. You must therefore be content to
slubber[65] the gloss of your new fortunes with this
more stubborn and boisterous expedition.   245

Othello   The tyrant custom, most grave senators,

---

[58] Than have one of his own

Brabantio gives Desdemona to Othello with all my heart, since he has taken her already, but he wishes with all his heart that he could keep her from him. He is glad he has no other children, because he would practically imprison them to prevent them betraying him in the manner Desdemona has betrayed him

[59] Refer to a proverb

[60] Step

[61] You only hurt yourself when you refuse to accept what cannot be changed

[62] If you can smile after being robbed, the thief has taken nothing from you

Brabantio turns the Duke's words against him, saying that, if this is the case, they should smile when the Turks steal Cyprus, and that it is easy to smile at these platitudes when you haven't suffered the loss that he has

[63] Defence

[64] The officer in charge is very competent

Public opinion is that Othello is the best man for the job

[65] Spoil

Othello is so used to war, he considers it as easy to partake in it as to lie on a soft bed

⁶⁶ *Recognise*

⁶⁷ *Briskness*

⁶⁸ *Appropriate accommodation*

⁶⁹ *Attendants*

⁷⁰ *Please listen to me*

⁷¹ *Permission*

⁷² *Shout*

⁷³ *True face*

⁷⁴ *Tie to him for ever*

⁷⁵ *Uselessly*

⁷⁶ *She will be deeply sad*

⁷⁷ *Lust*

⁷⁸ *Othello's sexual urges have declined with age*

⁷⁹ *The right of a married couple to be sexually active*

Hath made the flinty and steel couch of war
My thrice-driven bed of down: I do agnize⁶⁶
A natural and prompt alacrity⁶⁷
I find in hardness, and do undertake   250
These present wars against the Ottomites.
Most humbly therefore bending to your state,
I crave fit disposition⁶⁸ for my wife,
Due reference of place and exhibition,
With such accommodation and besort⁶⁹   255
As levels with her breeding.

Duke   Why, at her father's!

Brabantio   I will not have it so.

Othello   Nor I.

Desdemona   Nor I; I would not there reside,   260
To put my father in impatient thoughts
By being in his eye. Most gracious Duke,
To my unfolding lend your prosperous ear;⁷⁰
And let me find a charter⁷¹ in your voice,
T'assist my simpleness.   265

Duke   What would you, Desdemona?

Desdemona   That I did love the Moor to live with him,
My downright violence and storm of fortunes
May trumpet⁷² to the world. My heart's subdued
Even to the very quality of my lord.   270
I saw Othello's visage⁷³ in his mind,
And to his honours and his valiant parts
Did I my soul and fortunes consecrate;⁷⁴
So that, dear lords, if I be left behind,
A moth of peace,⁷⁵ and he go to the war,   275
The rites for which I love him are bereft me,
And I a heavy interim shall support⁷⁶
By his dear absence. Let me go with him.

Othello   Let her have your voice.
Vouch with me heaven, I therefore beg it not   280
To please the palate of my appetite
Nor to comply with heat⁷⁷– the young affects
In me defunct⁷⁸ – and proper satisfaction,⁷⁹

But to be free and bounteous to[80] her mind;
And heaven defend your good souls, that you think   285
I will your serious and great business scant[81]
When she is with me. No, when light-wing'd toys
Of feather'd Cupid[82] seal with wanton dullness
My speculative and officed instruments,[83]
That my disports[84] corrupt and taint my business,   290
Let housewives make a skillet[85] of my helm,[86]
And all indign[87] and base adversities
Make head against my estimation.[88]

Duke　　　Be it as you shall privately determine,
Either for her stay or going. Th'affair cries haste,   295
And speed must answer it.

1st Senator　　You must away tonight.

Othello　　With all my heart.

Duke　　　At nine i'th' morning here we'll meet again.
Othello, leave some officer behind,   300
And he shall our commission bring to you,
With such things else of quality and respect
As doth import you.[89]

Othello　　So please your grace, my ensign.[90]
A man he is of honesty and trust.   305
To his conveyance[91] I assign my wife,
With what else needful your good grace shall think
To be sent after me.

Duke　　　Let it be so.
Good night to every one.   310
[To Brabantio]
And, noble signor,
If virtue no delighted beauty lack,[92]
Your son-in-law is far more fair than black.

1st Senator　　Adieu, brave Moor. Use[93] Desdemona well.

Brabantio　　Look to her, Moor, if thou hast eyes to see.   315
She has deceived her father, and may thee.

Exit Duke, Senators, Officers, etc.

[80] To have access to

[81] Neglect

[82] The god of love

[83] Eyes (Cupid blinded lovers, hence the expression 'love is blind')

[84] Diversions

[85] Frying pan　[86] Helmet

[87] Unworthy

[88] Reputation

[89] Concern you

[90] Iago

[91] Care

[92] If virtue is beautiful

[93] Treat

Othello   My life upon her faith. Honest Iago,
My Desdemona must I leave to thee.
I prithee let thy wife attend on her,

⁹⁴ As soon as you can

And bring them after in the best advantage.⁹⁴   320
Come, Desdemona. I have but an hour
Of love, of worldly matter and direction
To spend with thee. We must obey the time.

Exit Othello and Desdemona

Roderigo   Iago.

Iago   What say'st thou, noble heart?   325

Roderigo   What will I do, think'st thou?

Iago   Why, go to bed and sleep.

⁹⁵ Immediately

Roderigo   I will incontinently⁹⁵ drown myself.

⁹⁶ Respect

Iago   If thou dost, I shall never love⁹⁶ thee after. Why,
thou silly gentleman!   330

Roderigo   It is silliness to live when to live is torment; and
then have we a prescription to die when death

⁹⁷ Doctor

is our physician.⁹⁷

Iago   O villainous! I ha' looked upon the world for four
times seven years, and since I could distinguish   335

⁹⁸ Between

betwixt⁹⁸ a benefit and an injury I never found man
that knew how to love himself. Ere I would say I

⁹⁹ Prostitute

would drown myself for the love of a guinea-hen,⁹⁹
I would change my humanity with a baboon.

Roderigo   What should I do? I confess it is my shame to be so   340
fond, but it is not in my virtue to amend it.

¹⁰⁰ Nonsense!

Iago   Virtue? A fig!¹⁰⁰ 'Tis in ourselves that we are thus
or thus. Our bodies are our gardens, to the which
our wills are gardeners; so that if we will plant

¹⁰¹ A medicinal herb

nettles, or sow lettuce, set hyssop¹⁰¹ and weed up   345
thyme, supply it with one gender of herbs or
distract it with many, either to have it sterile
with idleness or manured with industry, why, the

power and corrigible[102] authority of this lies in our
wills. If the balance of our lives had not one   350
scale of reason to poise another of sensuality, the
blood and baseness of our natures would conduct us
to most preposterous conclusions. But we have
reason to cool our raging motions, our carnal
stings, our unbitted lusts, whereof I take this that   355
you call love to be a sect or scion.[103]

Roderigo   It cannot be.

Iago   It is merely a lust of the blood and a permission of the will.
Come, be a man. Drown thyself? Drown cats and blind
puppies. I have professed me thy friend, and I confess   360
me knit to thy deserving with cables of perdurable[104]
toughness; I could never better stead thee than now.
Put money in thy purse. Follow thou the wars, defeat thy
favour[105] with an usurped[106] beard. I say, put money in
thy purse. It cannot be that Desdemona should long   365
continue her love to the Moor, – put money in thy purse,
– nor he his to her. It was a violent commencement,[107] and
thou shalt see an answerable sequestration[108] – put but
money in thy purse. These Moors are changeable in
their wills – fill thy purse with money. The food that to   370
him now is as luscious as locusts shall be to him shortly
as bitter as coloquintida.[109] She must change for youth.
When she is sated with his body, she will find the error
of her choice: she must have change, she must: therefore
put money in thy purse. If thou wilt needs damn thyself,   375
do it a more delicate way than drowning. Make all the
money thou canst. If sanctimony and a frail[110] vow
betwixt an erring[111] barbarian and a super-subtle[112]
Venetian is not too hard for my wits and all the tribe of
hell, thou shalt enjoy her; therefore make money. A pox   380
o' drowning thyself – it is clean out of the way. Seek thou
rather to be hanged in compassing[113] thy joy than to be
drowned and go without her.

Roderigo   Wilt thou be fast to my hopes if I depend on the issue?

Iago   Thou art sure of me. Go, make money. I have told   385
thee often, and I re-tell thee again and again, I hate the
Moor. My cause is hearted,[114] thine hath no less reason.
Let us be conjunctive[115] in our revenge against him. If

---

[102] Questionable

Iago explains that our bodies are like gardens, and our willpower is the gardener. So we have to use our self-control to stop unwanted emotions taking us over, just as weeds can easily take over a garden if you are not constantly vigilant

[103] Sideshoot

The repetition of the phrase 'put money in thy purse' shows exactly where Iago's priorities lie, and can also be delivered in a humorous manner

[104] Imperishable

[105] Disguise yourself [106] Fake

[107] They married in haste

[108] They will separate in haste

[109] Bitter apple which has purgative properties, a typically crude comment from Iago

[110] Weak

[111] Lustful [112] Well-mannered

[113] Achieving

[114] Heartfelt

[115] Join forces

thou canst cuckold[116] him, thou dost thyself a pleasure, me a sport. There are many events in the womb of time, 390 which will be delivered. Traverse,[117] go, provide thy money. We will have more of this tomorrow. Adieu.

Roderigo   Where shall we meet i'th' morning?

Iago   At my lodging.

Roderigo   I'll be with thee betimes.   395

Iago   Go to, farewell – Do you hear, Roderigo?

Roderigo   What say you?

Iago   No more of drowning, do you hear?

Roderigo   I am changed: I'll go sell all my land.

Exit

Iago   Thus do I ever make my fool my purse –   400
For I mine own gain'd knowledge should profane[118]
If I would time expend with such a snipe[119]
But for my sport and profit. I hate the Moor
And it is thought abroad, that 'twixt my sheets
He has done my office,[120] I know not if't be true;   405
But I, for mere suspicion in that kind,
Will do as if for surety. He holds me well:[121]
The better shall my purpose work on him.
Cassio's a proper[122] man. Let me see now,
To get his place, and to plume up[123] my will   410
In double knavery – How, how? Let's see.
After some time, to abuse[124] Othello's ears
That he is too familiar with his wife;
He hath a person and a smooth dispose[125]
To be suspected, framed to make women false.   415
The Moor is of a free and open nature,
That thinks men honest that but seem to be so,
And will as tenderly be led by th' nose
As asses are.
I ha't. It is engender'd.[126] Hell and night   420
Must bring this monstrous birth to the world's light.

Exit

Marginal notes:

[116] Make him a cuckold (by sleeping with Desdemona)

[117] Get going

[118] He would be wasting his talents

[119] Idiot

[120] He has done Iago's job, i.e. slept with his wife

[121] Othello thinks well of him

[122] Handsome

[123] Satisfy

[124] Offend

[125] Charming disposition

[126] Begun

THE SCENE BEGINS with the Duke discussing the Turkish advance. The Turkish fleet is trying to confuse the Venetian army by appearing to advance towards Rhodes rather than Cyprus, but the senate soon realises that it is Cyprus it is after.

It is clear that Othello is heavily relied upon, and of immense value to the Duke. The wealthy Venetian state depended upon the resources of its colonies, which allowed the Venetians to live a prosperous lifestyle. So, when Brabantio entreats the senate for help (it could, for example, annul the marriage), the audience already knows whose side the senators will be on.

Brabantio is convinced Othello seduced Desdemona with some foreign witchcraft, but Othello simply replies that Desdemona loves him for his exotic background, for the trials he has endured and the adventures he has experienced. In short, she loves him for who he truly is. The Duke is more than satisfied that Othello did nothing wrong, and claims his own daughter would have fallen in love with such a courageous man too. Desdemona asserts herself in front of her father, stating that she married Othello of her own free will, and that now her duty and loyalty is to her husband.

Desdemona is given permission to accompany her husband to Cyprus, although her father warns Othello that she may betray him too.

Iago tells a depressed Roderigo to pull himself together. He tells Roderigo to get hold of as much money as he can, and to journey to Cyprus too. He convinces Roderigo that he still has a chance with the newly wed Desdemona, and the gullible Roderigo believes him.

Iago's soliloquy at the end of Scene III lets the audience know that he plans to destroy Othello's happiness. He claims that he thinks Othello slept with Emilia – a curious comment that he fails to back up.

> *they do restem*
> *Their backward course, bearing with*
> *frank appearance*
> *Their purposes toward Cyprus*
>
> – MESSENGER

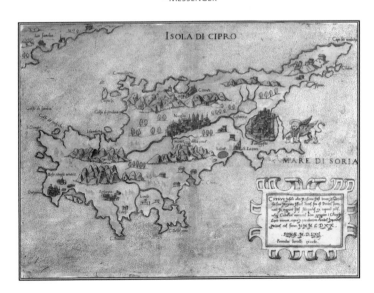

KEY **POINTS**

- *The Senate takes Othello's side against Brabantio.*

- *Desdemona chooses Othello over her father.*

- *The action of the play will now move to Cyprus, away from Venice.*

- *Iago reveals his plot is to ruin Othello's peace of mind by making him jealous.*

FOCUS ON ACT 1

'Othello is a prized general, but he is also an outsider, and he can only survive in this culture if he plays by rules that he does not really understand'

VENICE IS the setting for the first part of the play. It is an exotic place for Shakespeare's audience, and the hero, Othello, is more exotic still, as he is from North Africa. He is an outsider in this complex culture obsessed with breeding and etiquette. Some members of Shakespeare's audience might never have seen a black person, although it is thought that slaves may have been arriving in England from 1550 onwards. These were not multicultural times, however, and neither were they politically correct. The play abounds with offensive references to Othello's racial features. Othello is a prized general, but he is also an outsider, and he can only survive in this culture if he plays by rules that he does not really understand.

The play opens with an animated conversation between Iago and Roderigo. Roderigo is wealthy, but weak and gullible, and is disgusted that the object of his affections, Desdemona, has married Othello. Iago claims to hate Othello because he did not make him his second in command, choosing Michael Cassio instead. Iago is resentful of Cassio, too. Iago did not get his promotion, despite the fact that three great ones of the city interceded on his behalf. He bitterly remarks that it is who you know, not what you know, that matters: ***Preferment goes by letter and affection***. Iago is seemingly unaware of the irony of this statement: he also tried to use his connections to gain promotion; it just didn't work.

Iago assures Roderigo that he means to stay close to Othello, but only in order to get his revenge. The audience might assume that Iago is merely trying to placate the scorned lover, but in a stroke of genius, Shakespeare has Iago reveal his true nefarious intentions right from the start: ***I follow him to serve my turn upon him***. Iago speaks his mind in front of Roderigo because he knows that Roderigo poses absolutely no threat to him, and, of course, he wants Roderigo's money (Roderigo is essentially paying Iago to help him gain access to Desdemona). But he also states that he will not be so open with everyone else:

> *For when my outward action doth demonstrate*
> *The native act and figure of my heart*
> *In compliment extern, 'tis not long after*
> *But I will wear my heart upon my sleeve*
> *For daws to peck at. I am not what I am.*

To wear one's heart upon one's sleeve is to be honest and open, but also to be vulnerable. In a way, this describes both Othello and Desdemona.

Egged on by Iago, who is careful to lurk in the shadows so as not to be associated with him (even though he roars inflammatory comments, such as *an old black ram / Is tupping your white ewe*), Roderigo shouts up at Brabantio's apartments from the street. There is a history between the two: *I have charged thee not to haunt about my doors. / In honest plainness thou hast heard me say / My daughter is not for thee.* It seems that Brabantio couldn't think of a worse suitor for his daughter than Roderigo, but this changes when he learns who Desdemona has married. The unseen (but not unheard) Iago winds Brabantio up as much as possible: *Because we come to do you service and you think we are ruffians, you'll have your daughter covered with a Barbary horse, you'll have your nephews neigh to you, you'll have coursers for cousins and gennets for germans.* Iago also describes the consummation of the marriage in bestial terms: *your daughter and the Moor are now making the beast with two backs.* Then, when Roderigo tells Brabantio of his daughter's elopement,

I follow him to serve my turn upon him

– IAGO (ACT I SCENE I)

stealing away in the night with only a gondolier for her protection, to marry Othello –

> *... your fair daughter,*
> *At this odd-even and dull watch o'th' night,*
> *Transported with no worse nor better guard*
> *But with a knave of common hire, a gondolier,*
> *To the gross clasps of a lascivious Moor*

– Brabantio's reaction is as appalled as Iago had hoped: *It is too true an evil. Gone she is, / And what's to come of my despised time / Is nought but bitterness.*

At this juncture, Iago vanishes into the night. He may be a villain, but he is also an astute judge of character and circumstance. He knows Othello is too valuable to the Venetian state to be punished for the elopement. He also knows that it would not be prudent to reveal his hand just yet:

> *It seems not meet nor wholesome to my place*
> *To be produced – as, if I stay, I shall –*
> *Against the Moor, for I do know the state,*
> *However this may gall him with some check,*
> *Cannot with safety cast him.*

Iago's philosophy is 'keep your friends close and your enemies closer'.

Brabantio is convinced that black magic and enchantments are to blame for his daughter's marriage. *Is there not charms / By which the property of youth and maidhood / May be abused?* This is the first sign that, although Othello may seem to occupy a high status in this society, there will always be an underlying assumption that he is capable of things a white man simply would not do.

In Shakespeare's day, women were treated as the property of men. A daughter was her father's possession until marriage, when she became her husband's. A young woman might elope under circumstances in which she knew her father would never agree to the marriage, but there was very little he could do about it once it had happened, for marriage was a sacred, indissoluble bond. It took a very brave woman to go against her family's wishes in this way, so we already know a lot about Desdemona's character before we even meet her.

The second scene of the play presents us with a completely different side to Iago. Now he is Othello's friend and colleague, saying that he was so disgusted at Brabantio's remarks that he almost killed him, but didn't because he has such respect for human life!

> *Though in the trade of war I have slain men,*
> *Yet do I hold it very stuff o'th' conscience*
> *To do no contrived murder. I lack iniquity*
> *Sometime, to do me service. Nine or ten times*
> *I had thought to've yerk'd him here, under the ribs.*

Shakespeare's audiences always reacted enthusiastically to dramatic irony, and Iago's words provide many examples of this.

Othello, holding the rank of general, is clearly very confident of his worth to the Venetian state, its Duke and the senate. He claims that he is not one to boast, but he could if he wished to. As with many characters (and people in real life), Othello's need to sing his own praises is symptomatic of an underlying insecurity:

> *Let him do his spite.*
> *My services which I have done the signory*
> *Shall out-tongue his complaints. 'Tis yet to know –*
> *Which, when I know that boasting is an honour,*
> *I shall promulgate – I fetch my life and being*
> *From men of royal siege, and my demerits*
> *May speak unbonneted to as proud a fortune*
> *As this that I have reach'd.*

Othello does not realise that, in this world of courtly code and intrigue, little value is put on another culture's aristocracy. Shakespeare may once again be commenting on his own society, and its treatment of outsiders.

What is also significant is that Othello clearly didn't marry for the sake of it. He enjoyed being free and single, but true love compelled him to give up a life that he plainly relished. *For know, Iago, / But that I love the gentle Desdemona, / I would not my unhoused free condition / Put into circumscription and confine / For the seas' worth.*

Iago pretends to be protective of Othello, advising him to go inside the inn when they see men with torches approaching. Here again Othello's self-confidence seems remarkable: *My parts, my title, and my perfect soul / Shall manifest me rightly.*

In Act II the setting of the play changes to Cyprus, and we are prepared for this change of scene when the first group of men turn out to be a search party from the senate, seeking the invaluable Othello. Among them is Cassio, against whom Iago also professed a vendetta in the first scene: *Something from Cyprus, as I may divine; / It is a business of some heat. ... You have been hotly call'd for ...*

Brabantio and his men arrive hot on the heels of the Duke's men, and an incensed Brabantio repeats his accusations of black magic:

> *O thou foul thief, where hast thou stow'd my*
> > *daughter?*
> *Damn'd as thou art, thou hast enchanted her,*
> *For I'll refer me to all things of sense,*
> *If she in chains of magic were not bound,*
> *Whether a maid so tender, fair, and happy,*
> *So opposite to marriage that she shunned*
> *The wealthy curled darlings of our nation,*
> *Would ever have, t'incur a general mock,*
> *Run from her guardage to the sooty bosom*
> *Of such a thing as thou – to fear, not to delight.*

Othello's reaction is measured and courteous: he simply asks Brabantio where he wishes to put the charges to him. Clearly, Othello thinks the Venetian senate will take his side. Brabantio is equally convinced they will take his, and Scene II ends on a note of suspense:

Mine's not an idle cause. The Duke himself,
Or any of my brothers of the state,
Cannot but feel this wrong as 'twere their own;
For if such actions may have passage free,
Bondslaves and pagans shall our statesmen be.

Scene III begins with the late night meeting of the senate to discuss the Turkish offensive. Reports are mixed, both as to the number of Turkish vessels and the actual direction of the Turkish fleet. Some reports say that it is in fact headed towards Rhodes. The senate know that this is unlikely: *'tis a pageant / To keep us in false gaze.*

These conflicting reports create suspense, and they also give Shakespeare an opportunity to establish the cultural context. His English audience would have been fascinated by warfare, and by the mention of these strange and exotic places. When confirmed sightings of the Turkish fleet's real destination are reported (**bearing with frank appearance / Their purposes toward Cyprus**), the senate conclude that there is really only one person for the job: Othello. **Valiant Othello, we must straight employ you / Against the general enemy Ottoman.**

It is interesting to note that when Brabantio first tells the Duke of the theft of his daughter, the Duke could not be more sympathetic, promising that even if the guilty party were his own son, he would be severely punished:

Whoe'er he be that in this foul proceeding
Hath thus beguiled your daughter of herself

*That I did love the Moor to
live with him,
My downright violence and
storm of fortunes
May trumpet to the world*

– DESDEMONA (ACT I SCENE III)

*And you of her, the bloody book of law
You shall yourself read in the bitter letter
After your own sense, yea, though our proper son
Stood in your action.*

This all changes when the invaluable Othello is named as the culprit. The Duke gives Othello a chance to answer the charges against him, for Brabantio is quite unequivocal in his accusation that some sort of witchcraft must have been employed: *I therefore vouch again / That with some mixtures powerful o'er the blood, / Or with some dram conjured to this effect, / He wrought upon her.*

His portrayal of Desdemona does in fact seem quite at odds with such a daring elopement and choice of husband:

*A maiden never bold,
Of spirit so still and quiet, that her motion*

*Blush'd at herself – and she in spite of nature,
Of years, of country, credit, everything,
To fall in love with what she fear'd to look on!*

Othello suggests that Desdemona herself be questioned about the methods he used to seduce her, showing that theirs was a rather atypical marriage for the time. He is happy to bet his life upon her words: *If you do find me foul in her report, / The trust, the office I do hold of you / Not only take away, but let your sentence / Even fall upon my life.*

While the senate waits for Desdemona to arrive, Othello explains how they came to fall in love. The first surprise is that it is clear that he and Brabantio were once close: *Her father loved me, oft invited me …* Thus, Brabantio befriended Othello, to an extent, though that does not mean that he wanted him to marry his daughter. In a way, this is how everyone treats Othello. They think very well of him, but only up to a point. There is a boundary to their affection, but Othello fails to see this. Othello's exoticism seems to attract and repel in equal measure. Desdemona is the exception. Othello reports how avidly she listened to the stories of his exploits: *And of the cannibals that each other eat, / The Anthropophagi, and men whose heads / Do grow beneath their shoulders. These things to hear / Would Desdemona seriously incline.* He also paints a rather different portrait of Desdemona from the modest girl Brabantio had depicted:

> *... she wish'd*
> *That heaven had made her such a man. She thanked me,*
> *And bade me, if I had a friend that loved her,*
> *I should but teach him how to tell my story.*
> *And that would woo her.*

Desdemona seems to have been quite forthcoming in her affection for Othello, and although Othello claims to lack eloquence, his erudition is striking. He explains that Desdemona loved him for being so brave, and he loved her for understanding him: *She loved me for the dangers I had pass'd, / And I loved her that she did pity them.*

Rather touchingly, Othello adds that the only witchcraft he used was his adventurous past. It is clear that Desdemona was not enchanted or exploited in any way; she and Othello simply fell in love. The effect of Othello's stories on those who hear them is evident when the Duke says, *I think this tale would win my daughter, too.* Yet Brabantio is still absolutely convinced that his daughter would never have married Othello of her own free will, and would certainly never have betrayed her father in such an uncharacteristic manner: *If she confess that she was half the wooer, / Destruction on my head if my bad blame / Light on the man!*

Our first positive impression of Desdemona is formed when she stands up to her father, but in a respectful way:

> *I do perceive here a divided duty.*
> *To you I am bound for life and education.*
> *My life and education both do learn me*
> *How to respect you. You are the lord of duty,*
> *I am hitherto your daughter. But here's my husband,*
> *And so much duty as my mother show'd*
> *To you, preferring you before her father,*
> *So much I challenge that I may profess*
> *Due to the Moor my lord.*

Brabantio is astonished that he could have been so wrong about his daughter. The Duke tries to comfort him – or perhaps to smooth things over, so as to get on with the real business at hand – but Brabantio is not to be comforted. He compares the loss of Desdemona, and what this means to him, to how Venice would feel if it lost Cyprus to the Turks.

Othello agrees to go to Cyprus immediately. His value as a military general is seen in his nonchalance about going to this foreign place with all the challenges that poses: *The tyrant custom, most grave senators, / Hath made the flinty and steel couch of war / My thrice-driven bed of down.*

The next surprise comes when Desdemona refuses to stay in Venice with her father and asks to go with her husband. Women at this time, especially women of Desdemona's class, were kept well away from such a dangerous place, but Desdemona plainly loves her new husband more than she loves her own safety. She explains to the senate that she has not given up everything to marry Othello only to be parted from him so quickly: *That I did love the Moor to live with him, / My downright violence and storm of fortunes / May trumpet to the world.* Desdemona's loyalty is striking,

*I think this tale would
win my daughter, too*

– DUKE (ACT I SCENE III)

and so too is Othello's regard for her. He even explains that he wants her to accompany him, not out of a need for her physical presence, but because he wants her good company and conversation:

I therefore beg it not

To please the palate of my appetite

Nor to comply with heat – the young affects

In me defunct – and proper satisfaction,

But to be free and bounteous to her mind ...

Ironically, it is Iago to whom Othello entrusts his most precious possession, and this is one of the many times he describes him with the adjective 'honest'. The Duke tries to appease Brabantio one last time, although to no avail: *If virtue no delighted beauty lack, / Your son-in-law is far more fair than black.* Brabantio's parting shot to Othello is spoken out of his wounded pride, but it will have fatal repercussions later in the play: *Look to her, Moor, if thou hast eyes to see. / She has deceived her father, and may thee.*

The first act concludes as it began, with a conversation between Iago and Roderigo. Roderigo thinks that his pursuit of Desdemona has been in vain, and wants to kill himself. Iago talks him out of suicide, not out of concern, but because he loves Roderigo's money. He tells Roderigo to sell everything he can so as to get access to ready cash, and to use this money to travel to Cyprus so that he can win Desdemona back. Iago is convincing in his assertion that Desdemona will soon tire of Othello physically. He may be lying; or he may simply be judging others by his own standards: *She must change for youth. When she is sated with his body, she will find the error of her choice.*

Iago soliloquises at the end of this scene. A soliloquy can always be viewed as the absolute truth, so Iago's soliloquy alerts us to his true villainy. Iago calls Roderigo a fool, and makes a rather throwaway comment about Othello and his own wife, Emilia, having had an affair: *I hate the Moor / And it is thought abroad, that 'twixt my sheets / He has done my office.*

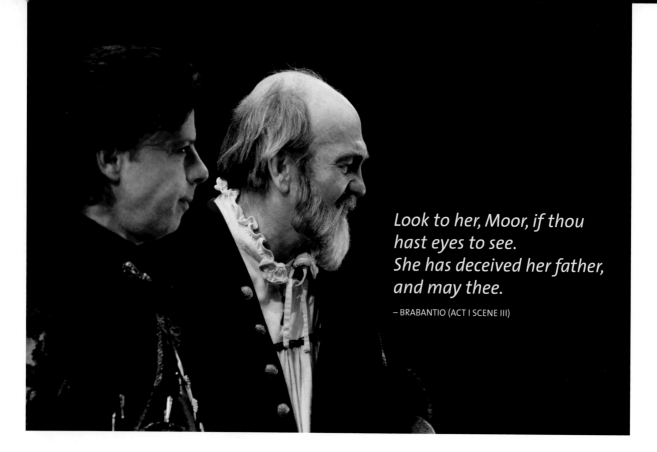

*Look to her, Moor, if thou
hast eyes to see.
She has deceived her father,
and may thee.*

– BRABANTIO (ACT I SCENE III)

Iago reveals his entire plan, which seems so simple as to be positively futile. He is going to make Othello jealous of Cassio and Desdemona: *to abuse Othello's ears / That he* [Cassio] *is too familiar with his wife.* Ironically, Iago's nefarious plan might actually work because

> *The Moor is of a free and open nature,*
> *That thinks men honest that but seem to be so,*
> *And will as tenderly be led by th' nose*
> *As asses are.*

IMPORTANT THEMES IN ACT I

• The theme of revenge is seen in Iago's quest to destroy Othello, for what he sees as Othello's slight in appointing Cassio over him.

• The theme of love is seen in Othello and Desdemona's elopement. Their marriage seems to be a true meeting of minds, their friendship having formed a solid basis for their relationship.

• The theme of racism is seen in Roderigo and Iago's derogatory terms for Othello's racial features, and also in Brabantio being quite happy to have Othello as a friend, but not as a son-in-law.

CHARACTER DEVELOPMENT IN ACT I

• The antagonist Iago is clearly a manipulative and conscienceless villain. He sees other people merely as obstacles or aids to his ambition. He is often considered to be the most villainous of all Shakespeare's villains.

• Roderigo is a pathetic creature, trying to buy the affections of a woman who has repeatedly refused him. Many actors playing Roderigo play him for laughs, and this adds much-needed comic relief to the play.

• Othello, once a slave, has risen to the highest ranks of the Venetian military. He is a stereotypical hero in every way but one: his colour.

• Desdemona shows considerable courage in defying her father. Her absolute love for Othello is clear right from the start.

• Brabantio is deeply hurt by his daughter's betrayal and outraged by her choice of husband. A general would normally be considered excellent husband material, but Brabantio is fearful of Othello's exotic roots, and worried for his daughter.

QUESTIONS ON ACT 1

1. **Do you think that Iago has any justification for his vendetta against Othello? Support your answer with reference to the text.**

2. **Write a diary entry for Roderigo in which he shares his feelings about Desdemona, Othello and Iago.**

3. **Write a love letter from Othello to Desdemona or from Desdemona to Othello written at any time prior to their marriage.**

4. **Write a list of five insulting terms that Iago and/or Roderigo use about Othello.**

5. **Why do you think Shakespeare supplies so much military detail in this act? Refer to the original audience in your answer.**

6. **Why, in your opinion, did Desdemona elope with Othello rather than have the traditional wedding that most young women would opt for?**

7. **You are a secretary recording the night's events in the senate. Write a formal report on what you witnessed, using details from the text (Brabantio's accusations, Othello's response, etc.).**

8. **Write a newspaper report for the Venetian Times with the title 'Othello and Desdemona's Secret Nuptials'.**

9. **Iago has more soliloquies than any other character in Othello. Read his soliloquy at the end of Scene III, and then explain why you think it is so crucial for this character to soliloquise.**

10. **Individually or in pairs, pick out what you think are the ten best quotations from Act I, explaining in each case why you have chosen that quotation. Make sure they cover a range of characters and themes.**

OTHELLO **ACT** **2**

A SEA-PORT IN CYPRUS. AN OPEN PLACE NEAR THE QUAY

Enter Montano and two Gentlemen

Montano   What from the cape can you discern at sea?

1st Gentleman   Nothing at all. It is a high-wrought flood.
I cannot, 'twixt the heaven and the main[1]
Descry[2] a sail.

Montano   Methinks the wind hath spoke aloud at land.[3]   5
A fuller blast ne'er shook our battlements,
If it ha' ruffian'd[4] so upon the sea,
What ribs of oak,[5] when mountains melt on them,
Can hold the mortise?[6] What shall we hear of this?

2nd Gentleman   A segregation of the Turkish fleet;   10
For do but stand upon the foaming shore,
The chidden billow[7] seems to pelt the clouds,
The wind-shaked surge,[8] with high and monstrous mane
Seems to cast water on the burning Bear[9]
And quench the guards of th'ever-fixed Pole.   15
I never did like molestation[10] view
On the enchafed[11] flood.

Montano   If that the Turkish fleet
Be not enshelter'd and embay'd,[12] they are drown'd.
It is impossible they bear it out.   20

Enter a 3rd Gentleman

3rd Gentleman   News, lads! Our wars are done.
The desperate tempest hath so bang'd[13] the Turks,
That their designment[14] halts. A noble ship of Venice
Hath seen[15] a grievous wreck and sufferance
On most part of their fleet.   25

Montano   How, is this true?

3rd Gentleman   The ship is here put in,
A Veronesa.[16] Michael Cassio,
Lieutenant to the warlike Moor Othello,
Is come on shore; the Moor himself at sea,   30

---

[1] Between the sky and the sea
[2] See
[3] It is also windy inland
[4] Raged
[5] Wooden ships
[6] Can stay joined together
[7] Angry waves
[8] Stormy waters
[9] The Little Bear (Ursa Minor) is a constellation of stars that was used to guide sailors
[10] Vexing
[11] Angry
[12] In a safe port
[13] Destroyed
[14] Enterprise
[15] Witnessed
[16] From Verona

	And is in full commission here for Cyprus.	
Montano	I am glad on't; 'tis a worthy governor.	
3rd Gentleman	But this same Cassio, though he speak of comfort	
	Touching the Turkish loss, yet he looks sadly,	
	And prays the Moor be safe, for they were parted	35
	With foul and violent tempest.	
Montano	Pray heavens he be,	
	For I have served him, and the man commands	
	Like a full soldier. Let's to the sea-side, ho! –	
	As well to see the vessel that's come in	40
	As to throw out our eyes for brave Othello,	
	Even till we make the main[17] and th'aerial blue[18]	
	An indistinct regard.[19]	
3rd Gentleman	Come, let's do so,	
	For every minute is expectancy	45
	Of more arrivance.[20]	

Enter Cassio

Cassio	Thanks, you the valiant of this warlike isle	
	That so approve the Moor! O, let the heavens	
	Give him defence against the elements,	
	For I have lost him on a dangerous sea.	50
Montano	Is he well shipp'd?[21]	
Cassio	His barque is stoutly timber'd,[22] his pilot	
	Of very expert and approved allowance.[23]	
	Therefore my hopes, not surfeited to death,[24]	
	Stand in bold cure.[25]	55

A cry within 'A sail, a sail, a sail!'
Enter a 4th Gentleman

Cassio	What noise?
4th Gentleman	The town is empty. On the brow o'th' sea
	Stand ranks of people, and they cry 'A sail!'
Cassio	My hopes do shape him for the governor.

[17] Sea [18] Sky
[19] Indistinguishable

[20] One might arrive at any moment

[21] Is his ship a good one?

[22] His ship is well built
[23] Experience
[24] Not overly optimistic
[25] Are realistic of success

Guns heard

2nd Gentlemen   They do discharge their shot of courtesy[26]–   60
Our friends, at least.

Cassio   I pray you, sir, go forth,
And give us truth who 'tis that is arrived.

2nd Gentleman   I shall.

Exit

Montano   But, good lieutenant, is your general wived?[27]   65

Cassio   Most fortunately. He hath achieved a maid
That paragons[28] description and wild fame,
One that excels the quirks of blazoning pens,
And in th'essential vesture of creation
Does tire the engineer.   70

Re-enter 2nd Gentleman

How now, who has put in?

2nd Gentleman   'Tis one Iago, ensign to the general.

Cassio   He's had most favourable and happy speed.
Tempests themselves, high seas, and howling winds,
The gutter'd[29] rocks and congregated sands –   75
Traitors ensteep'd[30] to clog the guiltless keel,[31] –
As having sense of beauty do omit
Their mortal natures, letting go safely by
The divine Desdemona.

Montano   What is she?   80

Cassio   She that I spake of, our great captain's captain,
Left in the conduct of the bold Iago,
Whose footing here anticipates our thoughts
A se'nnight's[32] speed. Great Jove,[33] Othello guard,
And swell his sail with thine own powerful breath,   85
That he may bless this bay with his tall ship,
Make love's quick pants in Desdemona's arms,
Give renew'd fire to our extincted[34] spirits
And bring all Cyprus comfort.

[26] A traditional greeting to show that the ship is friendly

[27] Married

[28] Surpasses

Cassio says that Desdemona's beauty and character are too great to be expressed in mere words by any poet, no matter how hard he tries to describe her excellence

[29] Jagged

[30] Submerged   [31] Part of a ship's hull

[32] Week (seven nights)   [33] God

[34] Extinguished

Enter Desdemona, Emilia, Iago, Roderigo, and Attendants

O, behold,   90
The riches of the ship is come on shore!
Ye men of Cyprus, let her have your knees.
Hail to thee, lady, and the grace of heaven
Before, behind thee, and on every hand,
Enwheel thee round!   95

Desdemona   I thank you, valiant Cassio.
What tidings can you tell me of my lord?

Cassio   He is not yet arrived, nor know I aught
But that he's well and will be shortly here.

Desdemona   O, but I fear – how lost you company?   100

Cassio   The great contention[35] of the sea and skies
Parted our fellowship. But, hark! a sail.

Within 'A sail, a sail!' Guns heard

2nd Gentleman   They give their greeting to the citadel.[36]
This likewise is a friend.

Cassio   See for the news.   105

Exit Gentleman

Good ensign, you are welcome.
[To Emilia] Welcome, mistress.
Let it not gall your patience,[37] good Iago,
That I extend my manners. 'Tis my breeding
That gives me this bold show of courtesy.   110
Kissing her

Iago   Sir, would she give you so much of her lips
As of her tongue she oft bestows on me,
You would have enough.

Desdemona   Alas, she has no speech!

Iago   In faith, too much.   115
I find it still, when I ha' leave to sleep:

35 *Storm*

36 *Fortress*

37 *Annoy you*

Iago pretends to be a browbeaten husband, who gets frequent tongue lashings from Emilia

Marry,[38] before your ladyship, I grant,
She puts her tongue a little in her heart,[39]
And chides[40] with thinking.

Emilia   You ha' little cause to say so.   120

Iago   Come on, come on. You are pictures out of doors,
Bells in your parlours, wildcats in your kitchens,
Saints in your injuries, devils being offended,
Players in your housewifery, and hussies in your beds.

Desdemona   O, fie upon thee, slanderer!   125

Iago   Nay, it is true, or else I am a Turk.
You rise to play and go to bed to work.

Emilia   You shall not write my praise.

Iago   No, let me not.

Desdemona   What wouldst write of me, if thou shouldst praise me?   130

Iago   O gentle lady, do not put me to't;
For I am nothing if not critical.

Desdemona   Come on essay[41] – There's one gone to the harbour?

Iago   Ay, madam.

Desdemona   I am not merry, but I do beguile   135
The thing I am by seeming otherwise.[42]
Come, how wouldst thou praise me?

Iago   I am about it, but indeed my invention
Comes from my pate as birdlime does from frieze[43] –
It plucks out brains and all. But my muse[44] labours,   140
And thus she is deliver'd.
If she be fair and wise, fairness and wit,
The one's for use, the other useth it.

Desdemona   Well praised! How if she be black[45] and witty?

Iago   If she be black, and thereto have a wit,   145
She'll find a white that shall her blackness fit.

[38] By Mary
[39] She stays quiet in front of Desdemona
[40] Gives out

Iago claims that women look beautiful when they go outside, but in private they are noisy, they act like wildcats, make themselves sound like saints when they are complaining, but act like devils when they are offended, only play at doing their housework, and act like hussies in bed

[41] Try

[42] She is trying to distract herself from worry by bantering with Iago

[43] Iago claims to have a limited imagination: his thoughts stick to his brain as birdlime (a sticky substance used to trap birds) sticks to frieze, a heavy woollen material

[44] Imagination

If a woman is good-looking and clever, she can use her good looks to get what she wants

[45] 'Black' in this sense may mean ugly

Desdemona	Worse and worse.
Emilia	How if fair and foolish?
Iago	She never yet was foolish that was fair;
	For even her folly[46] help'd her to an heir. 150
Desdemona	These are old fond paradoxes[47] to make fools laugh i'th' alehouse. What miserable praise hast thou for her that's foul and foolish?
Iago	There's none so foul and foolish thereunto,
	But does foul pranks which fair and wise ones do. 155
Desdemona	O heavy ignorance! Thou praisest the worst best. But what praise couldst thou bestow on a deserving woman indeed – one that, in the authority of her merit, did justly put on the vouch of very malice itself?[48]
Iago	She that was ever fair and never proud, 160
	Had tongue at will and yet was never loud,
	Never lack'd gold and yet went never gay,
	Fled from her wish, and yet said 'Now I may';
	She that, being anger'd, her revenge being nigh,
	Bade her wrong stay and her displeasure fly; 165
	She that in wisdom never was so frail
	To change the cod's head for the salmon's tail;[49]
	She that could think and ne'er disclose her mind,
	See suitors following, and not look behind,
	She was a wight,[50] if ever such wights were – 170
Desdemona	To do what?
Iago	To suckle fools, and chronicle small beer.[51]
Desdemona	O most lame and impotent conclusion! Do not learn of him, Emilia, though he be thy husband. How say you, Cassio, is he not a most profane[52] and liberal 175 counsellor?
Cassio	He speaks home,[53] madam: You may relish him more in the soldier than in the scholar.
Iago	*[Aside]* He takes her by the palm. Ay, well said –

[46] Weakness

[47] Old wives' tales

[48] A truly good woman who is impervious to criticism

[49] To swap something useless for something valuable – this may be a sexual reference

[50] A super-human (meaning that such a woman could not exist)

[51] To be concerned with trivial matters

[52] Disrespectful

[53] Bluntly

whisper. With as little a web as this will I ensnare   180
as great a fly as Cassio. Ay, smile upon her, do. I will
gyve[54] thee in thine own courtship. You say true,
'tis so indeed. If such tricks as these strip you out
of your lieutenantry, it had been better you had
not kissed your three fingers so oft, which now   185
again you are most apt to play the sir in.
Very good, well kissed, an excellent curtsy, 'tis
so indeed; yet again your fingers to your lips?
Would they were clyster-pipes[55] for your sake.

Trumpet within

The Moor – I know his trumpet.   190

Cassio   'Tis truly so.

Desdemona   Let's meet him and receive him.

Cassio   Lo where he comes!

Enter Othello and Attendants

Othello   O my fair warrior!

Desdemona   My dear Othello!   195

Othello   It gives me wonder great as my content
To see you here before me. O my soul's joy!
If after every tempest come such calms,
May the winds blow till they have waken'd death,
And let the labouring barque[56] climb hills of seas   200
Olympus-high,[57] and duck again as low
As hell's from heaven. If it were now to die,
'Twere now to be most happy, for I fear
My soul hath her content so absolute
That not another comfort like to this   205
Succeeds in unknown fate.

Desdemona   The heavens forbid
But that our loves and comforts should increase
Even as our days do grow.

Othello   Amen to that, sweet powers!   210

I cannot speak enough of this content.
It stops me here, it is too much of joy.
And this, and this, the greatest discords[58] be

58 *Conflicts*

[*Kissing her*]
That e'er our hearts shall make.

Iago [*Aside*] O, you are well tuned now,   215
But I'll set down the pegs that make this music,
As honest as I am.

Othello Come, let us to the castle.
News, friends: our wars are done, the Turks are drown'd.
How does my old acquaintance of this isle? –   220
Honey, you shall be well desired in Cyprus;
I have found great love amongst them. O my sweet,
I prattle out of fashion,[59] and I dote

59 *Babble out of happiness*

In mine own comforts. I prithee, good Iago,

60 *Luggage*

Go to the bay and disembark my coffers.[60]   225
Bring thou the master to the citadel.
He is a good one, and his worthiness
Does challenge much respect. Come, Desdemona.
Once more, well met at Cyprus.

Exit Othello, Desdemona, and Attendants

Iago [*To attendant*] Do thou meet me presently at the harbour. 230
[*To Roderigo*] Come hither. If thou be'est valiant – as
they say base men being in love have then a nobility in

61 *Listen to*

their natures more than is native to them – list me.[61]
The lieutenant tonight watches on the court of guard.
First, I must tell thee this: Desdemona is directly in love   235
with him.

Roderigo With him? Why, 'tis not possible!

Iago Lay thy finger thus, and let thy soul be instructed.
Mark me with what violence she first loved the Moor,
but for bragging and telling her fantastical lies.   240

62 *Chattering*

To love him still for prating?[62] – let not thy discreet heart
think it. Her eye must be fed and what delight shall she
have to look on the devil? When the blood is made dull

63 *Sexual activity*

with the act of sport,[63] there should be again to inflame it

64 *Being sated (satisfied, not hungry any more)*

and to give satiety[64] a fresh appetite, loveliness in favour, 245
sympathy in years, manners, and beauties; all which

the Moor is defective in. Now, for want of these required
conveniences, her delicate tenderness will find itself
abused, begin to heave the gorge,[65] disrelish[66] and
abhor[67] the Moor. Very nature will instruct her in it and   250
compel her to some second choice. Now, sir, this
granted – as it is a most pregnant and unforced position
– who stands so eminent in the degree of this fortune as
Cassio does? – a knave very voluble,[68] no further
conscionable[69] than in putting on the mere form of civil   255
and humane[70] seeming for the better compass of his salt
and most hidden loose affection.[71] Why, none; why, none
– a slipper[72] and subtle knave, a finder of occasion,[73] that
has an eye can stamp and counterfeit advantages,[74]
though true advantage never present itself, a devilish   260
knave! Besides, the knave is handsome, young, and hath
all those requisites[75] in him that folly and green[76] minds
look after. A pestilent complete knave, and the woman
hath found him already.

Roderigo   I cannot believe that in her. She's full of most blessed   265
condition.[77]

Iago   Blessed fig's-end! The wine she drinks is made of
grapes. If she had been blessed, she would never
have loved the Moor. Blessed pudding! Didst thou
not see her paddle with the palm of his hand? Didst   270
not mark that?

Roderigo   Yes, that I did, but that was but courtesy.

Iago   Lechery, by this hand; an index and obscure prologue[78]
to the history of lust and foul thoughts. They met
so near with their lips that their breaths embraced   275
together. Villanous thoughts, Roderigo! When these
mutualities[79] so marshal the way, hard at hand comes
the master and main exercise, th'incorporate[80]
conclusion. Pish! But, sir, be you ruled by me. I
have brought you from Venice. Watch you tonight.   280
For the command, I'll lay't upon you. Cassio knows
you not. I'll not be far from you. Do[81] you find
some occasion to anger Cassio, either by speaking
too loud, or tainting[82] his discipline, or from what
other course you please, which the time shall more   285

65 *Feel sick*   66 *Dislike*
67 *Hate*

68 *Eloquent*
69 *Conscientious*
70 *Courteous*
71 *Iago claims that Cassio's excellent manners hide his lewdness*
72 *Slippery*   73 *Opportunist*
74 *Invent opportunities*

75 *Characteristics*   76 *Gullible*

77 *Qualities*

78 *A complicated beginning*

79 *Intimacies*
80 *Physical*

81 *If*

82 *Flouting*

favourably minister.

Roderigo Well.

Iago Sir, he's rash and very sudden in choler,[83] and haply
may strike at you. Provoke him that he may, for
even out of that will I cause these of Cyprus to   290
mutiny, whose qualification shall come into no true
taste again but by the displanting[84] of Cassio. So
shall you have a shorter journey to your desires by
the means I shall then have to prefer them, and the
impediment[85] most profitably removed, without the   295
which there were no expectation of our prosperity.[86]

Roderigo I will do this, if I can bring it to any opportunity.

Iago I warrant thee. Meet me by and by at the citadel.
I must fetch his necessaries ashore. Farewell.

Roderigo Adieu.   300

Exit

Iago That Cassio loves her, I do well believe it.
That she loves him, 'tis apt[87] and of great credit.[88]
The Moor – howbe't[89] that I endure him not –
Is of a constant, loving, noble nature,
And I dare think he'll prove to Desdemona   305
A most dear husband. Now I do love her too,
Not out of absolute lust, though peradventure[90]
I stand accountant for as great a sin –
But partly led to diet my revenge
For that I do suspect the lusty Moor   310
Hath leap'd into my seat,[91] the thought whereof
Doth, like a poisonous mineral, gnaw my inwards;
And nothing can or shall content my soul
Till I am even'd with him, wife for wife –
Or failing so, yet that I put the Moor   315
At least into a jealousy so strong
That judgement cannot cure, which thing to do,
If this poor trash of Venice whom I trace
For his quick hunting stand the putting on,
I'll have our Michael Cassio on the hip,   320
Abuse him to the Moor in the rank garb[92]–

83 *Quick to anger*
84 *Firing*
85 *Obstacle*
86 *Without which we cannot succeed*
87 *Likely* 88 *Credible*
89 *Even though*
90 *Perhaps*
91 *Has slept with Emilia*
92 *Coarse fashion*

For I fear Cassio with my nightcap, too[93] –
Make the Moor thank me, love me, and reward me
For making him egregiously[94] an ass,
And practising upon his peace and quiet   325
Even to madness. 'Tis here, but yet confused.
Knavery's plain face is never seen till used.[95]

Exit

[93] *Cassio has worn his nightcap (slept with his wife)*

[94] *Stand out as*

[95] *Plots should remain secret until their execution*

News, lads! Our wars are done.
The desperate tempest hath so bang'd the Turks,
That their designment halts

– 3RD GENTLEMAN

IN THIS SCENE, the action moves from Venice to Cyprus, which will be the setting for the rest of the play. Shakespeare's talent for creating vivid imagery is clearly seen in the descriptions of the storm. Within a few moments we learn that the Turkish fleet has been sunk, and the war is over before it has even begun. This is an interesting narrative choice by Shakespeare, made perhaps to keep the focus on domestic, rather than national, conflict.

We get to know Cassio much better in this scene. He is a loyal and capable lieutenant, and he has the highest opinion of both Desdemona and Othello. His concern for Othello's safely clearly indicates his loyalty: *O, let the heavens / Give him defence against the elements.*

Iago arrives with Desdemona and her lady-in-waiting, Emilia, Iago's wife. While everyone waits anxiously for Othello's ship to arrive, Iago and Desdemona engage in a bout of verbal jousting. Desdemona is witty and articulate, and more than able to deal with Iago's rather misogynist remarks. Iago's views on women (that good-looking, clever women use their brains to manipulate men, while good-looking, dull women use their looks, and ugly, dull women use their bodies) are presented in a humorous manner so as to ensure that everyone thinks he is joking. But Iago clearly does hate women, and he will go on to demonstrate this inexplicable hatred repeatedly throughout the play.

Cassio's exquisite manners are gleefully noted by Iago, as he realises that he can use Cassio's chivalrous attentions towards Desdemona to make Othello conclude that there is something more than friendship between them. Iago is jealous of Cassio's looks and breeding, and assumes Othello will be too.

Othello's ship arrives safely, and he and Desdemona are joyfully reunited. Othello eloquently expresses how happy he is: *It gives me wonder great as my content / To see you here before me. O my soul's joy!* Iago acknowledges that this couple could be very happy together, but is determined to destroy any possibility of this happening.

In contrast with the love we see between Othello and Desdemona, Iago's plotting with – and against – Roderigo seems quite repulsive. Iago tries to make Roderigo jealous of Cassio (which proves easy as Roderigo is so gullible), and orders him to anger Cassio in some way. Although Iago may have many negative qualities, he is an astute and accurate observer of human nature, and this is what makes him so very dangerous. He mentions that Cassio has a quick temper, and he will use this flaw against him, just as he will use Othello's flaw – jealousy – against him. The scene ends with another soliloquy from Iago, in which he unconvincingly tries to justify his behaviour towards Othello, and Cassio, by claiming to believe that they have both slept with Emilia. Iago is shrewd and intelligent, and his cruel plan creates tension and suspense.

KEY **POINTS**

- *The Turkish fleet sinks, and the war is called off.*

- *Despite a great storm, everyone arrives safely in Cyprus.*

- *Othello and Desdemona's deep love is apparent for all to see.*

- *Iago's plot expands to include Cassio's destruction.*

- *Roderigo is a mere pawn in Iago's game.*

- *Iago is not to be underestimated. He is extremely clever, charming, charismatic, funny and a consummate actor.*

A STREET

Enter a Herald with a proclamation; People following

Herald   It is Othello's pleasure – our noble and valiant
general – that, upon certain tidings now arrived
importing[1] the mere perdition[2] of the Turkish fleet,
every man put himself into triumph: some to dance,
some to make bonfires, each man to what sport and   5
revels[3] his addiction leads him; for besides these
beneficial news, it is the celebration of his
nuptial. So much was his pleasure should be
proclaimed. All offices[4] are open, and there is full
liberty of feasting from this present hour of five   10
till the bell have told eleven. Heaven bless the
isle of Cyprus and our noble general, Othello!

Exit

[1] *Reporting*   [2] *Destruction*

[3] *Festivities*

[4] *Kitchens*

SCENE **ANALYSIS**

THIS BRIEF SCENE consists of a Herald reading a proclamation from Othello. Because war has been averted, and he has recently married, he is ordering the whole island to celebrate the good news. Everyone can enjoy whatever takes their fancy, and free food will be supplied. The party is to last from five until eleven. This tells us that Othello is a benevolent general, generous and kind. But there is also a curfew, which suggests restraint too. He wants everyone to feel some of his own personal happiness. This scene, with its straightforward tone of celebration, contrasts with the intrigue of the previous one. We are also aware that people will let their guards down this evening – and this may suit Iago's purposes very well indeed.

KEY **POINTS**

• *Othello is a popular and generous ruler.*

• *The Cypriots are to feast and make merry.*

A HALL IN THE CASTLE

Enter Othello, Desdemona, Cassio, and Attendants

Othello Good Michael, look you to the guard tonight:
Let's teach ourselves that honourable stop[1]
Not to outsport discretion.[2]

Cassio Iago hath direction[3] what to do,
But notwithstanding, with my personal eye   5
Will I look to't.

Othello  Iago is most honest.
Michael, good night. Tomorrow with your earliest
Let me have speech with you.
[To Desdemona]
Come, my dear love,   10
The purchase made, the fruits are to ensue.
That profit's yet to come 'tween me and you.
Good night.

Exit Othello, Desdemona, and Attendants

Enter Iago

Cassio Welcome, Iago. We must to the watch.[4]

Iago Not this hour, lieutenant; 'tis not yet ten o'th'clock.   15
Our general cast[5] us thus early for the love of his
Desdemona, who let us not therefore blame. He hath
not yet made wanton the night with her,[6] and she is
sport for Jove.[7]

Cassio She's a most exquisite lady.   20

Iago And, I'll warrant her, fun of game.[8]

Cassio Indeed, she's a most fresh and delicate creature.

Iago What an eye she has! Methinks it sounds a parley of
provocation.[9]

Cassio An inviting eye, and yet, methinks, right modest.   25

Side notes (left margin):

[1] Let's know our limits
[2] Not to cross the line into drunkenness

[3] Orders

The marriage ceremony has taken place; now they will consummate their union

[4] We must go on duty as night guards

[5] Left

[6] Othello hasn't slept with Desdemona yet
[7] She is good enough for God

[8] Lust

[9] Iago claims that Desdemona's eyes are provocative and sexually inviting

Iago	And when she speaks, is it not an alarum[10] to love?	[10] *Signal*
Cassio	She is indeed perfection.	
Iago	Well, happiness to their sheets. Come, lieutenant. I have a stoup[11] of wine, and here without are a brace[12] of Cyprus gallants[13] that would fain have a measure[14] to the health of black Othello.	[11] *Beaker* [12] *Pair* [13] *Countrymen* [14] *Like to drink*

30

Cassio	Not tonight, good Iago. I have very poor and unhappy brains for drinking. I could well wish courtesy would invent some other custom of entertainment.	
Iago	O, they are our friends! But one cup. I'll drink for you.	

35

Cassio	I ha' drunk but one cup tonight, and that was craftily qualified,[15] too, and behold what innovation[16] it makes here! I am infortunate in the infirmity,[17] and dare not task my weakness with any more.	[15] *Well-diluted* [16] *Change* [17] *He gets drunk very easily*
Iago	What, man, 'tis a night of revels, the gallants desire it!	

40

Cassio	Where are they?
Iago	Here at the door. I pray you call them in.
Cassio	I'll do't, but it dislikes me.
	Exit

Iago	If I can fasten but one cup upon him, With that which he hath drunk tonight already He'll be as full of quarrel and offence As my young mistress' dog. Now my sick fool Roderigo, Whom love hath turn'd almost the wrong side out, To Desdemona hath tonight caroused[18] Potations pottle-deep,[19] and he's to watch. Three else of Cyprus – noble swelling spirits That hold their honours in a wary distance, The very elements of this warlike isle – Have I tonight fluster'd with flowing cups, And they watch too. Now 'mongst this flock of drunkards Am I to put our Cassio in some action That may offend the isle. But here they come.	[18] *Toasted* [19] *Large portions of strong liquor* ***Iago has made three Cypriots – whom he claims are very easy to offend – drunk***

45

50

55

[20] *If things turn out the way he wants*

[21] *His plan will work*

If consequence do but approve my dream,[20]
My boat sails freely[21] both with wind and stream.

*Re-enter Cassio; with him Montano and Gentlemen;
servants following with wine*

[22] *Large drink*

Cassio Fore God, they have given me a rouse[22] already. 60

Montano Good faith, a little one; not past a pint,
As I am a soldier.

Iago Some wine, ho! *[Sings]*
  And let me the cannikin[23] clink, clink,

[23] *Tankard*

  And let me the cannikin clink. 65
  A soldier's a man,
  O man's life but a span;
  Why then, let a soldier drink.
Some wine, boys!

Cassio Fore God, an excellent song. 70

Iago I learned it in England, where indeed, they are most
potent in potting.[24] Your Dane, your German, and your
swag-bellied[25] Hollander – drink, ho! – are nothing to
your English.

[24] *Expert at drinking*

[25] *Beer-bellied*

Cassio Is your Englishman so expert in his drinking? 75

[26] *No effort*

[27] *German*

[28] *Tankard*

Iago Why, he drinks you with facility[26] your Dane dead drunk.
He sweats not to overthrow your Almain.[27] He gives your
Hollander a vomit ere the next pottle[28] can be filled.

Cassio To the health of our general!

Montano I am for it, lieutenant, and I'll do you justice. 80

Iago *[Singing]*
  O sweet England!
  King Stephen was and a worthy peer,
  His breeches cost him but a crown;
  He held them sixpence all too dear,

[29] *A clown*

[30] *Man*

  With that he call'd the tailor lown.[29] 85
  He was a wight[30] of high renown,
  And thou art but of low degree.

'Tis pride that pulls the country down,
Then take thy auld cloak about thee.
Some wine, ho! 90

Cassio Fore God, this is a more exquisite song than the other.

Iago Will you hear't again?

Cassio No, for I hold him to be unworthy of his place that does
those things. Well, God's above all, and there be souls
must be saved, and there be souls must not be saved. 95

Iago It's true, good lieutenant.

Cassio For mine own part – no offence to the general, nor
any man of quality – I hope to be saved.

Iago And so do I too, lieutenant.

Cassio Ay, but, by your leave, not before me. The lieutenant is 100
to be saved before the ensign. Let's ha' no more of this.
Let's to our affairs. God forgive us our sins. Gentlemen,
let's look to our business. Do not think, gentlemen, I am
drunk. This is my ensign, this is my right hand, and this
is my left. I am not drunk now. I can stand well enough, 105
and speak well enough.

All Excellent well.

Cassio Why, very well then. You must not think then that
I am drunk.

Exit

Montano To th' platform, masters. Come, let's set the watch. 110

Iago You see this fellow that is gone before –
He is a soldier fit to stand by Caesar
And give direction; and do but see his vice.
'Tis to his virtue a just equinox,[31]
The one as long as th'other. 'Tis pity of him. 115
I fear the trust Othello puts him in,
On some odd time of his infirmity,[32]
Will shake this island.

[31] *The exact opposite*

[32] *Weakness*

33 *Timepiece (like a watch)*
34 *Go around twice (i.e. twenty-four hours)*

Montano	But is he often thus?	
Iago	'Tis evermore the prologue to his sleep.	120
	He'll watch the horologe[33] a double set[34]	
	If drink rock not his cradle.	
Montano	It were well	
	The general were put in mind of it.	
	Perhaps he sees it not, or his good nature	125
	Prizes the virtue that appears in Cassio,	
	And looks not on his evils. Is not this true?	

Enter Roderigo

Iago	*[Aside to him]* How now, Roderigo!	
	I pray you after the lieutenant, go.	

Exit Roderigo

35 *Endanger*
36 *Ingrained*

Montano	And 'tis great pity that the noble Moor	130
	Should hazard[35] such a place as his own second	
	With one of an ingraft[36] infirmity.	
	It were an honest action to say so	
	To the Moor.	
Iago	Not I, for this fair island!	135
	I do love Cassio well, and would do much	
	To cure him of this evil.	
	But hark, what noise?	

Cry within: 'Help! help!'

Re-enter Cassio, driving in Roderigo

Cassio	'Swounds, you rogue, you rascal!	
Montano	What's the matter, lieutenant?	140

37 *A bottle encased in wicker*

Cassio	A knave teach me my duty? –	
	I'll beat the knave into a twiggen bottle.[37]	
Roderigo	Beat me?	

38 *Talk*

Cassio	Dost thou prate,[38] rogue?

Striking Roderigo

Montano	Nay, good lieutenant,	145

Staying him

I pray you, sir, hold your hand.

Cassio Let me go, sir, or I'll knock you o'er the mazard.[39]   [39] *Head*

Montano Come, come, you're drunk.

Cassio Drunk?

They fight

Iago [*Aside to Roderigo*]
Away, I say. Go out and cry a mutiny.[40]   150   [40] *Rebellion or riot*

Exit Roderigo

Nay, good lieutenant. God's will, gentlemen!
Help, ho! Lieutenant! Sir! Montano! Sir!
Help, masters. Here's a goodly watch indeed!

Bell rings

Who's that which rings the bell? Diablo,[41] ho!   [41] *The devil*
The town will rise. God's will, lieutenant, hold.   155
You will be shamed for ever.

Re-enter Othello and Attendants

Othello What is the matter here?

Montano 'Swounds, I bleed still. I am hurt to th' death.

Faints

Othello Hold, for your lives!

Iago Hold, ho, lieutenant, sir, Montano, gentlemen!   160
Have you forgot all sense of place and duty?
Hold, the general speaks to you. Hold, hold, for shame.

Othello Why, how now, ho? From whence ariseth this?
Are we turn'd Turks, and to ourselves do that
Which heaven hath forbid the Ottomites?   165
For Christian shame, put by this barbarous brawl.
He that stirs next to carve for his own rage

42 The next man to make a move will be killed

Holds his soul light. He dies upon his motion.[42]
Silence that dreadful bell – it frights the isle

43 Peace

From her propriety.[43] What is the matter, masters?   170
Honest Iago, that looks dead with grieving,
Speak. Who began this? On thy love I charge thee.

Iago I do not know. Friends all but now, even now,

44 In their proper positions

In quarter,[44] and in terms like bride and groom

45 Undressing

Devesting[45] them for bed; and then but now –   175
As if some planet had unwitted men –
Swords out, and tilting one at other's breasts
In opposition bloody. I cannot speak

46 Stupid fight

Any beginning to this peevish odds,[46]
And would in action glorious I had lost   180
Those legs that brought me to a part of it.

Othello How comes it, Michael, you are thus forgot?

Cassio I pray you pardon me. I cannot speak.

Othello Worthy Montano, you were wont be civil.
The gravity and stillness of your youth   185
The world hath noted, and your name is great

47 Opinion

In mouths of wisest censure.[47] What's the matter,

48 Undo

That you unlace[48] your reputation thus,
And spend your rich opinion for the name
Of a night-brawler? Give me answer to it.   190

49 Seriously hurt

Montano Worthy Othello, I am hurt to danger.[49]
Your officer Iago can inform you,
While I spare speech – which something now

50 Hurts

            offends[50] me –
Of all that I do know; nor know I aught
By me that's said or done amiss this night,   195

51 Self-defence

Unless self-charity[51] be sometimes a vice,
And to defend ourselves it be a sin

52 Attacks

When violence assails[52] us.

Othello Now, by heaven,

	My blood begins my safer guides to rule,[53]	200	[53] *His temper is beginning to get the better of him*
	And passion, having my best judgement collied,[54]		[54] *Clouded*
	Essays[55] to lead the way. 'Swounds, if I stir,		[55] *Tries*
	Or do but lift this arm, the best of you		
	Shall sink in my rebuke. Give me to know		
	How this foul rout[56] began, who set it on,	205	[56] *Brawl*
	And he that is approved[57] in this offence,		[57] *Found guilty*
	Though he had twinn'd with me, both at a birth,		
	Shall lose me. What, in a town of war,		
	Yet wild, the people's hearts brimful of fear,		
	To manage private and domestic quarrel	210	
	In night, and on the court and guard of safety!		
	'Tis monstrous. Iago, who began't?		

Montano If partially affined[58] or leagued in office[59]
Thou dost deliver more or less than truth,
Thou art no soldier.

[58] *Biased*   [59] *Subservient to a higher rank*

Iago Touch me not so near.
I had rather ha' this tongue cut from my mouth
Than it should do offence to Michael Cassio.
Yet I persuade myself to speak the truth
Shall nothing wrong him. This it is, general.
Montano and myself being in speech,
There comes a fellow crying out for help,
And Cassio following him with determined sword
To execute upon him. Sir, this gentleman
Steps in to Cassio, and entreats his pause.[60]

[60] *Asks him to stop*

Myself the crying fellow did pursue,
Lest by his clamour,[61] as it so fell out,

[61] *Noise*

The town might fall in fright. He, swift of foot,
Outran my purpose, and I return'd, the rather
For that I heard the clink and fall of swords

[62] *Cursing*

And Cassio high in oath,[62] which till tonight
I ne'er might say before. When I came back –
For this was brief – I found them close together
At blow and thrust, even as again they were
When you yourself did part them.
More of this matter cannot I report.
But men are men. The best sometimes forget.
Though Cassio did some little wrong to him.
As men in rage strike those that wish them best,
Yet surely Cassio, I believe, received

[63] *Terrible insult*

From him that fled some strange indignity[63]

215

220

225

230

235

240

Which patience could not pass.

Othello I know, Iago,
Thy honesty and love doth mince⁶⁴ this matter,
Making it light to Cassio. Cassio, I love thee,   245
But never more be officer of mine.

Re-enter Desdemona, attended

Look, if my gentle love be not raised⁶⁵ up.
I'll make thee an example.⁶⁶

Desdemona What is the matter dear?

Othello All's well now, sweeting.⁶⁷   250
Come away to bed. Sir, for your hurts
Myself will be your surgeon.⁶⁸ Lead him off.
[To Montano, who is led off]
Iago, look with care about the town,
And silence those whom this vile brawl distracted.
Come, Desdemona. 'Tis the soldier's life   255
To have their balmy⁶⁹ slumbers waked with strife.

Exit all but Iago and Cassio

Iago What, are you hurt, lieutenant?

Cassio Ay, past all surgery.

Iago Marry, God forbid!

Cassio Reputation, reputation, reputation – O, I ha' lost my   260
reputation, I ha' lost the immortal part of myself,
and what remains is bestial!⁷⁰ My reputation, Iago,
my reputation.

Iago As I am an honest man, I thought you had received
some bodily wound. There is more sense in that than   265
in reputation. Reputation is an idle and most false
imposition, oft got without merit, and lost without
deserving. You have lost no reputation at all
unless you repute yourself such a loser. What, man,
there are more ways to recover⁷¹ the general again. You   270
are but now cast⁷² in his mood – a punishment more in

Side notes:
⁶⁴ Make less of/downplay
⁶⁵ Woken
⁶⁶ Make an example of him
⁶⁷ Sweetheart
⁶⁸ Othello will ensure that Montano gets the best care for his injuries
⁶⁹ Pleasant
⁷⁰ Like an animal
⁷¹ Reconcile with
⁷² Dismissed

policy[73] than in malice, even so as one would beat his offenceless dog to affright[74] an imperious[75] lion. Sue[76] to him again, and he's yours.

[73] *Official military policy*
[74] *Frighten*   [75] *Powerful*
[76] *Appeal*

Cassio   I will rather sue to be despised than to deceive so good   275
a commander with so slight, so drunken, and so
indiscreet an officer. Drunk, and speak parrot,[77] and
squabble? Swagger, swear, and discourse fustian[78] with
one's own shadow? O thou invisible spirit of wine, if
thou hast no name to be known by, let us call thee devil.   280

[77] *Speak nonsensically, like a parrot*
[78] *Talk rubbish*

Iago   What was he that you followed with your sword? What
had he done to you?

Cassio   I know not.

Iago   Is't possible?

Cassio   I remember a mass of things, but nothing distinctly;   285
a quarrel, but nothing wherefore. O God, that men
should put an enemy in their mouths to steal away
their brains! That we should, with joy, pleasance,[79]
revel, and applause transform ourselves into beasts!

[79] *Pleasure*

Iago   Why, but you are now well enough. How came you thus   290
recovered?

Cassio   It hath pleased the devil drunkenness to give place
to the devil wrath. One unperfectness[80] shows me
another, to make me frankly despise myself.

[80] *Flaw*

Iago   Come, you are too severe a moraller.[81] As the time,   295
the place, and the condition of this country
stands, I could heartily wish this had not befallen;[82]
but since it is as it is, mend it for your own good.

[81] *Moraliser*

[82] *Happened*

Cassio   I will ask him for my place again. He shall tell me
I am a drunkard! Had I as many mouths as Hydra,[83]   300
such an answer would stop them all. To be now a
sensible man, by and by a fool, and presently a
beast! O, strange! Every inordinate[84] cup is
unblessed, and the ingredient is a devil.

[83] *A serpent from Greek mythology with many heads*

[84] *Large*

Iago   Come, come. Good wine is a good familiar creature,   305

if it be well used. Exclaim no more against it.
And, good lieutenant, I think you think I love you.

Cassio   I have well approved it, sir. I drunk?

Iago   You or any man living may be drunk at a time, man.
I'll tell you what you shall do. Our general's wife   310
is now the general. I may say so in this respect, for
that he hath devoted and given up himself to the
contemplation, mark, and denotement[85] of her parts
and graces. Confess yourself freely to her. Importune[86]
her help to put you in your place again. She is of   315
so free, so kind, so apt, so blessed a disposition,
she holds it a vice in her goodness not to do more
than she is requested. This broken joint between
you and her husband entreat her to splinter,[87] and,
my fortunes against any lay[88] worth naming, this   320
crack of your love shall grow stronger than it was
before.

Cassio   You advise me well.

Iago   I protest, in the sincerity of love and honest kindness.

Cassio   I think it freely, and betimes[89] in the morning I will   325
beseech the virtuous Desdemona to undertake for me.
I am desperate of my fortunes if they check me here.

Iago   You are in the right. Good night, lieutenant. I must to
the watch.

Cassio   Good night, honest Iago.   330

Exit

Iago   And what's he then that says I play the villain.
When this advice is free I give, and honest,
Probal[90] to thinking, and indeed the course
To win the Moor again? For 'tis most easy
Th'inclining Desdemona to subdue   335
In any honest suit.[91] She's framed as fruitful[92]
As the free elements; and then for her
To win the Moor, were't to renounce his baptism,
All seals and symbols of redeemed sin,

---

[85] Study
[86] Plead for
[87] Fix
[88] Wager
[89] Early
[90] Probable
[91] Appeal   [92] Known to be as generous

His soul is so enfetter'd[93] to her love   340

That she may make, unmake, do what she list,

Even as her appetite shall play the god

With his weak function.[94] How am I then a villain,

To counsel Cassio to this parallel course

Directly to his good? Divinity of hell:[95]   345

When devils will the blackest sins put on,

They do suggest at first with heavenly shows,

As I do now; for whiles this honest fool

Plies[96] Desdemona to repair his fortune,

And she for him pleads strongly to the Moor,   350

I'll pour this pestilence into his ear:

That she repeals him[97] for her body's lust,

And by how much she strives to do him good

She shall undo her credit[98] with the Moor.

So will I turn her virtue into pitch,[99]   355

And out of her own goodness make the net

That shall enmesh them all.

Re-enter Roderigo

How now, Roderigo?

Roderigo   I do follow here in the chase, not like a hound that

hunts, but one that fills up the cry.[100] My money is   360

almost spent, I ha' been tonight exceedingly well

cudgeled,[101] and I think the issue will be I shall

have so much experience for my pains: and so, with

no money at all and a little more wit,[102] return again

to Venice.   365

Iago   How poor are they that ha' not patience!

What wound did ever heal but by degrees?[103]

Thou know'st we work by wit[104] and not by witchcraft,

And wit depends on dilatory[105] time.

Does't not go well? Cassio hath beaten thee.   370

And thou by that small hurt hast cashier'd[106] Cassio.

Though other things grow fair against the sun,

Yet fruits that blossom first will first be ripe.

Content thyself a while. By the mass, 'tis morning.

Pleasure and action make the hours seem short.   375

Retire thee. Go where thou art billeted.[107]

Away, I say. Thou shalt know more hereafter.

Nay, get thee gone.

---

[93] Chained

[94] Mind

[95] The cleverness of hell

[96] Entreats

[97] Appeals for Cassio

[98] Lose her standing

[99] Her goodness into a liability

[100] Pack

[101] Beaten

[102] Sense

[103] Slowly

[104] Intellect

[105] Slow

[106] Destroyed

[107] Lodging

108 *Appeal*

109 *At the very time*

110 *Scheme/trick*

Exit Roderigo

Two things are to be done.
My wife must move[108] for Cassio to her mistress.   380
I'll set her on.
Myself a while to draw the Moor apart,
And bring him jum[109] when he may Cassio find
Soliciting his wife. Ay, that's the way.
Dull not device[110] by coldness and delay.   385

Exit

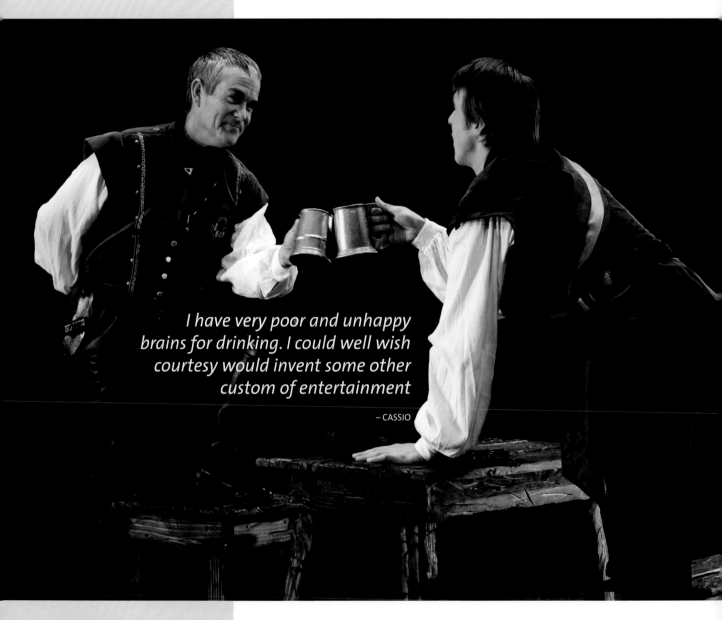

*I have very poor and unhappy
brains for drinking. I could well wish
courtesy would invent some other
custom of entertainment*

– CASSIO

MODERN ENGLISH VERSION

A HALL IN THE CASTLE

Enter Othello, Desdemona, Cassio, and Attendants

Othello   Michael, keep an eye on the guards tonight. Let's enjoy ourselves, but not get too carried away.

Cassio   Iago knows what to do, but I'll personally keep an eye on things too.

Othello   Iago's a good man. Michael, I'd like to have a private chat with you tomorrow. Come over as early as possible. *[To Desdemona]* Desdemona, love, we're married now, so let's enjoy our first night together as husband and wife. Good night, everyone.

Exit Othello, Desdemona, and Attendants
Enter Iago

Cassio   Hello, Iago. We have to keep a good eye on things tonight.

Iago   Ah, not yet, Lieutenant! It's not even ten o'clock! Othello ditched us so he could go to bed with Desdemona, although I don't blame him – he hasn't had the opportunity until now, and she is beautiful enough for God himself.

Cassio   She is absolutely gorgeous.

Iago   Yes, and sexy too.

Cassio   She is a beautiful, innocent girl.

Iago   And her eyes! They could give a man bad thoughts!

Cassio   Yes, she does have lovely eyes, but she is very ladylike and modest.

Iago   And doesn't her voice stir up feelings of lust?

Cassio   She is lovely. Just perfect.

Iago   Well, I hope the pair of them have a great time. Anyway, I have a good bottle of wine, and here's two Cypriots who want to drink to the health of black Othello.

Cassio   Not tonight, Iago. I'm not much of a drinker. It never agrees with me – I always end up doing something stupid. I wish people would find some other way to celebrate good news.

Iago   Our friends will be insulted if we don't have a drink with them. Just have one glass, I'll do the drinking for both of us.

Cassio   I've already had a glass – I was talked into that one as well, and look how drunk I am already. I can't handle my drink, and I don't want to risk it.

Iago   Don't be such a spoilsport – we can't let our friends down!

Cassio   Where are they?

Iago   Just by the door. Go on, tell them to come in.

Cassio   If I have to, but I really don't want to.

    Exit

Iago   If I can get him to drink just one more glass on top of what he's had already, he'll be as cranky and argumentative as Desdemona's yapping dog. That idiot Roderigo is madly in love with Desdemona, and he's been toasting her all night. The drink is flowing, all the guards are drunk, in fact the whole island is drunk. Now, if I can get Cassio to do something to offend the whole island of Cyprus, my dream of destroying him will definitely come true.

    Re-enter Cassio; with him Montano and Gentlemen; servants following with wine

Cassio   That is one large glass of wine you're giving me.

Montano   It's not that big – it's not even a pint!

Iago   Some more wine, eh?
    [Sings]   *And let me the glasses clink, clink;*
           And let me the glasses clink
           A soldier's just a man;
           Our lives just a short span;
           So let all the soldiers drink.
           More wine!

Cassio   My God ... that's a brilliant song!

Iago   I learned it in England, where else? The English love their alcohol. A Dane, or a German, or even a Dutchman, is a teetotaller compared to the English.

Cassio	Is an Englishman always an expert at drinking?
Iago	He can drink on when the Dane collapses; he doesn't even break a sweat out-drinking a German. When the Dutch are vomiting, the English are asking for refills!
Cassio	To Othello's health!
Montano	Hear hear!

Iago	*[Sings]* *O sweet England!*
	     King Stephen was a worthy peer,
	     His trousers cost him but a crown;
	     He held them sixpence all too dear,
	     With that he call'd the tailor lown.
	     He was a man of high renown,
	     And you are of low degree:
	     'Tis pride that pulls the country down;
	     Then take your old cloak about thee.
	More wine!

Cassio	*[Slurring his words]* That's the best song I ever heard.
Iago	Will I sing it again?
Cassio	No! We shouldn't be partying like this. God's looking down at us, and some of us are going to heaven, but some of us are going to hell.
Iago	That's true, Michael.
Cassio	Speaking for myself – no offence to Othello – but I hope I'm going to heaven.
Iago	Me too.
Cassio	Well, alright, but not before me! I'm a lieutenant, and you're just a flag-bearer. Anyway, let's get back to business. I'm not drunk – honestly! This is my right hand, and this is Iago, and this is my, eh, left hand. Well, I can still stand. And I can still speak!
All	You can indeed!
Cassio	So, that proves that I'm not drunk, and I don't want anyone to think that I am!
	Exit
Montano	Okay, I hate to spoil the party, but I think we'd better get back to

work. Let's head to the guards' platform.

Iago   You see him? *[Nods in the direction of Cassio]* He's a great soldier, fit to stand by Caesar, but he has one major flaw. His one flaw cancels out all the great things about him. I'm worried about him. And Othello trusts in him so much, I hope the pressure doesn't make him crack. God help Cyprus if it does!

Montano   Is he often drunk?

Iago   Every night. He goes to bed drunk, and it's such a habit now that he can't sleep at all without being completely intoxicated.

Montano   My God! I think I'll tell Othello about this. I wonder why he doesn't see it himself? But then again, Othello thinks well of everyone, especially Cassio.

Enter Roderigo

Iago   *[Aside to him]* Roderigo! Quick, follow Cassio!

Exit Roderigo

Montano   It's a pity that Othello made an alcoholic his second in command. I think we really have to say something to him.

Iago   I'm not saying anything bad about Cassio. Not even if you gave me this whole island. He's my friend, and I'd do anything to cure him of his disease ... what's all the noise?

A distant cry for help is heard offstage
Re-enter Cassio, dragging in Roderigo

Cassio   You idiot! You fool!

Montano   What on earth is going on, Cassio?

Cassio   The cheek of this fellow, trying to tell me what to do! I'll beat the daylights out of him!

Roderigo   Beat me!

Cassio   Are you still talking?

Punches Roderigo

Montano   Whoa, Cassio!

Staying him

	Get off him – what the hell are you doing?
Cassio	Let go of me, Montano, unless you want me to break your face!
Montano	Calm down, you're drunk.
Cassio	Drunk? Me?

They fight

Iago	[Aside to Roderigo] Quick, run and tell everyone there's a big fight happening!

Exit Roderigo

Cassio, Montano, please stop! I am shocked, shocked, at your behaviour.

Bell rings

Who on earth is ringing the bell? Stop it, for God's sake, the whole town will revolt. Cassio, please control yourself. You'll be ashamed of this in the morning!

Re-enter Othello and Attendants

Othello	What is going on?
Montano	Jesus, I'm bleeding. I feel like I'm going to die!

Faints

Othello	Stop fighting! Believe me, your lives depend on it.
Iago	Cassio, Montano, have you forgotten who you are? The General is speaking, show some respect!
Othello	How did this start? Are we killing each other now? After God saved us from the Turks? For God's sake, stop acting like savages. The next man to make a move will die! Silence that awful bell, it's frightening everyone and destroying their peace. I want to know what happened right now this minute. Poor Iago looks terribly upset. Iago, how did this fight start?
Iago	I honestly don't know. We were all friends until just a minute ago. Everyone was as happy as a bride and groom stripping off for bed ... and then all hell broke loose. I can't excuse it, and I wish I had lost these legs in battle, rather than walk into this disgraceful situation.

Othello	How could you behave in such a contemptible manner, Michael?
Cassio	I'm so sorry. I don't know what to say.
Othello	And Montano, you are normally so civil and polite. Everyone has commented on your calm, collected personality, and you're usually the one people call on to calm disputes! So what on earth would make you throw away your good reputation, to brawl in the streets? Answer me!
Montano	Sir, I am badly hurt. Iago will tell you what happened. I'm too weak to talk. I didn't do anything wrong tonight, unless it is a crime to defend yourself when someone attacks you.
Othello	By God, my blood is beginning to boil. You really don't want to see me angry, so for the last time I want to know how this brawl began, and who began it. And whoever that man is, even if he is my twin brother, I will disown him. This town almost went to war, and everyone is still tense and frightened. And my guards, who are supposed to set an example, and keep everyone safe and secure, are fighting among themselves? It is despicable! Iago, for the last time, who started it?
Montano	If you don't tell the truth, no matter where your allegiance lies, you are not worthy to be called a soldier.
Iago	You're hitting a raw nerve, Montano. I would rather have my tongue cut from my mouth than offend Michael Cassio. But I have to believe that it is always best to tell the truth. Othello, I was chatting with Montano, and a man appeared shouting for help, and Cassio was chasing him with a sword. Montano just asked Cassio to behave, while I chased the man to stop him from screaming and waking up the entire town. He was pretty fast, and outran me, and when I came back here I heard the swords clinking, and Cassio cursing at Montano – something I've never seen before tonight. I found them brawling just as you did, so I have nothing more to add. Except that men are men and even the best of us sometimes make mistakes, as Cassio did when he attacked Montano, who was only trying to help him. But I'm sure the man Cassio was chasing did something really bad to wind him up in the first place.
Othello	Iago, I know you're trying to make the best of a bad situation, out of loyalty to Cassio. Cassio, I love you, but you are never working for me again.
	Re-enter Desdemona, attended

You've even woken my wife! I have to make an example of you, Cassio.

Desdemona   What's the matter?

Othello   Nothing, sweetheart, go back to bed. Montano, I will personally ensure that you get the best medical attention. Bring him away. Iago, check the town, and calm everyone down. Come, Desdemona. Unfortunately, this is what it's like being a soldier's wife – your husband is always on call, night and day.

Exit all but Iago and Cassio

Iago   Are you hurt, Cassio?

Cassio   Yes. There is no surgery that can help me.

Iago   Don't say that!

Cassio   My reputation! My reputation ... I have lost the most important part of me, my reputation. So many years to build up, and lost in an instant. I am a mere animal without my reputation.

Iago   For God's sake, I thought you meant you were physically hurt! Reputation doesn't really mean anything. People often get good reputations when they don't deserve them, and likewise, some people get bad reputations for no reason either. You have lost nothing, unless you consider yourself a loser. There are ways you can make it up to Othello. He was just in a bad mood, and he had to be seen to punish you. It's kind of like how a man beats his dog in order to make him obedient, and then people respect him for it. You can get back into Othello's good books, I'm sure of it.

Cassio   I'd rather Othello hated me than that he was burdened with such a terrible lieutenant. One who was drunk and babbling and brawling? Someone who picks a fight with his own shadow? Wine is a terrible spirit. It should be called the devil, because it made me act in such a disgraceful way.

Iago   What about the man you were chasing? What exactly did he do to you?

Cassio   I can't even remember.

Iago   Really?

Cassio   I remember bits and pieces, but nothing distinctly. I remember some sort of argument, but it's all a blur. Oh God, why do we make such a thing as alcohol? The way we act when we're drunk is always shameful, so why do we drink something that will make us behave like animals?

Iago But you sobered up pretty quickly?

Cassio The shame I'm feeling was like a cold shower. God, I hate myself.

Iago Ah, come on. You're being way too hard on yourself. I wish this hadn't happened, not at this time, in this place, considering all you have lost as a result. But you can clean this mess up, if you put your mind to it.

Cassio If I ask Othello to reinstate me, he will just call me an alcoholic. And if I had many mouths, that word would shut all of them up. I hate wine. One minute, you're a sensible man, you have some wine, and then you're a fool. You have some more, and then you act like an animal. The devil must have created alcohol, it couldn't have been the work of God.

Iago Wine is also a friend when you use it properly. And Cassio, I hope you know that I'm your friend too.

Cassio I know that, Iago. Me, drunk!

Iago We all get drunk from time to time. I'll tell you my plan. Our general's wife is now the general. I say this in all seriousness, because Othello has given his heart to Desdemona, and so she controls him now. And she is such a kind, understanding woman that she would do anyone a favour. Ask her to mend this rift between you and her husband, and she will do everything in her power to do so. And I bet you'll end up better friends than you ever were before.

Cassio That is good advice.

Iago Well, it's given because I care about you, and I want to see you happy again.

Cassio I know that, and in the morning, I will ask Desdemona for her help to reconcile me with her husband. I am in deep trouble.

Iago You're doing the right thing. Good night, Lieutenant, I must go on duty.

Cassio Good night, honest friend.

Exit

Iago   Who could call me a villain now? I've given him good advice: it makes sense to use Desdemona to get back into Othello's good books. She's a generous soul, and won't be able to say no. She has Othello wrapped around her little finger, and she can make him do whatever she wants, even if she's doing it for a good cause. So, how could I be the bad guy, when I'm telling Cassio to do something which will help rather than hinder him? Well, that is how the devil works. First, you appear to be good and honest, like me. It may seem like I've helped Cassio, but I'm only helping myself. While he is asking Desdemona to help him, I'm going to poison Othello with thoughts and ideas of her being in love with Cassio. He'll wince every time she mentions his name, and if I know Desdemona, she'll mention his name a lot until they are reconciled. I'll turn her kindness against her, and use her generosity to make a net to trap all three of them.

Re-enter Roderigo

Hey, Roderigo!

Roderigo   I'm chasing my own tail here, Iago. My money's nearly gone, I got the stuffing knocked out of me tonight, and I think I'm going to go home to Venice with my tail between my legs, and penniless too!

Iago   You are truly poor if you've used up all your patience already! Does a wound heal immediately? No, it takes time. We are using our brains, not witchcraft, and it takes time to succeed. Haven't we done well so far? True, Cassio beat you up, but he lost his job by doing so. It only cost you a few bruises, and you've destroyed the competition. Be patient, our plan is already blossoming, and soon it will turn into the most delicious fruit. Lord, it's morning already. Time flies when you're having fun. Go to your lodgings and get some sleep. I'll fill you in on the rest of the plan later.

Exit Roderigo

I've a couple of things to sort out. First, I'll get Emilia to talk to Desdemona about Cassio. Second, I need to stay close to Othello and bring him home right at the moment that Cassio is talking to his wife. Yes, my plan is pretty clever. No point in delaying its execution.

Exit

FOCUS ON ACT 2

'To the original audience, Cyprus would have seemed exotic, but also, perhaps, a place where civilised values could be forgotten'

THE SECOND act begins as dramatically as the first. The setting in this first scene is the shores of Cyprus. To the original audience, Cyprus would have seemed exotic, but also, perhaps, a place where civilised values could be forgotten. Most members of the Globe Theatre's audience (the groundlings at least) would rarely have ventured outside of London, let alone England, and most of them would also have had a deep mistrust of foreign people and places.

Curiously, given that so much of the first act was taken up with thoughts of impending war with Turkey over Cyprus, the threat of war quickly vanishes with news that all the soldiers from the Turkish fleet have been drowned in the previous night's storms: ***Our wars are done. / The desperate tempest hath so bang'd the Turks, / That their designment halts. A noble ship of Venice / Hath seen a grievous wreck and sufferance / On most part of their fleet.*** We can assume that Shakespeare wished to focus entirely on domestic and personal conflict, rather than national and international.

A notable feature of this act is the imagery. The storm is described in evocative images, and the audience would have been able to picture it vividly from lines such as these: ***A segregation of the Turkish fleet; / For do but stand upon the foaming shore, / The chidden billow seems to pelt the clouds, / The wind-shaked surge, with high and monstrous mane / Seems to cast water on the burning Bear.***

Suspense is created when characters whom the audience is waiting to meet again are delayed. We learn of Cassio's loyalty to, and concern for, Othello, and also his esteem for Desdemona: ***He hath achieved a maid / That paragons description and wild fame, / One that excels the quirks of blazoning pens, / And in th'essential vesture of creation / Does tire the engineer.*** When

Iago's ship, carrying Desdemona, docks safely, Cassio romantically suggests that the storm itself could not hurt one as beautiful as Desdemona: *Tempests themselves ... As having sense of beauty do omit / Their mortal natures, letting go safely by / The divine Desdemona.* Cassio's open veneration of Desdemona is transparent: it is clear that he has no hidden feelings for her.

As everyone awaits the safe arrival of Othello, Iago, Desdemona and Emilia banter humorously. Iago shows a cynical, even misogynistic view of women here, but it is disguised as friendly teasing: *She never yet was foolish that was fair; / For even her folly help'd her to an heir.* The original audience would have found such ribald humour hilarious, and it also gives the audience a chance to see how Desdemona deals with Iago's bawdy words. She is dismissive and unfazed, again displaying her intelligence: *These are old fond paradoxes to make fools laugh i'th' alehouse.*

Iago knows that Cassio's regard for Desdemona, coupled with his gentlemanly etiquette, will be enough to incorporate Cassio into his plan: *With as little a web as this will I ensnare as great a fly as Cassio.*

Othello's safe arrival sees a touching and joyous reunion between the lovers, but Othello foreshadows pain to come when he says:

If it were now to die,
'Twere now to be most happy, for I fear
My soul hath her content so absolute

That not another comfort like to this
Succeeds in unknown fate.

In contrast to Othello's fear that it simply doesn't get better than this (and may disimprove), Desdemona is touchingly convinced that their happiness will grow and grow: *The heavens forbid / But that our loves and comforts should increase / Even as our days do grow.* The newlyweds' happiness, which most people would find touching, has the opposite effect on Iago. He compares their present happiness as being like an instrument in tune; but he will ruin the music of their love: *O, you are well tuned now, / But I'll set down the pegs that make this music.* Again, Iago's malevolence lacks any real motivation, aside from Cassio's promotion, and a rather weak suggestion that Othello slept with Emilia. Iago seems to delight in meddling because he can't stand to see anyone else happy. Indeed, a simple explanation for everything Iago does is that he is fundamentally unhappy. He is more than aware that, if he just leaves them alone, Othello and Desdemona are likely to have a long and happy marriage: *The Moor – howbe't that I endure him not – / Is of a constant, loving, noble nature, / And I dare think he'll prove to Desdemona / A most dear husband.*

Roderigo does not only supply Iago with money and jewels, but with an accomplice to ensure that he always keeps his own hands clean. Roderigo may not seem to have an important dramatic function, but, as Iago's willing dupe, he contributes to the unfolding of the plot. Iago instructs Roderigo to antagonise Cassio (whom Iago intends to get drunk) at the festivities that evening and, when he is alone, justifies it by saying: *For I fear Cassio with my nightcap, too.* It is hard to know what to make of these vague ideas that both Othello and Cassio have slept with Iago's wife. Jealousy, however, is often completely irrational, and no one knows more about jealousy than Iago.

Othello's professionalism is seen when he does not begin his wedding night without first giving orders to ensure that Cyprus will remain safe. The festivities are to conclude at a suitable hour, and Othello even reminds Cassio of the importance of knowing when to stop the celebrations. This is the night on which the marriage will be consummated – *The purchase made, the fruits are to ensue. / That profit's yet to come 'tween me and you* – and Iago knows that, tonight of all nights, Othello will not welcome any disruption.

Iago first attempts to entice Cassio into saying something inappropriate about Desdemona by making crude comments himself – *What an eye she has! Methinks it sounds a parley of provocation* – but Cassio will only speak chivalrously about her: *An inviting eye, and yet, methinks, right modest.* But Iago uses Cassio's good manners against him when he persuades him to have another cup of wine, despite Cassio's protestations that he has *very poor and unhappy brains for drinking.* Iago makes Cassio feel that it would be bad manners not to drink, and would insult the Cypriots' hospitality. It is a simple ruse, the age-old tactic of peer pressure, but it works. Soon the men are singing merrily, and Iago even throws in a few gags about what prodigious drinkers the English are – a comment designed to draw cheers from the audience in the Globe: *in England, where, indeed, they are most potent in potting. Your Dane, your German, and your swag-bellied Hollander – drink, ho! – are nothing to your English.*

When – predictably – Cassio becomes drunk, Iago has the opportunity to malign his character further, telling Montano that he is nothing less than an alcoholic! *'Tis*

*'Tis my breeding
That gives me this bold show of courtesy*

– CASSIO (ACT II SCENE I)

*I learned it in England, where, indeed, they are most potent
in potting. Your Dane, your German, and your swag-bellied
Hollander – drink, ho! – are nothing to your English*

– IAGO (ACT II SCENE III)

evermore the prologue to his sleep. / He'll watch the horologe a double set / If drink rock not his cradle. Just as we, the audience, might wonder if it will be a stretch too far for Montano to believe this, Cassio, riled up by Roderigo, arrives, shouting and roaring, and when Montano tries to calm him down, Cassio attacks him and the two men fight. The brawl leaves Montano badly injured. There is no doubt that good timing and happy accident contribute to Iago's plots as much as any of his skills. Othello, roused from his wedding bed by the brawl, is absolutely disgusted to see that it is his officers (who were supposed to be guarding the island) who are at fault. The tension is increased by Iago's convincing reluctance to name Cassio as the perpetrator. He waits until Othello almost explodes with fury, repeatedly demanding the name of the transgressor, and even seems to need to be prodded by Montano to name Cassio. Iago's show of hesitation is compelling. *I had rather ha' this tongue cut from my mouth / Than it should do offence to Michael Cassio. / Yet I persuade myself to speak the truth / Shall nothing wrong him.*

Othello's reaction is immediate and severe. He fires Cassio without hesitation, but it is hard to judge him harshly for this. Cassio is, after all, his second-in-command, and he is completely inebriated, even though Othello told him to set an example to the other men by not overdoing it. He has also injured a fellow nobleman: *I know, Iago, / Thy honesty and love doth mince this matter, / Making it light to Cassio. Cassio, I love thee, / But never more be officer of mine.*

Cassio sobers up immediately at this point, and when Othello leaves, he laments the loss of his reputation, clearly something he holds dear. Iago appears to comfort Cassio, while putting the next part of his plan in operation. He cunningly tells Cassio to appeal to Desdemona for help: *Importune her help to put you in your place again. She is of so free, so kind, so apt, so blessed a disposition, she holds it a vice in her goodness not to do more than she is requested.* Iago's analysis of Desdemona's character is extremely perceptive, reminding us once again how dangerous he is.

By the end of Act II, intrigue is created by Iago's confident prediction of how he will destroy all three lives. His role as apparent confidante and friend to every character (even Roderigo) contrasts sharply with the casual malevolence of his many soliloquies. For example:

... whiles this honest fool
Plies Desdemona to repair his fortune,
And she for him pleads strongly to the Moor,
I'll pour this pestilence into his ear:
That she repeals him for her body's lust,
And by how much she strives to do him good
She shall undo her credit with the Moor.
So will I turn her virtue into pitch,
And out of her own goodness make the net
That shall enmesh them all.

IMPORTANT THEMES IN ACT II

• The theme of jealousy is seen both in Iago's obvious jealousy of Othello and Cassio, and in his recognition that jealousy could be the way to destroy Othello.

• The theme of love is seen in the joyful union of Othello and Desdemona. They share a pure love, which may, despite Iago's best efforts, be impossible to destroy.

• The theme of hatred is seen in Iago's determination to destroy innocent people, for his own hateful reasons.

• The theme of remorse is seen in Cassio's utter desolation when he makes one mistake and loses everything.

Cassio, I love thee,
But never more be officer of mine

– OTHELLO (ACT II SCENE III)

CHARACTER DEVELOPMENT IN ACT II

• Iago continues to be breathtakingly malicious and spiteful, while quite brilliantly playing the part of a loyal and honest friend. His greatest attribute is his rhetoric. He can persuade anyone to believe anything. We now know that Iago is an expert manipulator, persuading every single person he encounters that he is the greatest and most honest of men. He is incredibly dangerous because of his combination of intelligence and evil impulses. Othello might be the titular character, but time and again, Iago's calculated cruelty and sheer audacity steal the show.

• Othello cuts as dignified a figure in Act II as in Act I. He speaks in a refined manner, clearly loves his new wife, and is not afraid or in any way hesitant in making difficult decisions: the demotion of Cassio, for example. He seems a balanced and steadfast man, and is clearly an excellent general. Even on his wedding night, he does not neglect his duties.

• Desdemona is beautiful, but also quick-witted, and there is no doubt that she is completely in love with her husband.

• Cassio is a young man who seems to have everything going for him, but his inability to handle his drink, a small flaw, is exploited by Iago. Cassio is in total awe of Desdemona, and clearly delighted for Othello that he has married such a wonderful person. To Cassio, reputation is everything. He is distraught at the end of this act, at the thought that one reckless act could cost him everything. Like Othello, he has complete trust in Iago.

QUESTIONS ON ACT 2

1. Write out the dialogue that Othello might have with the pilot of his ship as they attempt to land safely in Cyprus. Refer to details such as how the storm will affect both the Venetian and the Turkish fleets, Othello's concern for his wife's safety, his opinion of Cassio and of Iago, and, finally, his plan to hold a great celebration if they survive the voyage.

2. Write a newspaper article (tabloid or broadsheet) in which you report on the reasons for the war ending so quickly. You can adopt a modern or a Shakespearean style.

3. Cassio's character changes significantly throughout this act. Do you think he is an admirable young man, or is he a weak character who allows Iago to manipulate him into behaving badly? Support your answer with reference to the text.

4. What, in your opinion, is Iago's view of women? Support your answer with reference to the text.

5. Desdemona seems quite calm as she waits for Othello to arrive. Write out two or three paragraphs describing what she may be thinking as she stands on the shore in Scene I.

6. Write a diary entry for Iago, in which he explains why he hates Othello and Cassio so much.

7. Imagine you are a theatrical director. Describe how you would stage Act II Scene III with regards to props, costumes, lighting and sound effects.

8. Do you think that Othello was right to dismiss Cassio, or was he too harsh?

9. Iago can be quite funny at times. Pick out three examples from Act II where you thought he was humorous.

10. Pick out what you think are the ten best quotations from Act II, explaining in each case why you have chosen that quotation. Make sure they cover a range of characters and themes.

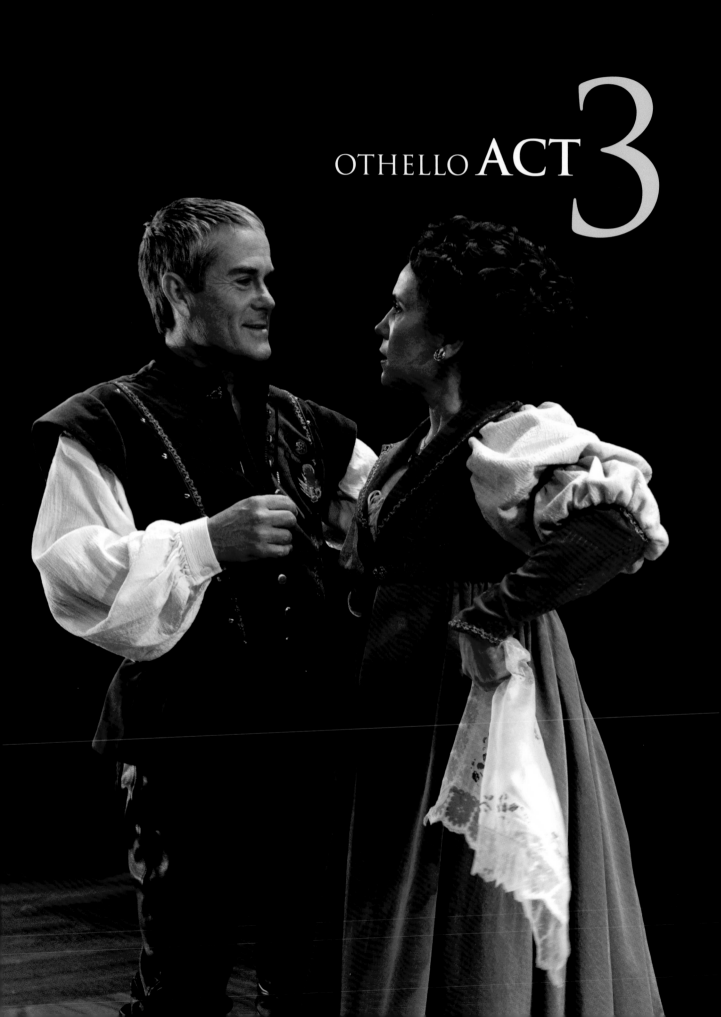

BEFORE THE CASTLE

Enter Cassio and some Musicians

Cassio	Masters, play here – I will content your pains[1] – Something that's brief, and bid 'Good morrow, general'.

Music
Enter Clown

Clown	Why, masters, ha' your instruments been in Naples, that they speak i'th' nose thus?[2]
1st Musician	How, sir, how?
Clown	Are these, I pray you, wind-instruments?
1st Musician	Ay, marry are they, sir.
Clown	O, thereby hangs a tail.[3]
1st Musician	Whereby hangs a tale, sir?
Clown	Marry, sir, by many a wind-instrument that I know. But masters, here's money for you, and the general so likes your music, that he desires you, for love's sake, to make no more noise with it.
1st Musician	Well, sir, we will not.
Clown	If you have any music that may not be heard, to't again; but, as they say to hear music the general does not greatly care.
1st Musician	We ha' none such, sir.
Clown	Then put up your pipes in your bag, for I'll away. Go, vanish into air, away!

Exit Musicians

Cassio	Dost thou hear, my honest friend?
Clown	No, I hear not your honest friend, I hear you.

5

10

15

20

[1] He will pay them

[2] The Naples accent was thought to be quite nasal

[3] 'Tail' means genitals here, a pun on 'tale'

4 *Quibble* 5 *Small*	**Cassio**	Prithee, keep up thy quillets.[4] There's a poor[5] piece of gold for thee. If the gentlewoman that attends the general's wife be stirring, tell her there's 25 one Cassio entreats her a little favour of speech. Wilt thou do this?
6 *He will tell her*	**Clown**	She is stirring, sir. If she will stir hither, I shall seem to notify unto her.[6]
	Cassio	Do, good my friend. 30

Exit Clown
Enter Iago

7 *Good*   In happy[7] time, Iago.

Iago   You ha' not been abed, then.

Cassio   Why, no. The day had broke
Before we parted. I ha' made bold, Iago,
To send in to your wife. My suit to her   35
Is, that she will to virtuous Desdemona
8 *Get*   Procure[8] me some access.

Iago   I'll send her to you presently,
And I'll devise a mean to draw the Moor
Out of the way, that your converse and business   40
May be more free.

Cassio   I humbly thank you for't.

Exit Iago

I never knew a Florentine more kind and honest.

Enter Emilia

Emilia   Good morrow, good lieutenant. I am sorry
For your displeasure, but all will sure be well.   45
The general and his wife are talking of it,
And she speaks for you stoutly. The Moor replies
9 *Importance*   That he you hurt is of great fame[9] in Cyprus,
10 *Nobility*   And great affinity,[10] and that in wholesome wisdom
He might not but refuse you. But he protests he loves you,50

And needs no other suitor but his likings
To take the saf'st occasion by the front
To bring you in again.

Cassio   Yet I beseech you,
If you think fit, or that it may be done,   55
Give me advantage of some brief discourse[11]
With Desdemona alone.

Emilia   Pray you come in.
I will bestow you where you shall have time
To speak your bosom freely.[12]   60

Cassio   I am much bound to you.

Exit

Because of Montano's influential standing, Othello has to be seen to punish Cassio appropriately, but he will reinstate him at a suitable opportunity

[11] *Conversation*

[12] *To say what is on his mind*

SCENE **ANALYSIS**

IN THIS SHORT scene, it is clear that Cassio is desperate to regain his position and Othello's favour. He has asked musicians to play under Othello's windows, but Othello has just sent them away. Iago seems to be the only friend Cassio has, and it is Iago's wife Emilia who comforts him, telling him that Montano's position in society made it necessary for Othello to punish him, but that he has every intention of reinstating him when the dust settles. Perhaps Cassio should be happy with this, but he is too agitated to let things run their own course, and entreats Emilia to arrange a meeting with Desdemona. This, of course, is exactly what Iago wants. As yet, it is not clear how much Emilia knows of her husband's true nature.

KEY **POINTS**

- *Cassio is devastated by his dismissal, and ripe for manipulation.*

- *Othello wishes to reinstate Cassio.*

- *Iago's plan is working as well as he had anticipated.*

A ROOM IN THE CASTLE

Enter Othello, Iago, and Gentlemen

Othello	These letters give, Iago, to the pilot,[1] And by him do my duties to the senate. That done, I will be walking on the works.[2] Repair there to me.[3]
Iago	Well, my good lord, I'll do't.
Othello	This fortification, gentlemen – shall we see't?
Gentleman	We'll wait upon your lordship.
	Exit

[1] *The pilot of the ship*

[2] *He will be walking on the battlements*

[3] *Come to me there*

5

SCENE **ANALYSIS**

ANOTHER SHORT SCENE, and another opportunity to see how thorough a general Othello is. Although war has been averted, he is still on the lookout for any danger, and he tells Iago that he will be checking the island's fortifications. Othello is oblivious to the fact that the danger he faces is much closer to home. We see yet again his trust in Iago, as he gives him letters for the Venetian senate.

KEY **POINTS**

- *Othello is professional and hard-working. However, this scene reminds us that he is used to dealing with military problems. He has no experience of married life, and no experience of dealing with personal problems. This scene suggests that Othello may deal with all the problems he encounters as a soldier, rather than as a husband.*

THE GARDEN OF THE CASTLE

Enter Desdemona, Cassio, and Emilia

Desdemona Be thou assured, good Cassio, I will do
All my abilities in thy behalf.[1]

Emilia Good madam, do. I warrant it grieves my husband
As if the case[2] were his.

Desdemona O, that's an honest fellow. Do not doubt, Cassio,   5
But I will have my lord and you again
As friendly as you were.

Cassio Bounteous[3] madam,
Whatever shall become of Michael Cassio
He's never anything but your true servant.   10

Desdemona I know't. I thank you. You do love my lord.
You have known him long, and be you well assured
He shall in strangeness stand no further off
Than in a polite distance.

Cassio Ay, but, lady,   15
That policy may either last so long,
Or feed upon such nice and wat'rish diet,
Or breed itself so out of circumstance,
That, I being absent and my place supplied,
My general will forget my love and service.   20

Desdemona Do not doubt that. Before Emilia here
I give thee warrant[4] of thy place. Assure thee,
If I do vow a friendship I'll perform it
To the last article.[5] My lord shall never rest.
I'll watch him tame and talk him out of patience.[6]   25
His bed shall seem a school, his board a shrift.[7]
I'll intermingle everything he does
With Cassio's suit. Therefore be merry, Cassio,
For thy solicitor[8] shall rather die
Than give thy cause away.[9]   30

Emilia Madam, here comes my lord.

Cassio Madam, I'll take my leave.

[1] She will do all she can for him

[2] Problem

[3] Generous

Othello is keeping his distance from Cassio for political reasons only

Cassio is fearful that the longer he is kept at a distance, the sooner he will be forgotten and someone else will take his place

[4] Guarantee

[5] Degree

[6] She will never give him a moment's rest until he reinstates Cassio

[7] Penance

[8] Supporter

[9] Than let his cause be forgotten

Desdemona Why, stay, and hear me speak.

Cassio Madam, not now. I am very ill at ease,
Unfit for mine own purposes.[10] 35

10 Unable to plead his case as he is too upset

Desdemona Well, do your discretion.[11]

11 Do what you think best

Exit Cassio

Enter Othello and Iago

Iago Ha! I like not that.

Othello What dost thou say?

Iago Nothing, my lord. Or if, I know not what.

Othello Was not that Cassio parted from my wife? 40

Iago Cassio, my lord? No, sure, I cannot think it,
That he would steal away so guilty-like
Seeing your coming.

Othello I do believe 'twas he.

Desdemona How now, my lord? 45
I have been talking with a suitor here,
A man that languishes in your displeasure.

Cassio is suffering due to Othello's bad opinion of him

Othello Who is't you mean?

Desdemona Why, your lieutenant, Cassio; Good my lord,
If I have any grace or power to move you, 50
His present reconciliation take;[12]
For if he be not one that truly loves you,
That errs in ignorance and not in cunning,
I have no judgement in an honest face.
I prithee[13] call him back. 55

12 Reinstate him immediately

13 Ask you

Othello Went he hence now?

Desdemona Yes, faith, so humbled
That he hath left part of his grief with me
To suffer with him. Good love, call him back.

Othello	Not now, sweet Desdemona. Some other time.	60

Desdemona But shall't be shortly?

Othello The sooner, sweet, for you.

Desdemona Shall't be tonight at supper?

Othello No, not tonight.

Desdemona Tomorrow dinner, then? 65

Othello I shall not dine at home.
I meet the captains at the citadel.

Desdemona Why then, tomorrow night, or Tuesday morn,
On Tuesday noon, or night, on Wednesday morn –
I prithee name the time, but let it not 70
Exceed three days. In faith, he's penitent,[14]
And yet his trespass,[15] in our common reason –
Save that, they say, the wars must make example
Out of her best – is not almost a fault
T'incur a private check. When shall he come? 75
Tell me, Othello. I wonder in my soul,
What you would ask me that I should deny,
Or stand so mamm'ring[16] on? What, Michael Cassio,
That came a-wooing[17] with you, and so many a time
When I have spoke of you dispraisingly[18] 80
Hath ta'en your part – to have so much to-do
To bring him in? Trust me, I could do much, –

Othello Prithee, no more. Let him come when he will.
I will deny thee nothing.

Desdemona Why, this is not a boon.[19] 85
'Tis as I should entreat you wear your gloves,
Or feed on nourishing dishes, or keep you warm,
Or sue to you to do a peculiar[20] profit
To your own person. Nay, when I have a suit
Wherein I mean to touch your love indeed, 90
It shall be full of poise and difficult weight,
And fearful to be granted.

Othello I will deny thee nothing,

14 Sorry

15 Mistake

Desdemona points out that Cassio's punishment is too severe

16 Wavering

17 Courting

18 Negatively

19 Favour

20 Particular

Desdemona points out that Othello is not doing her a favour in meeting Cassio, because it is he who will ultimately benefit from their reconciliation; but a real favour would be serious in nature and difficult to grant

²¹ *Leave him on his own for a while*

Whereon I do beseech thee grant me this:
To leave me but a little to myself.²¹   95

Desdemona Shall I deny you? No. Farewell, my lord.

Othello Farewell, my Desdemona. I'll come to thee straight.

²² *Do whatever you feel like*

Desdemona Emilia, come. Be as your fancies teach you.²²
Whate'er you be, I am obedient.

Exit Desdemona and Emilia

²³ *Eternal damnation*

Othello Excellent wretch! Perdition²³ catch my soul   100
But I do love thee, and when I love thee not,
Chaos is come again.

Iago My noble lord –

Othello What dost thou say, Iago?

Iago Did Michael Cassio, when you woo'd my lady,   105
Know of your love?

Othello He did, from first to last. Why dost thou ask?

Iago But for a satisfaction of my thought,
No further harm.

Othello Why of thy thought, Iago?   110

Iago I did not think he had been acquainted with her.

Othello O yes, and went between us very oft.

Iago Indeed?

²⁴ *Do you see anything in that?*

Othello Indeed? Ay, indeed. Discern'st thou aught in that?²⁴
Is he not honest?   115

Iago Honest, my lord?

Othello Honest? Ay, honest.

²⁵ *All*

Iago My lord, for aught²⁵ I know.

Othello	What dost thou think?
Iago	Think, my lord? 120
Othello	'Think, my lord?' By heaven, thou echo'st me, As if there were some monster in thy thought Too hideous to be shown![26] Thou dost mean something. I heard thee say even now, thou liked'st not that, When Cassio left my wife. What didst not like? 125 And when I told thee he was of my counsel[27] In my whole course of wooing, thou cried'st 'Indeed?' And didst contract and purse thy brow together[28] As if thou then hadst shut up in thy brain Some horrible conceit.[29] If thou dost love me, 130 Show me thy thought.
Iago	My lord, you know I love you.
Othello	I think thou dost; And for I know thou'rt full of love and honesty, And weigh'st thy words before thou giv'st them breath,[30] 135 Therefore these stops of thine fright me the more; For such things in a false disloyal knave Are tricks of custom,[31] but in a man that's just They're close dilations, working from the heart That passion cannot rule. 140
Iago	For Michael Cassio, I dare be sworn I think that he is honest.
Othello	I think so too.
Iago	Men should be what they seem, Or those that be not, would they might seem none. 145
Othello	Certain, men should be what they seem.
Iago	Why then, I think Cassio's an honest man.
Othello	Nay, yet there's more in this. I prithee speak to me as to thy thinkings, As thou dost ruminate, and give thy worst of thoughts 150 The worst of words.[32]

[26] Iago keeps repeating what Othello has said, as if he is afraid to reveal what he is really thinking, because it is too shocking

[27] Confidence

[28] Frowned

[29] Thought

[30] Thinks before he speaks

[31] Habits

Ironically, Othello trusts in Iago's facial expressions, because he considers him to be a man without guile, completely transparent

[32] Say what he is thinking, no matter how bad

33 *Even slaves can keep their thoughts to themselves*

Iago claimes that no one is so perfect that they cannot think a bad thought, but that thinking something does not make it true

34 *Legal records* **35** *The days courts sat*

Iago   Good my lord, pardon me.
Though I am bound to every act of duty,
I am not bound to that all slaves are free to.[33]
Utter my thoughts? Why, say they are vile and false,   155
As where's that palace whereinto foul things
Sometimes intrude not? Who has a breast so pure
But some uncleanly apprehensions
Keep leets[34] and law-days,[35] and in session sit
With meditations lawful?   160

Iago is not a true friend if he even thinks Othello has been wronged in some way and does not inform him of it

Othello   Thou dost conspire against thy friend, Iago,
If thou but think'st him wrong'd and mak'st his ear
A stranger to thy thoughts.

36 *It is a flaw in his nature*

37 *Imagines*
38 *From one who is not always right*

39 *Faulty observations*
40 *Peace*

Iago   I do beseech you,
Though I perchance am vicious in my guess –   165
As I confess it is my nature's plague[36] –
To spy into abuses, and oft my jealousy
Shapes[37] faults that are not – that your wisdom then,
From one that so imperfectly conceits,[38]
Would take no notice, nor build yourself a trouble   170
Out of his scattering and unsure observance.[39]
It were not for your quiet[40] nor your good,
Nor for my manhood, honesty, and wisdom,
To let you know my thoughts.

Othello   What dost thou mean?   175

41 *Most precious*

Iago is echoing what Cassio said earlier about the preciousness of one's good name and one's reputation

Iago   Good name in man and woman, dear my lord,
Is the immediate[41] jewel of their souls.
Who steals my purse steals trash; 'tis something, nothing;
'Twas mine, 'tis his, and has been slave to thousands.
But he that filches from me my good name   180
Robs me of that which not enriches him
And makes me poor indeed.

Othello   By heaven, I'll know thy thoughts.

Iago   You cannot, if my heart were in your hand;
Nor shall not, whilst 'tis in my custody.   185

Othello   Ha!

Iago   O, beware, my lord, of jealousy.

It is the green-eyed monster which doth mock
The meat it feeds on. That cuckold[42] lives in bliss
Who, certain of his fate, loves not his wronger.[43]   190
But O, what damned minutes tells he o'er
Who dotes[44] yet doubts, suspects, yet strongly loves!

Othello   O misery!

Iago   Poor and content is rich, and rich enough,
But riches fineless[45] is as poor as winter   195
To him that ever fears he shall be poor.
Good God the souls of all my tribe[46] defend
From jealousy!

Othello   Why, why is this?
Think'st thou I'd make a life of jealousy,   200
To follow still the changes of the moon
With fresh suspicions?[47] No, to be once in doubt
Is once to be resolved. Exchange me for a goat,
When I shall turn the business of my soul
To such exsufflicate[48] and blowed[49] surmises   205
Matching thy inference.[50] 'Tis not to make me jealous
To say my wife is fair, feeds well, loves company,
Is free of speech, sings, plays, and dances well.
Where virtue is, these are more virtuous,
Nor from mine own weak merits will I draw   210
The smallest fear or doubt of her revolt,[51]
For she had eyes and chose me. No, Iago,
I'll see before I doubt, when I doubt, prove;
And on the proof, there is no more but this:
Away at once with love or jealousy.   215

Iago   I am glad of this, for now I shall have reason
To show the love and duty that I bear you
With franker spirit.[52] Therefore, as I am bound,
Receive it from me. I speak not yet of proof.
Look to your wife. Observe her well with Cassio.   220
Wear your eyes thus: not jealous, nor secure.
I would not have your free and noble nature
Out of self-bounty[53] be abused. Look to't.
I know our country disposition well.
In Venice they do let heaven see the pranks[54]   225
They dare not show their husbands; their best conscience
Is not to leave't undone, but keep't unknown.[55]

[42] Husband of an adulteress

[43] The person who has wronged him, i.e. his wife

[44] Loves intensely

[45] Infinite riches

[46] Ancestors

[47] To grow more suspicious as the months pass

[48] Empty, frivolous [49] Overblown

[50] Insinuations

[51] Infidelity

[52] More honesty

[53] Kindness and generosity

[54] Only God knows what Venetian women get up to

[55] They still do bad things; they just try not to get caught

Othello	Dost thou say so?
Iago	She did deceive her father, marrying you,
	And when she seem'd to shake and fear your looks 230
	She loved them most.
Othello	And so she did.
Iago	Why, go to, then.
	She that so young could give out such a seeming,[56]
	To seel her father's eyes up close as oak,[57] 235
	He thought 'twas witchcraft! But I am much to blame.[58]
	I humbly do beseech you of your pardon
	For too much loving you.
Othello	I am bound[59] to thee for ever.
Iago	I see this hath a little dash'd your spirits. 240
Othello	Not a jot, not a jot.
Iago	I'faith, I fear it has.
	I hope you will consider what is spoke
	Comes from my love. But I do see you're moved.
	I am to pray you not to strain my speech 245
	To grosser[60] issues nor to larger reach
	Than to suspicion.
Othello	I will not.
Iago	Should you do so, my lord,
	My speech should fall into such vile success 250
	Which my thoughts aimed not. Cassio's my worthy friend.
	My lord, I see you're moved.
Othello	No, not much moved.
	I do not think but Desdemona's honest.
Iago	Long live she so, and long live you to think so! 255
Othello	And yet, how nature, erring from itself –
Iago	Ay, there's the point; as, to be bold[61] with you,
	Not to affect[62] many proposed matches

[56] A false appearance

[57] To deceive her father completely

[58] He has said too much

[59] Indebted

[60] Bigger/more serious

Iago cleverly claims that the last thing he wants is for Othello to start brooding about Desdemona and Cassio, and to conclude that they are having an affair – this was not his intention

[61] Frank

[62] Accept

Of her own clime,[63] complexion,[64] and degree,[65] 260
Whereto we see in all things nature tends.
Foh, one may smell in such a will most rank,[66]
Foul[67] disproportions, thoughts unnatural!
But pardon me. I do not in position
Distinctly speak of her, though I may fear
Her will, recoiling to her better judgement, 265
May fall to match you with her country forms
And happily repent.

Othello Farewell, farewell.
If more thou dost perceive,[68] let me know more.
Set on thy wife to observe. Leave me, Iago. 270

Iago *[Going]* My lord, I take my leave.

Othello Why did I marry? This honest creature doubtless
Sees and knows more, much more, than he unfolds.[69]

Iago *[Returning]* My lord, I would I might entreat your honour
To scan this thing no further. Leave it to time. 275
Although 'tis fit that Cassio have his place –
For sure he fills it up with great ability –
Yet, if you please to hold him off a while,
You shall by that perceive him and his means.[70]
Note if your lady strain his entertainment[71] 280
With any strong or vehement importunity.[72]
Much will be seen in that. In the mean time,
Let me be thought too busy in my fears[73] –
As worthy cause I have to fear I am –
And hold her free,[74] I do beseech your honour. 285

Othello Fear not my government.[75]

Iago I once more take my leave.

Exit

Othello This fellow's of exceeding honesty,
And knows all qualities with a learned spirit 290
Of human dealings.[76] If I do prove her haggard,[77]
Though that her jesses[78] were my dear heart-strings
I'd whistle her off[79] and let her down the wind
To prey at fortune.[80] Haply[81] for I am black,

---

[63] Country [64] Skin colour [65] Social rank

[66] Rebellious

[67] Dirty

*Desdemona may regret marrying
one so different from herself,
and seek someone more suitable
(such as Cassio)*

[68] See anything else

[69] Reveals

[70] His way of getting his job back

[71] Tries hard to get Othello to
reconcile with Cassio

[72] Persistence

[73] Over the top in his concerns

[74] Think her innocent

[75] Self-control

[76] Has great insight into human nature
[77] Wild (a hawking term)

[78] Ties to me (jesses are the leg straps
used for a hunting hawk)

[79] Send her away

[80] To fend for herself [81] Maybe

[82] *Dashing, gallant suitors (like Cassio)*

[83] *He's getting old*

[84] *Air*

[85] *Curse*

[86] *They are less privileged than those of inferior degree*

[87] *Cuckoldry*

[88] *Are born*

And have not those soft parts of conversation   295
That chamberers[82] have; or for I am declined
Into the vale of years[83] – yet that's not much –
She's gone. I am abused, and my relief
Must be to loathe her. O curse of marriage,
That we can call these delicate creatures ours   300
And not their appetites! I had rather be a toad,
And live upon the vapour[84] of a dungeon
Than keep a corner in the thing I love
For others' uses. Yet 'tis the plague[85] of great ones;
Prerogatived are they less than the base.[86]   305
'Tis destiny unshunnable, like death.
Even then this forked plague[87] is fated to us
When we do quicken.[88] Look where she comes.

Re-enter Desdemona and Emilia

If she be false, O then heaven mocks itself!
I'll not believe't.   310

Desdemona   How now, my dear Othello?
Your dinner, and the generous islanders
By you invited, do attend your presence.

Othello   I am to blame.

Desdemona   Why do you speak so faintly? Are you not well?   315

Othello   I have a pain upon my forehead here.

[89] *From lack of sleep*

Desdemona   Faith, that's with watching.[89] 'Twill away again.
Let me but bind it hard, within this hour
It will be well.

Othello   Your napkin is too little.   320
[He puts the handkerchief from him; and it drops]
Let it alone. Come, I'll go in with you.

Desdemona   I am very sorry that you are not well.

Exit Othello and Desdemona

Emilia   I am glad I have found this napkin.
This was her first remembrance[90] from the Moor.

[90] *Keepsake*

My wayward husband hath a hundred times   325
Woo'd[91] me to steal it, but she so loves the token –
For he conjured[92] her she should ever keep it –
That she reserves it evermore about her
To kiss and talk to. I'll ha' the work ta'en[93] out,
And give't Iago. What he will do with it   230
Heaven knows, not I.
I nothing, but to please his fantasy.[94]

Re-enter Iago

Iago	How now! What do you here alone?
Emilia	Do not you chide. I have a thing for you.
Iago	A thing for me? It is a common thing. 235
Emilia	Ha?
Iago	To have a foolish wife.
Emilia	O, is that all? What will you give me now For the same handkerchief?
Iago	What handkerchief? 340
Emilia	What handkerchief? Why, that the Moor first gave to Desdemona, That which so often you did bid me steal.
Iago	Hast stol'n it from her?
Emilia	No, faith, she let it drop by negligence,[95] 345 And, to th'advantage,[96] I, being here, took't up. Look, here 'tis.
Iago	A good wench! Give it me.
Emilia	What will you do with it, that you have been so earnest To have me filch[97] it? 350
Iago	*[Snatching it]* Why? What's that to you?
Emilia	If it be not for some purpose of import,[98]

91 Enticed

92 Told

93 Copy the embroidery

94 She tries to indulge his whims

95 Accident

96 Conveniently

97 Steal

98 Something important

Give't me again. Poor lady, she'll run mad
When she shall lack it.

Iago   Be not acknown on 't;[99] I have use for it.   355
Go, leave me.

Exit Emilia

I will in Cassio's lodging lose this napkin,
And let him find it. Trifles light as air[100]
Are to the jealous confirmations strong
As proofs of holy writ.[101] This may do something.   360
The Moor already changes with my poison.
Dangerous conceits[102] are in their natures poisons.
Which at the first are scarce found to distaste,[103]
But with a little act upon the blood,
Burn like the mines of Sulphur.[104] I did say so.   365
Look, where he comes!

Re-enter Othello

Not poppy[105] nor mandragora,[106]
Nor all the drowsy syrups[107] of the world
Shall ever medicine thee to that sweet sleep
Which thou owedst[108] yesterday.   370

Othello   Ha! Ha! False to me?

Iago   Why, how now, general? No more of that.

Othello   Avaunt, be gone. Thou hast set me on the rack.[109]
I swear 'tis better to be much abused
Than but to know't a little.   375

Iago   How now, my lord?

Othello   What sense had I of her stol'n hours of lust?
I saw't not, thought it not, it harm'd not me.
I slept the next night well, fed well, was free and merry.
I found not Cassio's kisses on her lips.   380
He that is robb'd, not wanting what is stol'n,
Let him not know't, and he's not robb'd at all.[110]

Iago   I am sorry to hear this.

Othello I had been happy if the general camp,
Pioneers[111] and all, had tasted her sweet body, 385
So I had nothing known. O, now for ever
Farewell the tranquil mind, farewell content,
Farewell the plumed troops[112] and the big wars,
That makes ambition virtue! O, farewell,
Farewell the neighing steed[113] and the shrill trump,[114] 390
The spirit-stirring drum, th'ear-piercing fife,[115]
The royal banner, and all quality,
Pride, pomp, and circumstance of glorious war!
And O, you mortal engines[116] whose rude throats
Th'immortal Jove's dead clamours counterfeit,[117] 395
Farewell! Othello's occupation's gone.

Iago Is't possible, my lord?

Othello Villain, be sure thou prove my love a whore.
Be sure of it. Give me the ocular proof,[118]
Or, by the worth of man's eternal soul, 400
Thou hadst been better have been born a dog
Than answer my waked wrath!

Iago Is't come to this?

Othello Make me to see't, or at the least so prove it
That the probation bear no hinge nor loop 405
To hang a doubt on,[119] or woe upon thy life.

Iago My noble lord.

Othello If thou dost slander her and torture me,
Never pray more; abandon all remorse,
On horror's head horrors accumulate, 410
Do deeds to make heaven weep, all earth amazed,
For nothing canst thou to damnation add
Greater than that.

Iago O grace, O heaven forgive me!
Are you a man? Have you a soul or sense? 415
God be wi' you; take mine office.[120] O wretched fool,
That lov'st to make thine honesty a vice!
O monstrous world, take note, take note, O world,
To be direct and honest is not safe!
I thank you for this profit, and from hence 420

---

[111] Lowest-ranking soldiers

[112] Troops in splendid uniforms

[113] Military horse   [114] Trumpet
[115] Small, shrill flute

[116] Deadly cannons

[117] The sound of the cannons imitates God's thunderbolts

[118] Proof of the eyes

[119] Prove it beyond any doubt

In an example of dramatic irony, Othello warns Iago that if he is lying, there is no point praying for mercy or asking forgiveness, that he might as well commit every terrible crime he could think of, because nothing could be worse than slandering Desdemona and torturing him

[120] Fire him

I'll love no friend, sith love breeds such offence.

Othello Nay, stay. Thou shouldst be honest.

Iago I should be wise, for honesty's a fool,
And loses that it works for.

Othello By the world,   425
I think my wife be honest, and think she is not.
I think that thou art just, and think thou art not.
I'll have some proof. Her name, that was as fresh
As Dian's[121] visage,[122] is now begrimed and black
As mine own face. If there be cords,[123] or knives,   430
Poison, or fire, or suffocating streams,
I'll not endure it. Would I were satisfied!

Iago I see, sir, you are eaten up with passion.
I do repent me that I put it to you.
You would be satisfied?   435

Othello Would? Nay, and I will.

Iago And may. But how, how satisfied, my lord?
Would you, the supervisor, grossly gape on,
Behold her topp'd?[124]

Othello Death and damnation! O!   440

Iago It were a tedious difficulty, I think,
To bring them to that prospect.[125] Damn them then
If ever mortal eyes do see them bolster[126]
More than their own! What then, how then?
What shall I say? Where's satisfaction?   445
It is impossible you should see this,
Were they as prime[127] as goats, as hot[128] as monkeys,
As salt as wolves in pride,[129] and fools as gross
As ignorance made drunk. But yet I say,
If imputation, and strong circumstances[130]   450
Which lead directly to the door of truth,
Will give you satisfaction, you may ha't.

Othello Give me a living reason she's disloyal.

Iago I do not like the office,[131]
But, sith I am enter'd in this cause so far,   455

121 *Diana was the goddess of chastity*
122 *Face*
123 *Ropes*

124 *Watch her having sexual relations*

125 *Situation (in bed together)*
126 *Go to bed*

127 *Eager* 128 *Lecherous*
129 *In heat*

130 *Evidence and circumstantial proof*

131 *The role*

Prick'd to't[132] by foolish honesty and love,
I will go on. I lay with Cassio lately,
And being troubled with a raging tooth,
I could not sleep. There are a kind of men
So loose of soul that in their sleeps   460
Will mutter their affairs. One of this kind is Cassio.
In sleep I heard him say 'Sweet Desdemona,
Let us be wary, let us hide our loves',
And then, sir, would he grip[133] and wring[134] my hand,
Cry 'O, sweet creature!' and then kiss me hard,   465
As if he pluck'd[135] up kisses by the roots,
That grew upon my lips, lay his leg o'er my thigh,
And sigh, and kiss, and then cry
'Cursed fate that gave thee to the Moor!'

Othello   O, monstrous, monstrous!   470

Iago   Nay, this was but his dream.

Othello   But this denoted a foregone conclusion.[136]
'Tis a shrewd doubt, though it be but a dream.

Iago   And this may help to thicken[137] other proofs
That do demonstrate thinly.[138]   475

Othello   I'll tear her all to pieces.

Iago   Nay, yet be wise; yet we see nothing done.
She may be honest yet. Tell me but this:
Have you not sometimes seen a handkerchief
Spotted with strawberries in your wife's hand?   480

Othello   I gave her such a one. 'Twas my first gift.

Iago   I know not that, but such a handkerchief –
I am sure it was your wife's – did I today
See Cassio wipe his beard with.

Othello   If it be that –   485

Iago   If it be that, or any that was hers,
It speaks against her with the other proofs.

Othello   O that the slave had forty thousand lives!

---

[132] Pushed into it

[133] Grab   [134] Squeeze

[135] Pulled

[136] It proves something has already happened

[137] Increase the validity of
[138] That seem insubstantial

One is too poor, too weak for my revenge.

Now do I see 'tis true. Look here, Iago.   490

All my fond[139] love thus do I blow to heaven – 'tis gone.

Arise, black vengeance, from thy hollow hell.

Yield up, O love, thy crown and hearted throne[140]

To tyrannous hate! Swell, bosom, with thy freight,[141]

For 'tis of aspics'[142] tongues!   495

Iago   Yet be content.

Othello   O, blood, blood, blood!

Iago   Patience, I say. Your mind may change.

Othello   Never, Iago. Like to the Pontic sea,[143]

Whose icy current and compulsive course[144]   500

Ne'er feels retiring ebb, but keeps due on

To the Propontic[145] and the Hellespont,[146]

Even so my bloody thoughts, with violent pace

Shall ne'er look back, ne'er ebb to humble love,

Till that a capable and wide[147] revenge   505

Swallow them up. Now, by yon marble heaven,

[Kneels]

In the due reverence of a sacred vow

I here engage my words.[148]

Iago   Do not rise yet.

[Kneels]

Witness, you ever-burning lights above,   510

You elements that clip[149] us round about,

Witness that here Iago doth give up

The execution of his wit, hands, heart

To wrong'd Othello's service. Let him command,

And to obey shall be in me remorse,   515

What bloody business ever.

They rise

Othello   I greet thy love,

Not with vain thanks, but with acceptance bounteous,[150]

And will upon the instant put thee to't:

Within these three days let me hear thee say   520

That Cassio's not alive.

Iago   My friend is dead.

139 *Foolish*

140 *Its seat in a person's heart*

141 *Burden*

142 *Snakes*

143 *The Black Sea*

144 *Relentless flow*

145 *Sea of Marmara*   146 *Dardanelles*

147 *All-encompassing*

148 *Pledge this promise*

149 *Surround*

150 *Wholehearted acceptance*

'Tis done at your request; but let her live.

Othello   Damn her, lewd minx![151] O, damn her!
Come, go with me apart. I will withdraw   525
To furnish me with some swift means of death
For the fair devil.[152] Now art thou my lieutenant.

Iago   I am your own for ever.

Exit

[151] Vile slut

[152] White devil (Desdemona)

Let me but bind it hard, within this hour It will be well

– DESDEMONA

MODERN ENGLISH VERSION

THE GARDEN OF THE CASTLE

Enter Desdemona, Cassio, and Emilia

Desdemona	Don't worry, Cassio. I'm going to do everything I can to help you.
Emilia	Please do, madam. I'll tell you, it upsets my husband so much, it is as if he was the one who was fired!
Desdemona	Oh, that is so sweet and kind of Iago. What an honest man! Don't worry, Cassio, I'll soon have your friendship with Othello back on track.
Cassio	You're such a kind lady. And whatever becomes of me, you have my undying loyalty for ever.
Desdemona	I know that, and I appreciate it. I also know that you love my husband; and you know him well enough to realise that he is only keeping his distance for the sake of appearances. He has his reputation to think of.
Cassio	Yes, but I'm worried that the longer he keeps me at a distance, the sooner he'll forget about me. He'll replace me with someone else, and my replacement will become his right-hand man instead of me.
Desdemona	Don't think that. As Emilia is my witness, I swear to help you get your job back. If I promise something, I keep my promise. Othello won't get a minute's peace until he reinstates you. I'll go on and on about it, I'll keep mentioning your name until he gives in. So smile, Cassio, because I'd rather die than let you down.
Emilia	Madam, here comes Othello.
Cassio	I had better go so.
Desdemona	No, stay, and you'll hear me defending you.
Cassio	Not now, I feel really uncomfortable, and I wouldn't be able to give a good account of myself. I'm a mess.
Desdemona	Alright, do whatever you think best.

Exit Cassio; Enter Othello and Iago

Iago Hmmm, that's a bit strange [*muttering*].

Othello What did you say?

Iago Oh ... nothing. I'm not sure what I saw.

Othello Wasn't that Cassio I just saw chatting to my wife?

Iago Cassio? Hardly! Why would Cassio, of all people, sneak away in that suspicious manner when he saw you coming?

Othello I think it was him.

Desdemona Darling, I've just been talking with a friend. A man who is devastated by your treatment of him.

Othello Who are you talking about?

Desdemona Cassio, of course! Dearest, if I have any influence on you, I ask you to reconcile with him. He truly loves you, and he just made a mistake. We all make mistakes, and it wasn't out of malice, just ignorance. Please call him back and make up with him.

Othello Did he go just now?

Desdemona Yes, and he was so upset that I'm upset for him. Please call him.

Othello Not now, love, but soon.

Desdemona How soon?

Othello For you, it will be soon.

Desdemona What about this evening? We could invite him for supper.

Othello No, not tonight.

Desdemona Will we invite him tomorrow so?

Othello I'm not home tomorrow. I'm dining with the captains at the citadel.

Desdemona Well then, tomorrow night, or Tuesday morning or Tuesday afternoon or Tuesday evening, or Wednesday morning ... Please just say when you'll see him, but it should be within the next couple of days. He's really sorry, and the punishment hardly fits the crime. I know you have to make an example of him, but don't you think you went too far? I wonder what you could possibly ask of me that I would be so hesitant about? Michael Cassio came with you when you courted me, and there were many times when I gave out about you but he took your part, and convinced me to give you another chance! Why won't you see him? Why are you making this so hard?

Othello   Okay, okay! Invite him whenever you wish. I can't say no to you!

Desdemona   Hey, you're not doing me a favour, you're doing yourself one. This is like me asking you to wear your gloves, or to eat nourishing food, or to keep yourself warm, or any other request that benefits only you. No, when I ask you for a favour, it will be a big one, it will be serious, and hard to grant!

Othello   I won't refuse you anything, but I would ask you for one favour: will you give me a little time to myself?

Desdemona   Would I deny you anything? Bye, sweetheart.

Othello   Bye, Desdemona, I'll come and find you in a while.

Desdemona   Come on, Emilia. Suit yourself, Othello – whatever you want, I want.

Exit Desdemona and Emilia

Othello   God, she is an amazing woman. I love her so much. The day I stop loving her will be a black one indeed.

Iago   General?

Othello   Yes?

Iago   Before you married Desdemona, did Cassio know about the two of you?

Othello   Yes, he knew about it from the very start. Why do you ask?

Iago   No reason.

Othello   You don't ask a question like that for no reason!

Iago   No, it's just that I didn't think that he knew her.

Othello   No, he knew her very well. In fact, he was our go-between.

Iago   Sure!

Othello	'Sure'? What's that supposed to mean? Cassio is very trustworthy!
Iago	Cassio – trustworthy!
Othello	Yes, he is, I think.
Iago	Well, for all I know he could be.
Othello	What do you think?
Iago	What do I think?
Othello	Yes, what do you think? Why do you keep repeating what I said as if you're thinking something so terrible you can't say what it is? Why did you say you didn't like to see Cassio talking to my wife? And when I told you he was our messenger you said 'Sure!' And you frowned, and looked as if there was something serious on your mind. If you're my friend, you'll tell me what you meant.
Iago	You know I'm your friend.
Othello	I know you are. And I also know how honest you are, and how thoughtful. I know you think things through before you speak. And that's why your reluctance to tell me what is on your mind is making me worry. If you were disloyal or one of those men who just pretend to be a friend, you could fake that worried expression, but you're so transparent, I know it must be genuine.
Iago	Ah no, I'd say Cassio is honest.
Othello	I think he is.
Iago	People should be exactly how they appear. But some people are pretty fake.
Othello	I agree, people should be honest and straightforward.
Iago	Well, if people should be, then I am sure Cassio is.
Othello	No, there's more to it than you are saying. Tell me what you're thinking, and don't be afraid to tell me, even if you're thinking something terrible.
Iago	Excuse me, boss, but I don't have to tell you everything that's on my mind. What if my thoughts are false? For we all think terrible

things of others sometimes: it doesn't mean that what we're thinking is true. Who is so pure that their mind doesn't sometimes wander and think impure thoughts?

Othello   You're betraying your friend if you even think he has been wronged in some way and you choose to stay quiet.

Iago   Please don't ask me to reveal what I am thinking. I have an overactive imagination, and sometimes I see faults that are not there. I'm not perfect. So you shouldn't take my thoughts too seriously. I don't want my undoubtedly exaggerated ideas to destroy your peace of mind, it wouldn't be right.

Othello   What are you talking about?

Iago   A person's good name is everything. It is the most precious jewel he or she could possess. If someone steals my money, it's nothing that can't be replaced. But if someone steals my good name, he robs me of something which won't benefit him, and without it I'll be very poor, because we are nothing without our reputation.

Othello   By God, I want to know what's going on in that mind of yours.

Iago   Well, I'm not telling you. I wouldn't, even if you were holding my heart in your hand, and I certainly won't while it is still in my chest!

Othello   For God's sake!

Iago   Beware of jealousy. It is a green-eyed monster, and it mocks the very meat it feeds on. There is no more painful emotion to feel. A betrayed husband lives in peace, so long as he doesn't know what his wife is up to. But it is a kind of living hell to be madly in love with someone you know is cheating on you.

Othello   Oh God!

Iago   To be poor but happy is all the wealth anyone needs. But infinite riches mean nothing to someone who is always afraid he will lose his wealth and be poor. God save us from jealousy.

Othello   Do you think I'd live a life of jealousy, always tormenting myself with new suspicions? I'd be an animal before I'd let my soul be ruined with groundless thoughts of betrayal. If someone compliments my wife, it is because she deserves to be complimented. Not because she has betrayed me. I won't let my own weakness make me think ill of her. No, I'm not going to get all upset until I actually see something to get upset over. She chose me, and that's an end to it.

Iago I'm glad to hear you say that, because now I can be completely honest with you. Observe your wife with Cassio, and if there is anything going on, you'll see it straight away. I'm protective of you because I know how nice you are, and I don't want anyone taking advantage of your good nature. I'm just suspicious because I know what Venetian women are like. Only God knows the kind of things they get up to – we don't, because they're too sly to get caught!

Othello Really?

Iago Well, Desdemona has already betrayed her father ...

Othello That's true.

Iago It just makes me wonder ... that such a young girl could fool her father so completely. Sorry, I've said too much, I'm being too honest now!

Othello I am forever indebted to you.

Iago I can see this has got you down a bit.

Othello Not at all. Not at all.

Iago I'm worried that I've upset you. I hope you know that I'm saying this out of friendship. But I can see you're upset. I want you to promise me that you're not going to dwell on this.

Othello I promise.

Iago I never intended to upset you, and Cassio is my friend too.

Othello I'm not upset. I know she is honest.

Iago Good for her, then, and good for you!

Othello Then again, sometimes people do unnatural things.

Iago True, and, not to be blunt, but she made an unnatural choice when she married you, someone of a different background, colour and rank. It would kind of make you wonder about her. Not that I mean to offend her ... but I worry that she might regret not choosing someone more like herself as a husband.

Othello	Well, goodbye for now. If you find out anything else, be sure and tell me. Ask Emilia to keep her eyes open.
Iago	*[Going]* Will do.
Othello	What the hell did I get married for? Iago obviously knows more than he is letting on.
Iago	*[Returning]* I just came back to ask you not to worry about this; things will work out. Maybe you should keep Cassio at a distance for the moment. If Desdemona keeps asking about him, it might be time to worry, but not before then. Please don't be too hard on her, whatever happens.
Othello	Don't worry about that.
Iago	Okay, bye then.
	Exit
Othello	Iago is so honest, and so perceptive. But if I find out that she has betrayed me, then I'll divorce her, and send her away to fend for herself. Maybe it is because I'm black and I don't act like the Venetians do. Maybe it is because I'm a little bit older. Maybe it is the curse of marriage that you can own someone, but not their feelings. I'd rather be a toad living in a filthy dungeon than be married to someone who is sleeping with someone else. It seems we great men are more prone to unfaithful wives than poor men. Here she comes.
	Re-enter Desdemona and Emilia
	But when I look at her face, it makes me feel she could never be false.
Desdemona	Othello, everyone is waiting for you to join them for dinner.
Othello	Sorry for being late.
Desdemona	You sound strange; are you feeling alright?
Othello	I have a headache.
Desdemona	That's from not sleeping. Here. I'll wrap my handkerchief around it, and you'll soon be well again.
Othello	Your handkerchief is too small. *[He puts the handkerchief from him; and it drops]*

Don't worry about it, I'll go in now.

Desdemona   I'm sorry you're not feeling well.

Exit Othello and Desdemona

Emilia   I'm glad I've found this. It was her first present from Othello. Iago has asked me to steal it a hundred times, but she loves it so much that I couldn't bring myself to do it. I'll copy the embroidery and give it to him. I wonder what he wants with it? I can't imagine, but I do so want to please him.

Re-enter Iago

Iago   What are you doing here on your own?

Emilia   Don't be cross, I have something for you.

Iago   I already have something – a silly wife!

Emilia   What would you do for me if I had got that handkerchief for you?

Iago   What handkerchief?

Emilia   What handkerchief? The one you've been asking me to steal for ages!

Iago   And did you?

Emilia   No, she dropped it, and I picked it up.

Iago   Good girl; give it me.

Emilia   Why do you want it so badly?

Iago   *[Snatching it]* What's it to you?

Emilia   If it's not for something important, give it back to me. Desdemona will be really upset that she has lost it.

Iago   Never mind why I need it, I just do. Now go away.

Exit Emilia

I'll plant this in Cassio's apartment and let him find it. Silly little things are significant to a jealous mind. I've poisoned Othello with jealousy, he is only a little bit sick with it now, but it's going to grow and grow until it is unbearable.

Re-enter Othello

[Whispers] There's no drug on earth that will let him enjoy the sweet envy-free dreams he had only yesterday.

Othello   You think she betrayed me?

Iago   Come on now, let's not talk about that again.

Othello   You're torturing me with little bits of information! I want to know everything!

Iago   Where has all this come from?

Othello   I had no idea what she was up to, and that ignorance was bliss. I wasn't tormented with thoughts of Cassio kissing her. If you don't notice something has been stolen, you haven't been robbed at all.

Iago   I hate to see you so upset.

Othello   Even if everyone in the camp had slept with her, I would have preferred not to know about it. I've said goodbye to my peaceful mind and my happy life! Everything is ruined!

Iago   Don't say that!

Othello   You had better be sure you can back up your accusations. Be sure you can prove my love is a whore, give me proof than I can see with my own eyes. If you've messed around with my peace of mind for nothing, you're going to have to deal with my ferocious anger!

Iago   Has it come to this?

Othello   Prove she has been unfaithful!

Iago   But ...

Othello   If you are just slandering her and torturing me, then don't even bother praying or repenting, commit any crime you wish, because you are going to hell!

Iago   So being honest is a crime, is it? Is this what I get for being a real friend?

Othello	No, that's not what I'm saying.
Iago	Only a fool is honest. It exacts too high a price.
Othello	I don't know what to think. I think my wife is honest, and then I think she's not. I think you're honest, and then I think you're a liar. I feel like killing myself, I'm so upset. I just want to know the truth.
Iago	I regret saying anything. I wish I hadn't upset you. Do you really want to know the truth?
Othello	I do!
Iago	But how will you know for sure? Do you plan on standing there and watching them in bed together?
Othello	Oh God, the thought of that makes me sick.
Iago	It would be hard to actually catch them in the act. They are not animals, after all. You might have to make do with logic and circumstantial proof. Would that be enough for you?
Othello	Tell me what evidence you have.
Iago	I really hate to be the one to do this, but I am your friend ... I had to share a bed with Cassio lately, and I was awake all night with a toothache. But Cassio talks in his sleep, and he was talking about Desdemona, and saying the two of them were in love. He was even stroking my face in his sleep, and calling me Desdemona and kissing me, and throwing his leg over me. He even cried out, 'I wish you hadn't married Othello!'
Othello	I can't believe it!
Iago	But it may just have been a harmless dream.
Othello	But he was obviously dreaming of something that had already happened!
Iago	Well, if we put all these small bits of proof together, we may end up with enough proof to convince you.
Othello	I'll rip her to shreds!
Iago	No, this isn't enough proof. But tell me, does she happen to have a handkerchief decorated with strawberries?

Othello	I gave her that. It was my first gift to her.
Iago	I don't know about that, but I saw Cassio wiping his beard with that handkerchief today.
Othello	What?
Iago	If it was her handkerchief, it is a clear sign she has betrayed you.
Othello	I wish he had forty thousand lives: killing him once won't satisfy my revenge. I don't love her any more, I hate her so much that I want to kill her.
Iago	Don't do anything hasty.
Othello	I want to kill them both.
Iago	You might change your mind?
Othello	I'll never change my mind. My thoughts of revenge are like a river that flows just one way, and I will not stop until I have my revenge! *[Kneels]* I swear to God, I mean what I say!
Iago	Don't rise yet. *[Kneels]* I swear that I will do everything I can to help Othello find justice! *They rise*
Othello	Thank you for your loyalty. The first thing I will ask of you is that you kill Cassio in the next three days.
Iago	I'll kill my friend for you. But don't hurt Desdemona.
Othello	Damn that filthy slut. Damn her. I'm going to think about how to punish that beautiful devil. Now you are my lieutenant.
Iago	I am your loyal servant. *Exit*

*She that so young could give
out such a seeming,
To seel her father's eyes up
close as oak*

– IAGO (ACT III SCENE III)

BEFORE THE CASTLE

Enter Desdemona, Emilia, and Clown

¹ Lodges	**Desdemona**	Do you know, sirrah, where Lieutenant Cassio lies?¹

Clown I dare not say he lies anywhere.

Desdemona Why, man?

Clown He's a soldier, and for one to say a soldier lies, 'tis stabbing. 5

Desdemona Go to. Where lodges he?

Clown To tell you where he lodges is to tell you where I lie.

Desdemona Can anything be made of this?

Clown I know not where he lodges, and for me to devise a lodging and say he lies here or he lies there, were 10 to lie in mine own throat.

² Informed

Desdemona Can you enquire him out, and be edified² by report?

³ Instruct someone by means of question and answer

Clown I will catechize³ the world for him; that is, make questions, and by them answer.

Desdemona Seek him, bid him come hither, tell him I have 15 moved⁴ my lord on his behalf, and hope all will be well.

⁴ Entreated

⁵ Limits

Clown To do this is within the compass⁵ of man's wit, and therefore I will attempt the doing it.

Exit

Desdemona Where should I lose that handkerchief, Emilia?

Emilia I know not, madam. 20

Desdemona Believe me, I had rather have lost my purse
Full of crusadoes,⁶ and but⁷ my noble Moor
Is true of mind, and made of no such baseness⁸
As jealous creatures are, it were enough

⁶ Gold coins ⁷ Except that

⁸ Bad character

	To put him to ill thinking.	25
Emilia	Is he not jealous?	
Desdemona	Who, he? I think the sun where he was born Drew all such humours[9] from him.	
Emilia	Look where he comes.	
Desdemona	I will not leave him now till Cassio Be call'd to him.	30

Enter Othello

	How is't with you, my lord?	
Othello	Well, my good lady. *[Aside]* O hardness to dissemble![10] – How do you, Desdemona?	35
Desdemona	Well, my good lord.	
Othello	Give me your hand. This hand is moist, my lady.	
Desdemona	It yet hath felt no age, nor known no sorrow.	
Othello	This argues fruitfulness[11] and liberal[12] heart. Hot, hot and moist – this hand of yours requires A sequester[13] from liberty; fasting, and prayer, Much castigation,[14] exercise devout, For here's a young and sweating devil here, That commonly rebels. 'Tis a good hand, A frank[15] one.	40 45
Desdemona	You may indeed say so, For 'twas that hand that gave away my heart.	
Othello	A liberal hand. The hearts of old gave hands, But our new heraldry[16] is hands, not hearts.	
Desdemona	I cannot speak of this. Come now, your promise.	50
Othello	What promise, chuck?[17]	

9 *Tendencies*

10 *Pretend*

11 *Fertility* 12 *Free/lustful*

13 *Break (from freedom), meaning she should be held captive*

14 *Reprimand*

15 *Free/lustful*

16 *Ceremony (marriage)*

17 *Chicken: a term of endearment*

	Desdemona	I have sent to bid Cassio come speak with you.
[18] *A bad cold*	**Othello**	I have a salt and sorry rheum[18] offends me.
		Lend me thy handkerchief.
	Desdemona	Here, my lord.
	Othello	That which I gave you.
	Desdemona	I have it not about me.
	Othello	Not?
	Desdemona	No, faith, my lord.
	Othello	That's a fault. That handkerchief
		Did an Egyptian to my mother give.
[19] *A fortune teller*		She was a charmer,[19] and could almost read
		The thoughts of people. She told her, while
		she kept it, 'twould make her amiable, and subdue
		my father
		Entirely to her love; but if she lost it,
		Or made a gift of it, my father's eye
		Should hold her loathed, and his spirits should hunt
		After new fancies. She, dying, gave it me,
[20] *Marry*		And bid me, when my fate would have me wived,[20]
		To give it her. I did so, and take heed on't;
		Make it a darling, like your precious eye.
[21] *Damnation*		To lose't or give't away were such perdition[21]
		As nothing else could match.
	Desdemona	Is't possible?
	Othello	'Tis true. There's magic in the web of it.
[22] *Prophetess*		A sibyl,[22] that had number'd in the world
[23] *She was two hundred years old*		The sun to course two hundred compasses[23]
		In her prophetic fury sew'd the work.
[24] *Sacred*		The worms were hallow'd[24] that did breed the silk,
		And it was dyed in mummy which the skilful
[25] *Liquid from the embalmed hearts of virgins*		Conserved of maidens' hearts.[25]
	Desdemona	I'faith, is't true?
[26] *True*	**Othello**	Most veritable.[26] Therefore look to't well.

Line references: 55, 60, 65, 70, 75, 80

Desdemona	Then would to God that I had never seen't!
Othello	Ha, wherefore? 85
Desdemona	Why do you speak so startingly and rash?
Othello	Is't lost? Is't gone? Speak, is't out o'th' way?
Desdemona	Heaven bless us!
Othello	Say you?
Desdemona	It is not lost, but what an if it were? 90
Othello	How?
Desdemona	I say it is not lost.
Othello	Fetch't, let me see't.
Desdemona	Why, so I can, sir, but I will not now. This is a trick to put me from my suit. 95 Pray you let Cassio be received again.
Othello	Fetch me the handkerchief. My mind misgives.[27]
Desdemona	Come, come, you'll never meet a more sufficient man.
Othello	The handkerchief.
Desdemona	I pray, talk me of Cassio. 100
Othello	The handkerchief.
Desdemona	A man that all his time Hath founded his good fortunes on your love, Shared dangers with you –
Othello	The handkerchief. 105
Desdemona	I'faith,[28] you are to blame.
Othello	'Swounds!
	Exit

[27] *Doubts*

[28] *In truth*

Emilia	Is not this man jealous?	

Desdemona

I ne'er saw this before.

Sure there's some wonder²⁹ in this handkerchief. 110

I am most unhappy in the loss of it.

²⁹ *Magic*

Emilia

'Tis not a year or two shows us a man.

They are all but stomachs, and we all but food.

To eat us hungrily, and when they are full,

They belch us. Look you, Cassio and my husband. 115

Men devour women – a comment on the inequality of Shakespeare's times

Enter Cassio and Iago

Iago

There is no other way. 'Tis she must do't,

And lo, the happiness!³⁰ Go and importune³¹ her.

³⁰ *Happy coincidence* ³¹ *Ask*

Desdemona

How now, good Cassio? What's the news with you?

Cassio

Madam, my former suit. I do beseech you

That by your virtuous means I may again 120

Exist and be a member of his love

Whom I, with all the office of my heart,

Entirely honour. I would not be delay'd.

If my offence be of such mortal kind

That nor my service past, nor present sorrows, 125

Nor purposed merit in futurity,³²

Can ransom³³ me into his love again,

But to know so must be my benefit.

So shall I clothe me in a forced content,

And shut myself up in some other course 130

To fortune's alms.³⁴

³² *The promise of loyal service in the future*
³³ *Redeem/restore*

³⁴ *Mercy*

Desdemona

Alas, thrice-gentle Cassio!

My advocation is not now in tune.³⁵

My lord is not my lord, nor should I know him

Were he in favour as in humour alter'd.³⁶ 135

So help me every spirit sanctified

As I have spoken for you all my best,

And stood within the blank³⁷ of his displeasure

For my free speech! You must a while be patient.

What I can do I will; and more I will 140

Than for myself I dare: let that suffice³⁸ you.

³⁵ *Her help is not available at this moment*

³⁶ *If his appearance had changed as much as his mood*

³⁷ *Target*

³⁸ *Satisfy*

Iago

Is my lord angry?

| Emilia | He went hence but now, |
| | And certainly in strange unquietness.[39] |

[39] Upset

Iago	Can he be angry? I have seen the cannon	145
	When it hath blown his ranks[40] into the air,
	And, like the devil, from his very arm
	Puff'd[41] his own brother; and is he angry?
	Something of moment[42] then. I will go meet him.
	There's matter in't indeed, if he be angry.	150

[40] Soldiers

[41] Blew up

[42] Significance

| Desdemona | I prithee do so. |

Exit Iago

	Something sure of state,
	Either from Venice or some unhatch'd practice[43]
	Made demonstrable[44] here in Cyprus to him,
	Hath puddled[45] his clear spirit; and in such cases	155
	Men's natures wrangle with inferior things,
	Though great ones are their object. 'Tis even so;
	For let our finger ache and it indues[46]
	Our other, healthful members even to that sense
	Of pain. Nay, we must think men are not gods,	160
	Nor of them look for such observancy[47]
	As fit the bridal.[48] Beshrew me much, Emilia,
	I was – unhandsome warrior as I am –
	Arraigning[49] his unkindness with my soul;
	But now I find I had suborn'd[50] the witness,	165
	And he's indicted falsely.[51]

[43] Plot

[44] Revealed

[45] Disturbed

[46] Endows

[47] Attention/respect

[48] Newly married

[49] Accusing

[50] Misjudged

[51] Wrongly accused

Emilia	Pray heaven it be
	State-matters, as you think, and no conception[52]
	Nor no jealous toy[53] concerning you.

[52] Idea

[53] Fancy

| Desdemona | Alas the day, I never gave him cause. | 170 |

Emilia	But jealous souls will not be answer'd so.
	They are not ever jealous for the cause,
	But jealous for they're jealous. It is a monster
	Begot upon itself, born on itself.

| Desdemona | Heaven keep that monster from Othello's mind. | 175 |

| Emilia | Lady, amen. |

Desdemona	I will go seek him. Cassio, walk here about.	
	If I do find him fit[54] I'll move your suit,	
	And seek to effect it to my uttermost.	

54 In a good mood

| **Cassio** | I humbly thank your ladyship. | 180 |

Exit Desdemona and Emilia
Enter Bianca

55 God save you

| **Bianca** | Save you,[55] friend Cassio. |

Cassio	What make you from home?
	How is't with you, my most fair Bianca?
	I'faith, sweet love, I was coming to your house.

Bianca	And I was going to your lodging, Cassio.	185
	What, keep a week away? Seven days and nights,
	Eightscore-eight hours, and lovers' absent hours

56 Clock
57 A very long wait

| | More tedious than the dial[56] eightscore times! |
| | O weary reckoning![57] |

| **Cassio** | Pardon me, Bianca, | 190 |

58 Heavy
59 Suitable
60 Make up for their long separation

	I have this while with leaden[58] thoughts been press'd,
	But I shall in a more continuate[59] time
	Strike off this score of absence.[60] Sweet Bianca,
	[Giving her Desdemona's handkerchief]

61 Copy the embroidery

| | Take me this work out.[61] |

| **Bianca** | O Cassio, whence came this? | 195 |
| | This is some token from a newer friend. |

62 Now she sees a reason for his absence

| | To the felt absence now I feel a cause.[62] |
| | Is't come to this? Well, well. |

63 Go away!

Cassio	Go to,[63] woman!
	Throw your vile guesses in the devil's teeth,	200
	From whence you have them. You are jealous now
	That this is from some mistress, some remembrance.

64 It is not, truthfully

| | No, by my faith,[64] Bianca. |

| **Bianca** | Why, whose is it? |

Cassio	I know not, neither. I found it in my chamber.	205
	I like the work well. Ere it be demanded –
	As like enough it will – I would have it copied.

Take it, and do't, and leave me for this time.

Bianca   Leave you? Wherefore?

Cassio   I do attend here on the general,   210
            And think it no addition,[65] nor my wish,
            To have him see me woman'd.[66]

Bianca   Why, I pray you?

Cassio   Not that I love you not.

Bianca   But that you do not love me.   215
            I pray you bring me on the way a little,
            And say if I shall see you soon at night.

Cassio   'Tis but a little way that I can bring you,
            For I attend here; but I'll see you soon.

Bianca   'Tis very good. I must be circumstanced.[67]   220

            Exit

[65] It would not help his cause

[66] With a woman

[67] Satisfy herself with their current situation

SCENE **ANALYSIS**

THIS SCENE BEGINS with Desdemona seeking out Cassio to inform him that she has spoken to Othello on his behalf. Desdemona also realises that her handkerchief is missing, and, while she is upset, she does not feel that her husband will really mind, commenting ironically that he is not the jealous type.

However, when Othello arrives, the very first thing he requests is the handkerchief, and a flustered Desdemona learns of its true value, a precious family heirloom with magical properties. It seems strange that Othello did not tell her of its significance before, especially when we know Desdemona loved to hear of his home and family. To make matters worse, Desdemona tries to distract Othello by once again pleading for Cassio! This is an important moment in the play, because it shows Othello's jealousy isn't entirely irrational. Seen from his point of view, Desdemona's loss of such an important gift, and her continual mention of Cassio, does seem suspicious.

Emilia wryly comments that Othello is jealous after all, as all men are.

The scene concludes with Cassio once again entreating Desdemona for her help, and we also see him give the handkerchief to Bianca, so she can copy the embroidery for him. The fact that a prostitute now has the handkerchief is no doubt something that will work in Iago's favour, and so Act III ends on a tense, expectant tone of suspense.

KEY **POINTS**

- *Desdemona learns that Othello is, in fact, jealous.*
- *Othello grows more convinced of Desdemona's guilt, and correspondingly, more crazed with jealousy.*
- *Cassio persists in his requests for Desdemona to intervene on his behalf.*
- *Cassio gives Bianca the handkerchief.*

'twas that hand that gave away my heart

– DESDEMONA

FOCUS ON ACT 3

'In real life, there are people who manipulate others by spreading gossip and innuendo, and do a great deal of damage, while appearing to be acting out of concern for a friend'

IN THIS, the central act of the play and its climax, everything, particularly Othello's character, changes dramatically.

The act begins with the woebegone Cassio sending musicians to sing under Othello's window, but the musicians are sent away. The music and humour of the Clown provide a few moments of comic relief in what is otherwise an emotionally charged act. Cassio speaks to Emilia, who tries to reassure him that he will be reinstated, once Othello has been seen to have punished him suitably. But Cassio, spurred on by Iago, is determined to press the matter. His persistence may be another example of how sheer luck plays a substantial role in Iago's plots, but it may also be the very reaction that Iago anticipated: *Give me advantage of some brief discourse / With Desdemona alone.*

Desdemona is more than eager to help Cassio. He is her good friend, after all: *be merry, Cassio, / For thy solicitor shall rather die / Than give thy cause away.* Her words may comfort Cassio, but her promise to bring Cassio's name up at every possible opportunity creates tension for the audience. This is just what Iago wants.

Cassio is not ready to face Othello, and makes a swift exit when he hears that he is almost home. In real life, there are people who manipulate others by spreading gossip and innuendo, and do a great deal of damage, while appearing to be acting out of concern for a friend. They wreak havoc in schools, workplaces, families, groups of friends, and so, while most of us will never be unfortunate enough to meet an Iago, at least some of his unscrupulous behaviour will almost certainly be familiar to us. For example, the way he makes Othello feel paranoid about Cassio's hasty departure: *I cannot think it, / That he would steal away so guilty-like / Seeing your coming.* Iago plants the seed of suspicion,

*What will you do with it, that
you have been so earnest
To have me filch it?*

– EMILIA (ACT III SCENE III)

and Desdemona's well-intended pleas for Cassio's reinstatement help to water it: *Michael Cassio, / That came a-wooing with you, and so many a time / When I have spoke of you dispraisingly, / Hath ta'en your part – to have so much to-do / To bring him in?*

Now that Othello has begun to feel the first pangs of jealousy, Iago continues to look worried, but he won't explain why he seems so unsettled. He makes Othello think he is reluctant to speak because he knows something. Othello seems to have to prise Iago's insinuations from him, and this leads him to conclude that Iago's reluctance is born out of genuine concern for him: *thou echo'st me, / As if there were some monster in thy thought / Too hideous to be shown!* Othello will only believe Iago if he truly trusts him, and, unfortunately, it is clear that he does: *I know thou'rt full of love and honesty, / And weigh'st thy words before thou giv'st them breath, / Therefore these stops of thine fright me the more.*

It seems that all Iago has to do is prevaricate and refuse to answer directly, and Othello will think the worst. It is hard not to admire Iago's devious skills. He even warns Othello that jealousy is *the green-eyed monster which doth mock / The meat it feeds on*, and he shrewdly plays on Othello's insecurity about being an outsider, claiming that Venetian women are known for their loose morals: *In Venice they do let heaven see   the pranks / They dare not show their husbands; their best conscience / Is not to leave't undone, but keep't unknown.* Iago really is an evil genius. He even mentions the fact that Desdemona 'betrayed' her father as proof that she is capable of deception: *She did deceive her father, marrying you*. Brabantio's parting words to Othello have clearly had a strong impact on him. (This reminds us yet again of the importance of seeing beyond

the script. On stage, Othello is often depicted as looking worried when Brabantio warns him about Desdemona's capacity for betrayal.) Othello fails to see that Desdemona's decision to marry him is proof of her love, not her treachery. Iago is adept at spotting a raw nerve: *She that so young could give out such a seeming, / To seel her father's eyes up close as oak*. Husbands adopted an almost paternalistic approach to their wives in Shakespeare's day, especially wives as young as Desdemona, and this accounts for Othello's sense that he is playing the same role in Desdemona's life as Brabantio did.

Iago gets lucky again when Desdemona, in her concern for Othello's headache, drops the handkerchief that was his first gift to her. In those days, a 'token' such as this was very significant. Very often, such a token was even a symbol of a betrothal. Emilia picks up the forgotten handkerchief, and decides to give it to her husband: *What he will do with it / Heaven knows, not I. / I nothing, but to please his fantasy*. This will propel the plot forward, but it also shows that Emilia has a deep need to please her husband. She loves Desdemona, and knows how important this gift is to her – *I am glad I have found this napkin. / This was her first remembrance from the Moor* – but the opportunity to be of service to Iago is clearly something she cannot pass up.

Iago already knows that one small insinuation has been enough of a catalyst for Othello's jealousy, and realises that he can further provoke his envy, with very little proof: *I will in Cassio's lodging lose this napkin, / And let him find it. Trifles light as air / Are to the jealous confirmations strong / As proofs of holy writ*. Iago refers to the act of making Othello jealous as akin to poisoning, and it is an apt comparison. Othello is changing before our eyes, becoming erratic and illogical.

Every now and then, his intuition seems to emerge as he wonders about Iago's motivation:

Villain, be sure thou prove my love a whore,

Be sure of it. Give me the ocular proof,

Or, by the worth of man's eternal soul,

Thou hadst been better have been born a dog

Than answer my waked wrath!

But Iago's feigned indignation at the suggestion that he is a liar – *take note, take note, O world, / To be direct and honest is not safe!* – convinces Othello that he is, indeed, honest.

Othello finally decides that he will not believe that Desdemona has been unfaithful until he has proof. Iago says it would be difficult to catch the lovers in bed together, but that if Othello would be satisfied with circumstantial proof, then he can supply plenty. Iago's proof is:

1) When Iago was sharing a bed with Cassio in the barracks, Cassio cried out Desdemona's name in his sleep, kissed Iago (thinking he was Desdemona) and cursed the fact that she was Othello's wife, not his: *'Cursed fate that gave thee to the Moor!'*

2) Iago has seen Cassio wiping his beard with *a handkerchief / Spotted with strawberries*.

This is all it takes for Othello to allow jealousy to consume him completely, and he swears that he will not rest until he gets revenge: *my bloody thoughts, with violent pace / Shall ne'er look back*. The fact that the proof is flimsy is the point Shakespeare is making about jealousy. It is very rarely rooted in truth; it grows according to the insecurities of the person feeling it. And Othello, for all his successes, is clearly very insecure. He orders Iago to kill Cassio within three days, and his decision to kill Desdemona makes for

a very shocking end to the third scene:

Damn her, lewd minx! O, damn her!

Come, go with me apart. I will withdraw

To furnish me with some swift means of death

For the fair devil.

In Scene IV, the first thing Othello asks Desdemona about is the handkerchief. Desdemona, flustered, tries to change the subject, but unfortunately her choice of subject is Cassio. Othello tells Desdemona the story of the handkerchief, and the not too subtle implication is that losing the handkerchief means losing the person who gave it to you:

That handkerchief

Did an Egyptian to my mother give.

She was a charmer, and could almost read

The thoughts of people. She told her, while

she kept it, 'twould make her amiable, and subdue

  my father

Entirely to her love; but if she lost it,

Or made a gift of it, my father's eye

Should hold her loathed, and his spirits should hunt

After new fancies.

Desdemona, understandably, does not know how to

account for this dramatic change in her husband's attitude towards her. When Cassio again entreats her for help, she is firm in her refusal to do any more for the moment: ***I have spoken for you all my best, / And stood within the blank of his displeasure / For my free speech!*** She seems to know that Othello's displeasure is linked to her friendship with Cassio, but doesn't realise the extent of it. She is eager to excuse his bad behaviour, and refuses to believe that he could act in this way unless something serious were preoccupying him: ***Something sure of state ... Hath puddled his clear spirit.*** Emilia correctly guesses that Othello is jealous, but doesn't seem to make the link between Othello's sudden jealousy and the recently 'lost' handkerchief, which is strange, as she is sharp enough to point out that jealousy is: ***a monster / Begot upon itself, born on itself.***

The final moments of this eventful act see Cassio giving his mistress, Bianca, the handkerchief that he found in his rooms. We are left wondering how this will tie in with Iago's plot.

IMPORTANT THEMES IN ACT III

• The theme of the role of women is seen throughout this act. We see a bright, intelligent woman such as Emilia betraying her instincts in order to please her husband. We see Othello discarding his beloved wife on the most circumstantial evidence. We see Desdemona desperately excusing her husband's altered attitude, and it is quite depressing when she says that men can't be expected to act like newlyweds for ever – they have only been married a couple of days! Finally, we see Bianca, a prostitute who has eyes for only one man: Cassio, and he is merely sowing his wild oats.

• Jealousy is the dominant theme in this act. There are many perceptive, pithy comments on the nature of jealousy, such as it being a monster which mocks the meat it feeds on. But the theme is most clearly seen in Othello's rapid descent into the grip of this destructive emotion. Iago's poison has done its work, and Othello is tormented with thoughts of Desdemona's infidelity, and his own lust for revenge. Iago is also jealous, improbably claiming that he fears both Othello and Cassio have bedded his wife, thus motivating his provocative actions.

CHARACTER DEVELOPMENT IN ACT III

• Desdemona and Cassio remain the same admirable characters we met in the previous acts. Desdemona responds to Othello's strange conduct with bewilderment, but her character remains exemplary. Cassio is determined to regain his rightful place as Othello's second-in-command, and his preoccupation with being a gentleman and a lieutenant remains constant.

• Emilia shows weakness when she decides to give Iago the handkerchief, despite knowing how important it is to Desdemona. She compounds her error by staying silent, even when she sees her mistress's distress.

• Iago continues to be as audaciously unscrupulous as in previous acts. What is most surprising is the fact that he never sways from his heinous course of action, and still hasn't shown the slightest remorse.

• It is in Othello's character that we see the greatest change. The upstanding military commander, eloquent speaker and loving husband of Acts I and II has apparently disappeared. In this act, he orders the death of Cassio, and horrifies us with his decision to kill his innocent young wife.

QUESTIONS ON ACT 3

1. **Draw a diagram or sketch a picture of Desdemona's handkerchief, and write a paragraph on its significance in the plot, and to Othello personally.**

2. **Cassio decides to write to Othello, begging to be reinstated. Write the text of this letter.**

3. **What are the stages by which Iago convinces Othello that Desdemona has been unfaithful?**

4. **Iago often repeats what other characters have said to him, but pretends that he is speaking from his own heart. Can you find an example of this in Act III?**

5. **Now that you know the characters quite well, what contemporary actors would you choose to play the parts of Desdemona, Othello, Cassio, Iago and Emilia? Explain your choices with reference to the play.**

6. **In Emilia's journal, she writes of her guilt over giving the handkerchief to Iago. Compose this journal entry.**

7. **What excuses does Desdemona make for Othello's behaviour? Refer to the text in support of your answer.**

8. **Othello changes dramatically in this act. Do you have any sympathy for him at this point, or do you think that a man of his age and experience should be able to see through Iago?**

9. **There are only three female characters in this play. How similar and how different do you think Desdemona, Emilia and Bianca are to/from each other?**

10. **Pick out what you think are the ten best quotations from Act III, explaining in each case why you have chosen that quotation. Make sure they cover a range of characters and themes.**

OTHELLO **ACT**4

CYPRUS. BEFORE THE CASTLE

Enter Othello and Iago

Iago	Will you think so?

Othello	Think so, Iago?

Iago	What, to kiss in private?

Othello	An unauthorized[1] kiss.

Iago	Or to be naked with her friend in bed	5
	An hour or more, not meaning any harm?	

Othello	Naked in bed, Iago, and not mean harm?	
	It is hypocrisy against the devil.	
	They that mean virtuously[2] and yet do so,	
	The devil their virtue tempts, and they tempt heaven.	10

Iago	If they do nothing, 'tis a venial slip.[3]	
	But if I give my wife a handkerchief –	

Othello	What then?

Iago	Why then, 'tis hers, my lord, and being hers,	
	She may, I think, bestow't on any man.	15

Othello	She is protectress[4] of her honour, too.	
	May she give that?	

Iago	Her honour is an essence that's not seen.	
	They have it very oft that have it not.[5]	
	But for the handkerchief –	20

Othello	By heaven, I would most gladly have forgot it.	
	Thou said'st – it comes o'er my memory	
	As doth the raven o'er the infectious house,	
	Boding to all! – he had my handkerchief.	

Iago	Ay, what of that?	25

Othello	That's not so good now.

---

[1] Forbidden

[2] To behave in a moral manner

[3] Pardonable sin

[4] Guardian

[5] Some people who have a good reputation don't deserve it

A raven was a bad omen, signifying death or disease. During the plague, a raven flying overhead was considered proof that the household was infected

Iago   What, if I had said I had seen him do you wrong,
Or heard him say – as knaves be such abroad,
Who having by their own importunate suit[6]
Or voluntary dotage[7] of some mistress,   30
Convinced or supplied them, cannot choose
But they must blab –

6 *Persistent wooing*

7 *Infatuation*

Some men cannot help but brag about their sexual conquests

Othello   Hath he said anything?

Iago   He hath, my lord. But, be you well assured,
No more than he'll unswear.   35

Othello   What hath he said?

Iago   Faith, that he did – I know not what he did.

Othello   What? What?

Iago   Lie –

Othello   With her?   40

Iago   With her, on her, what you will.

Othello   Lie with her? Lie on her? We say 'lie on her' when
they belie[8] her. Lie with her? 'Swounds, that's fulsome![9]
Handkerchief – confessions – handkerchief. To
confess and be hanged for his labour. First to be   45
hanged and then to confess! I tremble at it.
Nature would not invest herself in such shadowing
passion without some instruction. It is not words
that shakes me thus. Pish! Noses, ears, and lips.
Is't possible? Confess? Handkerchief? O devil!   50

Falls in a trance

8 *Slander*   9 *Disgusting*

Othello believes that his visceral reaction is proof that he is correct in his suspicions. He is confusing his worst fears with his gut instinct

Iago   Work on; my medicine works. Thus credulous fools
    are caught,
And many worthy and chaste dames even thus,
All guiltless, meet reproach. What ho, my lord!
My lord, I say. Othello!

Enter Cassio

	How now, Cassio!	55
Cassio	What's the matter?	
Iago	My lord is fall'n into an epilepsy.	
	This is his second fit. He had one yesterday.	
Cassio	Rub him about the temples.	
Iago	No, forbear.	60
	The lethargy[10] must have his quiet course.	
	If not, he foams at mouth, and by and by	
	Breaks out to savage madness. Look, he stirs.	
	Do[11] you withdraw yourself a little while,	
	He will recover straight. When he is gone	65
	I would on great occasion[12] speak with you.	

Exit Cassio

	How is it, general? Have you not hurt your head?	
Othello	Dost thou mock me?	
Iago	I mock you not, by heaven.	
	Would you would bear your fortune like a man.	70
Othello	A horned man's[13] a monster and a beast.	
Iago	There's many a beast then in a populous city,	
	And many a civil[14] monster.	
Othello	Did he confess it?	
Iago	Good sir, be a man.	75
	Think every bearded fellow that's but yoked[15]	
	May draw with you. There's millions now alive	
	That nightly lie in those unproper[16] beds	
	Which they dare swear peculiar.[17] Your case is better.	
	O, 'tis the spite of hell, the fiend's arch-mock,	80
	To lip[18] a wanton[19] in a secure couch	
	And to suppose her chaste! No, let me know,	
	And knowing what I am, I know what she shall be.	
Othello	O, thou art wise, 'tis certain.	

[10] *Fit*

[11] *If*

[12] *An important matter*

[13] *A cuckold*

[14] *City dwelling*

[15] *Married (derogatory term)*

[16] *Unfaithful*

[17] *Faithful*

[18] *Kiss* [19] *Promiscuous woman*

Iago   Stand you awhile apart.   85
Confine yourself but in a patient list.[20]
Whilst you were here, o'erwhelmed with your grief –
A passion most unsuiting such a man –
Cassio came hither. I shifted him away,
And laid good 'scuse upon your ecstasy,[21]   90
Bade him anon return and here speak with me,
The which he promised. Do but encave[22] yourself,
And mark the fleers,[23] the gibes and notable scorns
That dwell in every region of his face.
For I will make him tell the tale anew,   95
Where, how, how oft, how long ago, and when
He hath and is again to cope[24] your wife.
I say, but mark his gesture. Marry, patience,
Or I shall say you're all-in-all in spleen,[25]
And nothing of a man.   100

Othello Dost thou hear, Iago?
I will be found most cunning in my patience,
But – dost thou hear? – most bloody.

Iago   That's not amiss,
But yet keep time[26] in all. Will you withdraw?   105

Othello retires

Now will I question Cassio of Bianca,
A hussy that by selling her desires
Buys herself bread and clothes: it is a creature
That dotes on Cassio – as 'tis the strumpet's plague[27]
To beguile[28] many and be beguiled by one.   110
He, when he hears of her, cannot refrain
From the excess of laughter. Here he comes.

Re-enter Cassio

As he shall smile, Othello shall go mad;
And his unbookish[29] jealousy must conster[30]
Poor Cassio's smiles, gestures, and light behaviour,   115
Quite in the wrong. How do you now, lieutenant?

Cassio   The worser that you give me the addition[31]
Whose want[32] even kills me.

Iago	Ply Desdemona well and you are sure on't.
	[Speaking lower] Now, if this suit lay in Bianca's power, 120
	How quickly should you speed!
Cassio	Alas, poor wretch!
Othello	*[Aside]* Look how he laughs already.
Iago	I never knew woman love man so.
Cassio	Alas, poor rogue! I think, i'faith she loves me. 125
Othello	*[Aside]* Now he denies it faintly, and laughs it out.
Iago	Do you hear, Cassio?
Othello	*[Aside]* Now he importunes him
	To tell it o'er. Go to, well said, well said.
Iago	She gives it out that you shall marry hey. 130
	Do you intend it?
Cassio	Ha, ha, ha!
Othello	*[Aside]* Do ye triumph, Roman, do you triumph?
Cassio	I marry! What, a customer?[33] Prithee, bear some
	charity to my wit – do not think it so unwholesome.[34] 135
	Ha, ha, ha!
Othello	*[Aside]* So, so, so, so. They laugh that wins.
Iago	Faith, the cry goes that you marry her.
Cassio	Prithee, say true.
Iago	I am a very villain else. 140
Othello	Ha' you scored[35] me? Well.
Cassio	This is the monkey's own giving out. She is
	persuaded I will marry her out of her own love and
	flattery, not out of my promise.

[33] *Prostitute*

[34] *Give his intelligence some credit*

[35] *Injured*

Othello   *[Aside]* Iago beckons me. Now he begins the story.   145

Cassio   She was here even now. She haunts me in every place. I was the other day talking on the sea-bank with certain Venetians, and thither comes the bauble,[36] and, she falls me thus about my neck.

36 *Pretty plaything*

Othello   Crying 'O dear, Cassio!' as it were. His gesture imports[37] it. 150

37 *Suggests*

Cassio   So hangs and lolls and weeps upon me, so hales[38] and pulls me – ha, ha, ha!

38 *Grabs*

Othello   *[Aside]* Now he tells how she plucked him to my chamber. O, I see that nose of yours, but not that dog I shall throw it to!   155

Cassio   Well, I must leave her company.

Iago   Before me, look where she comes.

Cassio   'Tis such another fitchew![39] Marry, a perfumed one.

39 *Polecat*

Enter Bianca

What do you mean by this haunting of me?

Bianca   Let the devil and his dam[40] haunt you. What did you 160 mean by that same handkerchief you gave me even now? I was a fine fool to take it. I must take out the work – a likely piece of work, that you should find it in your chamber and know not who left it there. This is some minx's token, and I must take out the 165 work. There, give it your hobby-horse.[41] Wheresoever you had it, I'll take out no work on't.

40 *Mother*

41 *Loose woman*

Cassio   How now, my sweet Bianca, how now, how now?

Othello   By heaven, that should be my handkerchief.

Bianca   An you'll come to supper to-night, you may; an you 170 will not, come when you are next prepared for.[42]

42 *If Cassio doesn't go to her that evening, he need never go to her again*

Exit

Iago	After her, after her.
Cassio	Faith, I must, she'll rail[43] in the street else.
Iago	Will you sup there?
Cassio	Faith, I intend so.
Iago	Well, I may chance to see you, for I would very fain[44] speak with you.
Cassio	Prithee, come; will you?
Iago	Go to, say no more.

Exit Cassio

Othello	*[Advancing]* How shall I murder him, Iago?
Iago	Did you perceive how he laughed at his vice?
Othello	O Iago!
Iago	And did you see the handkerchief?
Othello	Was that mine?
Iago	Yours, by this hand. And to see how he prizes the foolish woman your wife. She gave it him, and he hath given it his whore.
Othello	I would have him nine years a-killing.[45] A fine woman, a fair woman, a sweet woman.
Iago	Nay, you must forget that.
Othello	Ay, let her rot, and perish, and be damned tonight, for she shall not live. No, my heart is turned to stone; I strike it, and it hurts my hand. O, the world hath not a sweeter creature! She might lie by an emperor's side and command him tasks.
Iago	Nay, that's not your way.

Margin notes:

175

180

185

190

195

43 *Shout and roar*

44 *Like to*

45 *He could spend nine years murdering Cassio*

Othello   Hang her, I do but say what she is – so delicate
with her needle, an admirable musician. O, she
will sing the savageness out of a bear! Of so high
and plenteous wit[46] and invention.[47]   200

Iago   She's the worse for all this.

Othello   O, a thousand, a thousand times! And then of so
gentle a condition!

Iago   Ay, too gentle.

Othello   Nay, that's certain. But yet the pity of it, Iago.   205
O, Iago, the pity of it, Iago!

Iago   If you are so fond over her iniquity,[48] give her patent[49]
to offend; for, if it touch not you, it comes near nobody.

Othello   I will chop her into messes.[50] Cuckold me!

Iago   O, 'tis foul in her.   210

Othello   With mine officer.

Iago   That's fouler.

Othello   Get me some poison, Iago, this night. I'll not
expostulate[51] with her, lest her body and beauty
unprovide[52] my mind again. This night, Iago.   215

Iago   Do it not with poison. Strangle her in her bed, even
the bed she hath contaminated.

Othello   Good, good, the justice of it pleases, very good.

Iago   And for Cassio, let me be his undertaker.[53] You
shall hear more by midnight.   220

Othello   Excellent good.

A trumpet within

What trumpet is that same?

46 *Intelligence*   47 *Creativity*

48 *Ready to forgive her sins*   49 *Permission*

50 *Small pieces*

51 *Argue*
52 *Dissuade*

53 *Killer*

Iago	I warrant, something from Venice. sure. 'Tis Lodovico. This comes from the Duke. See, your wife's with him.
	Enter Lodovico, Desdemona, and Attendants
Lodovico	God save the worthy general. 225
Othello	With all my heart, sir.
Lodovico	The Duke and the senators of Venice greet you.
	Gives him a letter
Othello	I kiss the instrument of their pleasures.
	Opens the letter, and reads
Desdemona	And what's the news, good cousin Lodovico?
Iago	I am very glad to see you, signor. Welcome to Cyprus. 230
Lodovico	I thank you. How does Lieutenant Cassio?
Iago	Lives, sir.
Desdemona	Cousin, there's fall'n between him and my lord An unkind breach.[54] But you shall make all well.
Othello	Are you sure of that? 235
Desdemona	My lord.
Othello	*[Reads]* 'This fail you not to do as you will' –
Lodovico	He did not call, he's busy in the paper.[55] Is there division 'twixt my lord and Cassio?
Desdemona	A most unhappy one. I would do much 240 T'atone[56] them, for the love I bear to Cassio.
Othello	Fire and brimstone!
Desdemona	My lord?

[54] *Unfortunate rift*

[55] *Reading*

[56] *Reconcile*

57 *Crazy*	**Othello**	Are you wise?[57]
	Desdemona	What, is he angry? 245
	Lodovico	Maybe the letter moved him,
		For, as I think, they do command him home,
58 *Putting Cassio in his place*		Deputing Cassio in his government.[58]
	Desdemona	By my troth, I am glad on't.
	Othello	Indeed! 250
	Desdemona	My lord?
	Othello	I am glad to see you mad.
	Desdemona	Why, sweet Othello!
	Othello	*[Striking her]* Devil!
	Desdemona	I have not deserved this. 255
	Lodovico	My lord, this would not be believed in Venice,
		Though I should swear I saw't. 'Tis very much.
		Make her amends, she weeps.
	Othello	O devil, devil!
59 *Be filled with*		If that the earth could teem[59] with woman's tears, 260
60 *Women's tears are crocodile tears, i.e. fake*		Each drop she falls would prove a crocodile.[60]
		Out of my sight!
	Desdemona	I will not stay to offend you.
		Going
	Lodovico	Truly, an obedient lady.
		I do beseech your lordship call her back. 265
	Othello	Mistress!
	Desdemona	My lord?
	Othello	What would you with her, sir?

Lodovico	Who, I, my lord?	

Othello   Ay, you did wish that I would make her turn.[61]   270
Sir, she can turn and turn, and yet go on
And turn again, and she can weep, sir, weep,
And she's obedient, as you say, obedient,
Very obedient.
[To Desdemona] Proceed you in your tears.   275
[To Lodovico] Concerning this, sir –
[To Desdemona] O well painted passion![62]
[To Lodovico] I am commanded home.
[To Desdemona] Get you away.
I'll send for you anon.   280
[To Lodovico] Sir, I obey the mandate,
And will return to Venice.
[To Desdemona] Hence, avaunt![63]

Exit Desdemona

Cassio shall have my place, and, sir, tonight
I do entreat that we may sup together.   285
You are welcome, sir, to Cyprus. Goats and monkeys![64]

Exit

Lodovico   Is this the noble Moor whom our full senate
Call all-in-all sufficient?[65] Is this the nature
Whom passion could not shake,[66] whose solid virtue
The shot of accident nor dart of chance   290
Could neither graze nor pierce?[67]

Iago   He is much changed.

Lodovico   Are his wits safe? Is he not light of brain?[68]

Iago   He's that he is. I may not breathe my censure[69]
What he might be. If what he might he is not,   295
I would to heaven he were.

Lodovico   What, strike his wife!

Iago   Faith, that was not so well.[70] Yet would I knew
That stroke would prove the worst.[71]

---

[61] Return, also a pun on 'turn' as in being false

[62] Well-acted show of sadness

[63] Be gone!

[64] Refers to earlier comments comparing Desdemona and Cassio's supposed lechery to goats and monkeys

[65] Competent in every way

[66] Who never lost control

[67] The solid personality that nothing could affect

[68] Going insane

[69] He is unwilling to criticise Othello

[70] That was not good

[71] He fears Othello will do worse to Desdemona

<table>
<tr><td>72 Habit</td><td>**Lodovico**</td><td>Is it his use,[72]</td><td>300</td></tr>
<tr><td>73 Did the letters upset him</td><td></td><td>Or did the letters work upon his blood[73]
And new-create this fault?</td><td></td></tr>
<tr><td></td><td>**Iago**</td><td>Alas, alas.
It is not honesty in me to speak
What I have seen and known. You shall observe him,</td><td>305</td></tr>
<tr><td>74 Expose</td><td></td><td>And his own courses will denote[74] him so</td><td></td></tr>
<tr><td></td><td></td><td>That I may save my speech. Do but go after,</td><td></td></tr>
<tr><td>75 Observe</td><td></td><td>And mark[75] how he continues.</td><td></td></tr>
<tr><td></td><td>**Lodovico**</td><td>I am sorry that I am deceived in him.</td><td></td></tr>
<tr><td></td><td></td><td>*Exit*</td><td></td></tr>
</table>

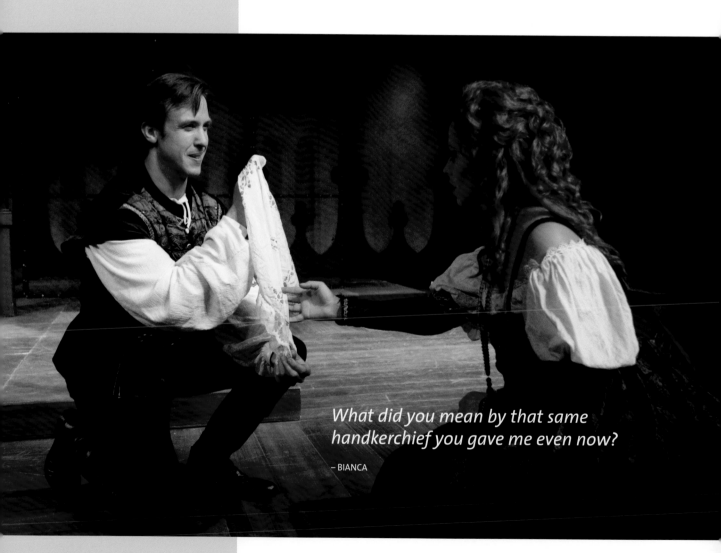

What did you mean by that same handkerchief you gave me even now?

– BIANCA

THE BREATHTAKING SPEED of Othello's plummet into jealous madness continues in this act. Othello is so upset that he has an epileptic fit, and, when he recovers, Iago is sure to mention that Cassio witnessed his unmanly weakness. This humiliates Othello, and riles his emotions up to such an extent he cannot appear his normal, chivalrous self to Lodovico, newly arrived from Venice to summon Othello home.

Iago has cleverly contrived to have Othello in place to eavesdrop on his conversation with Cassio. The conversation is about Bianca, but it appears to Othello that Cassio is talking about Desdemona. He is enraged to hear how crazy Desdemona is about Cassio, how she follows him around, and how he sees her as a common prostitute. Then Bianca herself arrives, something which could have ruined Iago's plan, but luck is on his side yet again, because Bianca is waving the handkerchief in Cassio's face and demanding to know the 'minx' who gave it to him. To Othello, this is further proof of an illicit relationship.

When Desdemona mentions to Lodovico the rift between Cassio and Othello, the incensed Othello lashes out and strikes her. Lodovico is astounded at his atrocious behavior, and asks Iago – of all people – if Othello has gone mad. The fact that the war ended before it had even begun was quite puzzling: but now it becomes clear that Shakespeare had a compelling reason for creating a peaceful Cyprus. Othello has no distractions whatsoever, and this gives him time to obsess about Desdemona and Cassio. His powerful emotions have been expertly channeled in the wrong direction by Iago.

The tone of this scene is ominous and foreboding, with Othello making the horrible decision to kill Desdemona that night, and Iago promising to kill Cassio. Yet the summons to Venice gives the audience hope that the couple may yet escape Iago's interference.

*it comes o'er my memory
As doth the raven o'er the
infectious house,
Boding to all! – he had my
handkerchief*

—OTHELLO

KEY **POINTS**

- *Othello overhears Iago and Cassio's disparaging conversation about Bianca, and believes they are discussing Desdemona.*

- *Lodovico arrives to summon Othello back to Venice.*

- *Othello strikes Desdemona in front of everyone.*

- *Iago's plot expands to include Cassio's destruction.*

- *Iago tells Othello to smother Desdemona in the marital bed, while he kills Cassio.*

A ROOM IN THE CASTLE

Enter Othello and Emilia

Othello   You have seen nothing then?

Emilia   Nor ever heard, nor ever did suspect.

Othello   Yes, you have seen Cassio and she together.

Emilia   But then I saw no harm, and then I heard
Each syllable that breath made up between 'em.   5

Othello   What, did they never whisper?

Emilia   Never, my lord.

Othello   Nor send you out o'th' way?

Emilia   Never.

¹ *A face mask that you might wear to a masked ball, common in Venetian dress*

Othello   To fetch her fan, her gloves, her mask,¹ nor nothing?   10

Emilia   Never, my lord.

Othello   That's strange.

² *Dare*

Emilia   I durst,² my lord, to wager she is honest,
Lay down my soul at stake. If you think other,
Remove your thought; it doth abuse your bosom.³   15

³ *It insults your intuition*

If any wretch ha' put this in your head,
Let heaven requite it with the serpent's curse,⁴

⁴ *Let God punish him with eternal damnation*

For if she be not honest, chaste, and true,
There's no man happy; the purest of their wives
Is foul as slander.   20

Othello   Bid her come hither. Go.

Exit Emilia

⁵ *Brothel-keeper*
⁶ *Clever*
⁷ *Terrible*

She says enough, yet she's a simple bawd⁵
That cannot say as much. This is a subtle⁶ whore,
A closet lock and key of villanous⁷ secrets,
And yet she'll kneel and pray – I ha' seen her do't.   25

Enter Desdemona with Emilia

Desdemona My lord, what is your will?

Othello Pray you, chuck, come hither.

Desdemona What is your pleasure?

Othello Let me see your eyes.
Look in my face. 30

Desdemona What horrible fancy's this?

Othello *[To Emilia]* Some of your function,[8] mistress;
Leave procreants[9] alone and shut the door,
Cough or cry 'Hem' if anybody come.
Your mystery,[10] your mystery – nay, dispatch.[11] 35

[8] Do your nasty job
[9] People who are having sexual relations
[10] Job [11] Leave us now

Exit Emilia

Desdemona Upon my knees, what doth your speech import?[12]
I understand a fury in your words.
But not the words.

[12] Mean

Othello Why? What art thou?

Desdemona Your wife, my lord, your true and loyal wife. 40

Othello Come, swear it, damn thyself,
Lest, being like one of heaven,[13] the devils themselves
Should fear to seize thee. Therefore be double-damn'd:
Swear thou art honest.

[13] An angel

Desdemona Heaven doth truly know it. 45

Othello Heaven truly knows that thou art false as hell.

Desdemona To whom, my lord? With whom? How am I false?

Othello Ah, Desdemona, away! Away! Away!

Desdemona Alas, the heavy day! Why do you weep?
Am I the motive of these tears, my lord? 50
If haply[14] you my father do suspect

[14] It happens that

An instrument of this your calling back,
Lay not your blame on me. If you have lost him,
I have lost him too.

Othello   Had it pleased God   55
To try me with affliction; had they rain'd
All kinds of sores and shames on my bare head,
Steep'd me in poverty to the very lips,
Given to captivity me and my utmost hopes,
I should have found in some place of my soul   60
A drop of patience. But, alas, to make me
A fixed figure for the time of scorn
To point his slow unmoving finger at –
Yet could I bear that too, well, very well.

[15] Gathered   But there where I have garner'd[15] up my heart,   65
Where either I must live or bear no life,
[16] Life   The fountain from the which my current[16] runs
Or else dries up – to be discarded thence,
[17] Tank   Or keep it as a cistern[17] for foul toads
[18] Reproduce [19] Face   To knot and gender[18] in! Turn thy complexion[19] there,   70
[20] Angel   Patience, thou young and rose-lipp'd cherubin,[20]
Ay, here look grim as hell.

[21] Believes me to be   **Desdemona**   I hope my noble lord esteems me[21] honest.

[22] Slaughterhouse, where eggs that flies   **Othello**   O, ay – as summer flies are in the shambles,[22]
lay on rotten meat turn into maggots   That quicken even with blowing.[23] O thou weed,   75
[23] Lay eggs every time the wind blows   Who art so lovely fair, and smell'st so sweet,
That the sense aches at thee – would thou hadst
ne'er been born!

[24] Sin that she is unaware of   **Desdemona**   Alas, what ignorant sin[24] have I committed?

Othello   Was this fair paper, this most goodly book,
Made to write 'whore' upon? What committed?   80
[25] Common prostitute   Committed? O thou public commoner![25]
I should make very forges of my cheeks,
That would to cinders burn up modesty,
[26] If he was Desdemona, his cheeks would   Did I but speak thy deeds.[26] What committed?
be fiery red with embarrassment   Heaven stops the[27] nose at it, and the moon winks;[28]   85
[27] Holds its [28] Closes its eyes   The bawdy wind that kisses all it meets,
Is hush'd within the hollow mine of earth,
And will not hear't. What committed?
[29] Insolent whore!   Impudent strumpet![29]

Desdemona	By heaven, you do me wrong.	90

Othello   Are you not a strumpet?

Desdemona   No, as I am a Christian.
If to preserve this vessel[30] for my lord
From any other foul unlawful touch
Be not to be a strumpet, I am none.   95

30 Body

Othello   What, not a whore?

Desdemona   No, as I shall be saved.

Othello   Is't possible?

Desdemona   O, heaven forgive us!

Othello   I cry you mercy then.   100
I took you for that cunning whore of Venice
That married with Othello.
[Raising his voice] You, mistress,
That have the office opposite to Saint Peter[31]
And keep the gate of hell,   105

31 Saint Peter guards the gates of heaven

Re-enter Emilia

you, you, ay, you.
We ha' done our course,[32] there's money for your pains.
I pray you, turn the key and keep our counsel.[33]

32 Business
33 Secret

Exit Othello

Emilia   Alas, what does this gentleman conceive?[34]
How do you, madam? How do you, my good lady?   110

34 Believe

Desdemona   Faith, half asleep.

Emilia   Good madam, what's the matter with my lord?

Desdemona   With who?

Emilia   Why, with my lord, madam.

Desdemona   Who is thy lord?   115

Emilia   He that is yours, sweet lady.

Desdemona   I ha' none. Do not talk to me, Emilia.
I cannot weep, nor answers have I none
But what should go by water.[35] Prithee tonight
Lay on my bed my wedding sheets, remember.   120
And call thy husband hither.

Emilia   Here's a change indeed.

Exit

Desdemona   'Tis meet[36] I should be used so, very meet.
How have I been behaved, that he might stick
The small'st opinion[37] on my least misuse?[38]   125

Re-enter Emilia with Iago

Iago   What is your pleasure, madam? How is't with you?

Desdemona   I cannot tell. Those that do teach young babes
Do it with gentle means and easy tasks.
He might ha' chid me so, for, in good faith,
I am a child to chiding.[39]   130

Iago   What's the matter, lady?

Emilia   Alas, Iago, my lord hath so bewhored her,[40]
Thrown such despite[41] and heavy terms upon her,
As true hearts cannot bear it.

Desdemona   Am I that name, Iago?   135

Iago   What name, fair lady?

Desdemona   Such as she said my lord did say I was.

Emilia   He call'd her whore. A beggar in his drink
Could not have laid such terms upon his callet.[42]

Iago   Why did he so?   140

Desdemona   I do not know. I am sure I am none such.

Sidenotes:

[35] She can only cry

[36] Fair

[37] Criticism   [38] Perfect conduct

[39] She is not used to such treatment

[40] Humiliated her and called her a whore

[41] Contempt, scorn

[42] A drunken beggar wouldn't have used the kind of language Othello did

Iago	Do not weep, do not weep. Alas the day!
Emilia	Hath she forsook so many noble matches,
	Her father and her country and her friends,
	To be call'd whore? Would it not make one weep? 145
Desdemona	It is my wretched fortune.
Iago	Beshrew[43] him for't!
	How comes this trick upon him?
Desdemona	Nay, heaven doth know.
Emilia	I will be hang'd, if some eternal villain, 150
	Some busy and insinuating rogue,
	Some cogging,[44] cozening[45] slave, to get some office,
	Have not devised this slander. I will be hang'd else.
Iago	Fie, there is no such man. It is impossible.
Desdemona	If any such there be, heaven pardon him. 155
Emilia	A halter[46] pardon him, and hell gnaw his bones!
	Why should he call her whore? Who keeps her company?
	What place? What time? What form? What likelihood?
	The Moor's abused by some most villanous knave,
	Some base, notorious knave, some scurvy fellow. 160
	O heaven, that such companions thou'dst unfold,[47]
	And put in every honest hand a whip
	To lash the rascals naked through the world,
	Even from the east to th' west!
Iago	Speak within door.[48] 165
Emilia	O, fie upon them. Some such squire he was
	That turn'd your wit the seamy side without,[49]
	And made you to suspect me with the Moor.
Iago	You are a fool. Go to.[50]
Desdemona	O God, Iago, 170
	What shall I do to win my lord again?
	Good friend, go to him; for by this light of heaven,
	I know not how I lost him. Here I kneel.

[43] Curse him!
[44] Lying [45] Deceiving
[46] Hangman
[47] Villains should be revealed
[48] Be careful what she says
[49] Wrong way round
[50] Be quiet

If e'er my will did trespass 'gainst his love,

Either in discourse[51] of thought or actual deed,   175

Or that mine eyes, mine ears, or any sense

Delighted them[52] in any other form,

Or that I do not yet, and ever did,

And ever will – though he do shake me off

To beggarly divorcement – love him dearly,   180

Comfort forswear[53] me. Unkindness may do much,

And his unkindness may defeat[54] my life,

But never taint my love. I cannot say 'whore'

It does abhor me now I speak the word.

To do the act that might the addition[55] earn,   185

Not the world's mass of vanity could make me.[56]

Iago   I pray you, be content. 'Tis but his humour.[57]

The business of the state does him offence,

And he does chide with you.

Desdemona   If 'twere no other!   190

Iago   It is but so, I warrant.

Trumpets within

Hark how these instruments summon to supper.

The messengers of Venice stays the meat.[58]

Go in, and weep not. All things shall be well.

Exit Desdemona and Emilia

Enter Roderigo

How now, Roderigo?   195

Roderigo   I do not find that thou deal'st justly[59] with me.

Iago   What in the contrary?

Roderigo   Every day thou daff'st[60] me with some device,[61] Iago,

and rather, as it seems to me now, keep'st from me

all conveniency[62] than suppliest me with the least   200

advantage of hope. I will indeed no longer endure

it, nor am I yet persuaded to put up in peace what

already I have foolishly suffered.[63]

Iago	Will you hear me, Roderigo?	
Roderigo	Faith, I have heard too much, for your words and performances[64] are no kin together.[65]	205

[64] Actions [65] Don't add up

Iago	You charge me most unjustly.	

| Roderigo | With naught but truth. I have wasted myself out of my means.[66] The jewels you have had from me to deliver to Desdemona would half have corrupted a votarist.[67] You have told me she hath received 'em and returned me expectations and comforts of sudden respect and acquaintance, but I find none. | 210 |

[66] Money

[67] Monk

Iago	Well, go to, very well.	

| Roderigo | 'Very well', 'go to'! I cannot go to, man, nor 'tis not very well. Nay, I think it is scurvy,[68] and begin to find myself fopped[69] in it. | 215 |

[68] Trickery
[69] Fooled

Iago	Very well.	

| Roderigo | I tell you 'tis not very well. I will make myself known to Desdemona. If she will return me my jewels, I will give over my suit and repent my unlawful solicitation.[70] If not, assure yourself I will seek satisfaction[71] of you. | 220 |

[70] He will not attempt to court her further
[71] Repayment

Iago	You have said now.	

| Roderigo | Ay, and said nothing but what I protest intendment of doing. | 225 |

| Iago | Why, now I see there's mettle[72] in thee, and even from this instant to build on thee a better opinion than ever before. Give me thy hand, Roderigo. Thou hast taken against me a most just exception,[73] but yet, I protest, I have dealt most directly in thy affair. | 230 |

[72] Strength

[73] Grievance

Roderigo	It hath not appeared.	

| Iago | It hath not appeared, and your suspicion is not without wit and judgement. But, Roderigo, if thou hast that in thee indeed which I | 235 |

have greater reason to believe now than ever – I mean purpose, courage, and valour – this night show it. If thou the next night following enjoy not Desdemona, take me from this world with treachery, and devise engines[74] for my life. 240

74 *Plots against*

75 *Scope*

Roderigo Well, what is it? Is it within reason and compass?[75]

Iago Sir, there is especial commission come from Venice to depute Cassio in Othello's place.

Roderigo Is that true? Why then, Othello and Desdemona return again to Venice. 245

Iago O no, he goes into Mauritania, and takes away with him the fair Desdemona, unless his abode be lingered[76] here by some accident, wherein none can be so determinate[77] as the removing of Cassio.

76 *Prolonged*
77 *Effective*

Roderigo How do you mean 'removing' of him? 250

Iago Why, by making him uncapable of Othello's place – knocking out his brains.

Roderigo And that you would have me to do.

Iago Ay, if you dare do yourself a profit and a right. He sups tonight with a harlotry,[78] and thither will I 255 go to him. He knows not yet of his honourable[79] fortune. If you will watch his going thence, which I will fashion[80] to fall out between twelve and one, you may take him at your pleasure. I will be near, to second[81] your attempt, and he shall fall between 260 us. Come, stand not amazed at it, but go along with me. I will show you such a necessity in his death that you shall think yourself bound to put it on him. It is now high supper-time, and the night grows to waste. About it. 265

78 *Prostitute*
79 *Good*

80 *Contrive*

81 *Support*

Roderigo I will hear further reason for this.

Iago And you shall be satisfied.

Exit

Why, by making him uncapable of Othello's place –
knocking out his brains

– IAGO

THE SCENE OPENS with Othello questioning Emilia about Desdemona's relationship with Cassio. Emila swears faithfully that they have never been alone, much less inappropriate, and it seems as if Othello is having second thoughts, as he even says: *That's strange.* For a brief moment, the truth seems tantalisingly close, but then he reasons that Emilia, Desdemona's lady-in-waiting, would naturally lie for her mistress: *She says enough, yet she's a simple bawd / That cannot say as much. This is a subtle whore.* He calls Emilia a bawd (a woman in charge of a brothel) and tells her to stand guard while he sleeps with Desdemona, whom he calls a subtle whore – a conniving prostitute. Othello's language is extremely offensive, and unrecognisable from the eloquence with which he spoke in Acts I and II.

Desdemona tries to convince Othello that she is no 'strumpet' and that she is chaste, but nothing will appease him now. When he leaves, Emilia laments his crude language to her young mistress, and Iago is once again serendipitously on hand to console and advise. Desdemona even kneels before him, begging him to believe in her innocence, but even this does not make him question his terrible actions. Desdemona is a young, vulnerable girl, literally on her knees, and Iago is completely indifferent to her suffering. It is natural to assume that a human being will have some degree of conscience, and that is what is so disturbing about Iago. When Emilia suggests that some terrible person has turned Othello against Desdemona, Iago says *Fie, there is no such man. It is impossible.* This is yet another moment of dramatic irony. Iago is so believeable. He is that terrible man, yet he claims to be disgusted at the very idea that such a character could exist. Is it any wonder that everyone believes in Iago? He is a brilliant and convincing actor, as well as an acute and perceptive observer. He really is a consummate villain and he preys relentlessly on the weaknesses and human frailty of others, with no conscience to restrain him, much less stop him.

The arrival of Roderigo at the end of the scene is a key moment which makes us feel that an obstacle to Iago's ambitions may yet appear. Roderigo has finally concluded that Iago has been stringing him along, and wants to make himself known to Desdemona and return to Venice. Iago has no real trouble convincing Roderigo to trust in him again, and even gets him to agree to kill Cassio. Granted, Roderigo may not be an intelligent character, but Iago has an amazing ability to make everyone believe him – no one questions him.

*If to preserve this vessel for my lord
From any other foul unlawful touch
Be not to be a strumpet, I am none*

– DESDEMONA

KEY **POINTS**

- *Othello acts hatefully towards Desdemona, and refuses to believe her protestations of innocence.*

- *Emilia hates Othello, and wishes that Desdemona had not chosen him.*

- *Iago has Roderigo primed to kill Cassio that very night.*

ANOTHER ROOM IN THE CASTLE

Enter Othello, Lodovico, Desdemona, Emilia, and
Attendants

Lodovico	I do beseech you, sir, trouble yourself no further.
Othello	O, pardon me, 'twill do me good to walk.
Lodovico	Madam, good night. I humbly thank your ladyship.
Desdemona	Your honour is most welcome.
Othello	Will you walk, sir? 5 O, Desdemona!
Desdemona	My lord?
Othello	Get you to bed on th'instant. I will be returned forthwith.[1] Dismiss your attendant there. Look't be done.
Desdemona	I will, my lord. 10

Exit Othello, Lodovico, and Attendants

Emilia	How goes it now? He looks gentler than he did.
Desdemona	He says he will return incontinent.[2] He hath commanded me to go to bed, And bid me to dismiss you.
Emilia	Dismiss me? 15
Desdemona	It was his bidding. Therefore, good Emilia, Give me my nightly wearing, and adieu. We must not now displease him.
Emilia	I would you had never seen him.
Desdemona	So would not I. My love doth so approve him 20 That even his stubbornness, his checks, his frowns – Prithee unpin me – have grace and favour in them.
Emilia	I have laid those sheets you bade me on the bed.

[1] Shortly

[2] Immediately

Desdemona can't share in Emilia's regret that she ever met Othello, because she loves him unconditionally, and so she loves even his criticisms and his displeasure

Desdemona All's one. Good faith, how foolish are our minds!
         If I do die before thee, prithee shroud[3] me   25
         In one of those same sheets.

Emilia Come, come, you talk.

Desdemona My mother had a maid call'd Barbary:[4]
         She was in love, and he she loved proved mad
         And did forsake her. She had a song of willow.[5]   30
         An old thing 'twas, but it express'd her fortune,
         And she died singing it. That song tonight
         Will not go from my mind. I have much to do,
         But to go hang my head all at one side[6]
         And sing it, like poor Barbary. Prithee, dispatch.   35

Emilia Shall I go fetch your nightgown?

Desdemona No. Unpin[7] me here.
         This Lodovico is a proper[8] man.

Emilia A very handsome man.

Desdemona He speaks well.   40

Emilia I know a lady in Venice would have walked barefoot
         to Palestine for a touch of his nether[9] lip.

Desdemona *[Singing]*
         'The poor soul sat sighing by a sycamore tree,
         Sing all a green willow.
         Her hand on her bosom, her head on her knee,   45
         Sing willow, willow, willow:
         The fresh streams ran by her and murmur'd her moans,
         Sing willow, willow, willow.
         Her salt tears fell from her and soften'd the stones,
         Sing willow' –   50

         Lay by these. –

         'willow, willow.'

         Prithee, hie thee. He'll come anon.

         [Singing]
         'Sing all a green willow must be my garland.
         Let nobody blame him; his scorn I approve' –   55

         Nay, that's not next. Hark, who is't that knocks?

[3] Wrap me for burial

[4] The maid was from North Africa – like Othello

[5] The willow can be a symbol of death and loss, as in 'weeping willow'

[6] She can only hang her head in despair

[7] Unbutton her garments

[8] Handsome

[9] Lower

Emilia   It's the wind.

Desdemona *[Singing]*
'I call'd my love false love, but what said he then?
Sing willow, willow, willow.
If I court more women, you'll couch with more men.'   60

So, get thee gone. Good night. Mine eyes do itch.
Doth that bode weeping?

Emilia   'Tis neither here nor there.

Desdemona I have heard it said so. O, these men, these men!
Dost thou in conscience think – tell me, Emilia –   65

10 Deceive   That there be women do abuse[10] their husbands
11 Immoral ways   In such gross kind?[11]

Emilia   There be some such, no question.

Desdemona Wouldst thou do such a deed for all the world?

Emilia   Why, would not you?   70

Desdemona No, by this heavenly light.

Emilia   Nor I neither by this heavenly light;
I might do't as well i' the dark.

Desdemona Wouldst thou do such a deed for all the world?

Emilia   The world's a huge thing. It is a great price for   75
a small vice.

Desdemona In truth, I think thou wouldst not.

12 Regret it   **Emilia**   In truth, I think, I should, and undo't[12] when I had
done. Marry, I would not do such a thing for a
13 Fancy ring *14 Fine linens*   joint ring,[13] nor for measures of lawn,[14] nor for   80
gowns, petticoats, nor caps, nor any petty
15 Trivial thing   exhibition;[15] but for the whole world? Why, who would
not make her husband a cuckold to make him a
16 Risk   monarch? I should venture[16] purgatory for't.

17 Curse   **Desdemona** Beshrew[17] me, if I would do such a wrong   85
For the whole world.

Emilia   Why the wrong is but a wrong i'th' world, and
having the world for your labour,[18] 'tis a wrong in your
own world, and you might quickly make it right.

Desdemona   I do not think there is any such woman.   90

Emilia   Yes, a dozen, and as many
To th' vantage as would store the world they played for.[19]
But I do think it is their husbands' faults
If wives do fall. Say that they slack their duties,
And pour our treasures into foreign laps,[20]   95
Or else break out in peevish jealousies,
Throwing restraint[21] upon us; or say they strike us,
Or scant our former having in despite:[22]
Why, we have galls;[23] and though we have some grace,
Yet have we some revenge. Let husbands know   100
Their wives have sense[24] like them. They see, and smell,
And have their palates[25] both for sweet and sour,
As husbands have. What is it that they do
When they change us for others? Is it sport?
I think it is. And doth affection breed[26] it?   105
I think it doth. Is't frailty[27] that thus errs?
It is so, too. And have not we affections,
Desires for sport,[28] and frailty, as men have?
Then let them use[29] us well, else let them know
The ills we do, their ills instruct us so.[30]   110

Desdemona   Good night, good night. God me such uses send
Not to pick bad from bad, but by bad mend!

Exit

[18] Work

[19] Many more would do it if the world was the prize

[20] Sleep with other women

[21] Restrictions

[22] Cut down on what they previously gave their wives out of spite

[23] Tempers

[24] Feelings

[25] Tastes

[26] Cause it

[27] Weakness

[28] Fun

[29] Treat

[30] The sins women commit are caused by men

May God let her hear of such women, not so that she can emulate them, but so she can learn from their mistakes

MODERN ENGLISH VERSION

ANOTHER ROOM IN THE CASTLE

Enter Othello, Lodovico, Desdemona, Emilia, and Attendants

Lodovico   Please sir, don't go to any more trouble for me.

Othello   It is no trouble, it will do me good to walk.

Lodovico   Thank you for a lovely evening, madam.

Desdemona   You are welcome, sir.

Othello   Let's go. Oh, Desdemona?

Desdemona   Yes, dear?

Othello   Go straight to bed. I'll be back soon. Tell Emilia to leave for the night.

Desdemona   I will do as you say.

Exit Othello, Lodovico, and Attendants

Emilia   How is everything now? Othello seems to be in a slightly better mood.

Desdemona   He said he'll be back shortly, and he told me to dismiss you for the evening.

Emilia   Dismiss me?

Desdemona   That's what he said. So I'll say good night, Emilia. Please give me my nightdress, and then you'd better leave. I don't want to do anything to irritate him at the moment.

Emilia   I wish you had never met him!

Desdemona   I would never regret having met him. I love him unconditionally, so even when he is cross or mean, I still love him. Will you help me undress, please?

Emilia   I dressed your bed with your wedding sheets, as you told me.

Desdemona   Thank you, Emilia. I'm a silly woman, but if I die before you, will you wrap me in my wedding sheets for a shroud?

Emilia   Don't talk silly.

Desdemona   My mother had a maid called Barbary. She was madly in love with this man who went crazy and left her, and she used to sing a song called 'Willow'. For some reason, that song is going round and round in my head tonight. She died singing it. And I have lots to do, but all I can do is weep and sing that same song. You'd better go, Emilia.

Emilia   Will I get your nightdress?

Desdemona   No, just help me undo my buttons. Lodovico seems like a nice man.

Emilia   He is a very handsome man.

Desdemona   He has a lovely voice.

Emilia   I know a lady in Venice who would have walked barefoot to Palestine for a kiss of his bottom lip.

Desdemona   [Singing]
'The poor soul sat sighing by a sycamore tree,
Sing all a green willow:
Her hand on her bosom, her head on her knee,
Sing willow, willow, willow:
The fresh streams ran by her, and murmur'd her moans;
Sing willow, willow, willow;
Her salt tears fell from her, and soften'd the stones;
Sing willow' –

Lay these close by.

[Singing]
'willow, willow'.

Please, come here; he'll come soon.

[Singing]
'Sing all a green willow must be my garland.
Let nobody blame him; his scorn I approve,' –

No, I'm getting the words mixed up. Did someone knock on the door?

Emilia   It's just the wind.

Desdemona   [Singing]
'I call'd my love false love; but what said he then?
Sing willow, willow, willow:

If I court more women, you'll sleep with more men!'
You'd better leave, Emilia. My eyes are stinging: does that mean I'm going to cry?

Emilia   It doesn't mean anything.

Desdemona   I think I've heard it is a bad sign. But tell me, Emilia, do you think there are women out there who would do something as terrible and immoral as cheat on their husbands?

Emilia   Oh yes, there are plenty of unfaithful women.

Desdemona   Would you cheat on your husband for all the world?

Emilia   Why, wouldn't you?

Desdemona   There is no way in heaven that I would!

Emilia   I wouldn't do it by heaven's light either. Maybe at night, though!

Desdemona   I don't believe you would do such a thing for the whole world!

Emilia   The world is a big thing. It might be worth such a huge prize to commit one small sin.

Desdemona   I don't think you're serious?

Emilia   Actually, I think I would, and I'd make up for it later. I wouldn't do it for a nice ring, or expensive clothes or anything like that, but, yes, for the whole world I think I would. I would betray my husband if it meant I could make him a king! I'd take the risk.

Desdemona   I swear to God that I couldn't do such a thing for any price.

Emilia   Well, it would only be a crime in this world – if you owned the world by doing it, you could quickly make up for it.

Desdemona   I don't really believe any woman would betray her husband.

Emilia   There are loads of women who betray their men. But I think it is the husband's fault if a wife slips up. If they neglect their wives, or give their love to someone else, or get jealous for no reason, or limit our freedom, for example. Or if they beat their wives, or take away their affections, well then, we're justified in getting our needs met elsewhere. Husbands don't realise that their wives are people too. They see, smell and touch the same things, they live in the same world as their husbands. Why do our husbands go elsewhere? Is it for fun? I think it is. And is it for affection? I think so. Is it our weakness which makes us cheat? I think so too, and don't we want affection and fun too? And aren't we as weak as men too? So, men should treat us well. Or we will go elsewhere too.

Desdemona   Good night, Emilia. Your view of men and women just makes me all the more determined never to cheat on my husband!

Exit

My love doth so approve him
That even his stubbornness, his checks, his frowns –
... have grace and favour in them

– DESDEMONA (ACT IV SCENE III)

FOCUS ON ACT 4

'The raven was a potent symbol of death and disease in Shakespeare's day, and Othello's mention of it would certainly have filled the original audience with a sense of unease'

THIS is an emotional and highly charged act. We continue to see the devastating effect of jealousy on Othello, but we also learn more about Desdemona and Emilia. Iago continues to play the part of sociopathic puppet-master: this in itself is surprising, because it is natural for us to expect a pang of conscience or some evidence of remorse, but we certainly don't get that in this act.

Othello's language has changed too. Now his speech contains disturbing symbolism and imagery. When Iago reminds him of the handkerchief Desdemona supposedly gave to Cassio, Othello replies:

> *By heaven, I would most gladly have forgot it.*
> *Thou said'st – it comes o'er my memory*
> *As doth the raven o'er the infectious house,*
> *Boding to all! – he had my handkerchief.*

The raven was a potent symbol of death and disease in Shakespeare's day, and Othello's mention of it would certainly have filled the original audience with a sense of unease. Othello's emotional turbulence causes him to have an 'epileptic' fit (probably not epilepsy, in our modern understanding of the word, but rather a seizure, or even a tantrum, caused by being emotionally overwhelmed). Cassio witnesses this, and Iago is sure to tell Othello that his supposed rival saw him in this vulnerable state: *Whilst you were here, o'erwhelmed with your grief – / A passion most unsuiting such a man – / Cassio came hither*.

Information in those days was often gleaned from eavesdropping, and so Iago has Othello hide while he has a conversation with Cassio about Desdemona:

> *Do but encave yourself,*
> *And mark the fleers, the gibes and notable scorns*
> *That dwell in every region of his face.*
> *For I will make him tell the tale anew,*

Nature would not invest herself in such shadowing passion without some instruction. It is not words that shakes me thus. Pish! Noses, ears, and lips. Is't possible? Confess? Handkerchief? O devil!

– OTHELLO (ACT IV SCENE I).

Where, how, how oft, how long ago, and when
    He hath and is again to cope your wife.

In an aside, Iago reveals that the conversation will really concern Bianca, a prostitute who is madly in love with Cassio. But Othello, a man as concerned with reputation as it is possible to be, is enraged to hear of how 'Desdemona' chases after Cassio in public: *She was here even now. She haunts me in every place. I was the other day talking on the sea-bank with certain Venetians, and thither comes the bauble, and, she falls me thus about my neck.*

When Bianca herself arrives, it seems that Iago's ruse will be discovered, but in fact Bianca unwittingly helps Iago, by complaining about the handkerchief she assumes another woman gave to Cassio: *This is some minx's token, and I must take out the work. There, give it your hobby-horse.* So Othello thinks that a common prostitute is competing with his wife for Cassio's attention, and this naturally infuriates him, but it is more

than disconcerting to hear him say he will chop her into little pieces: *I will chop her into messes. Cuckold me!* Othello plans to kill Desdemona without allowing her to defend herself. He justifies this by saying he does not want to be swayed by her charms – *lest her body and beauty unprovide my mind again. This night, Iago –* but it is disturbing to hear that an innocent woman may die without even having the opportunity to prove her innocence. When Othello asks Iago to get him some poison, Iago callously suggests: *Do it not with poison. Strangle her in her bed, even the bed she hath contaminated.* This is arguably one of the most appalling things that Iago says in the entire play, for he knows that Desdemona has done nothing wrong, and he doesn't even want to give her a relatively painless death: he wants her to feel fear and terror as her beloved husband takes her life.

Lodovico's arrival from Venice brings significant news; Othello is to return to Venice and Cassio is to be deputed in his place. To Othello, this news

I have not deserved this

– DESDEMONA (ACT IV SCENE I)

must signify that Cassio has usurped him once again, and when Desdemona merely enquires as to his wellbeing, he hits her. Othello is known for his size and strength, and, especially in performance, it is shocking to see this powerful man hit a young girl in such a violent and public way. Desdemona's response is striking, because it is simple and truthful: *I have not deserved this.* The truth needs no adornment, and her heartfelt words contrast dramatically with Iago's use of complicated, convoluted language and schemes to twist events and ensnare people. Lodovico cannot quite believe what he sees. He asks Othello to apologise to his weeping wife, but Othello refuses. Lodovico is bewildered by such a dramatic change in Othello's nature, and questions none other than Iago about it:

> *Is this the noble Moor whom our full senate*
> *Call all-in-all sufficient? Is this the nature*
> *Whom passion could not shake, whose solid virtue*
> *The shot of accident nor dart of chance*

Once again, Iago is convincing as the loyal, concerned friend. Always thinking ahead to his next move, he also feigns concern for Desdemona, saying that he fears Othello will do more than just hit her: *Yet would I knew / That stroke would prove the worst.*

In a Shakespearean play, nothing is a foregone conclusion, so when Othello questions Emilia about whether she thinks Desdemona has been unfaithful, we, the audience, earnestly hope that Emilia's staunch declaration of her mistress's chastity will convince Othello to change his mind:

> *I durst, my lord, to wager she is honest,*
> *Lay down my soul at stake. If you think other,*
> *Remove your thought; it doth abuse your bosom.*
> *If any wretch ha' put this in your head,*
> *Let heaven requite it with the serpent's curse,*
> *For if she be not honest, chaste, and true,*
> *There's no man happy; the purest of their wives*
> *Is foul as slander.*

Emilia's impressive defence of Desdemona provides us with a glimmer of hope. Even Othello concedes that it is strange that Desdemona could have carried on an affair without Emilia's knowledge. However, our hopes are dashed when Othello concludes that it is out of loyalty that Emilia refuses to admit to Desdemona being unfaithful, and so he dismisses her words: *She says enough, yet she's a simple bawd / That cannot say as much.* Even though Othello refers to Emilia as a brothel-keeper (another way of calling Desdemona a prostitute), and verbally attacks Desdemona once again, she still tries to justify and excuse his behaviour, even though she is coming to the wrong conclusions: *If haply you my father do suspect / An instrument of this your calling back, / Lay not your blame on me.* The horrible imagery in Othello's speech – maggots, weeds and toads – is striking.

Yet Desdemona does not stop loving Othello for a moment. Shakespeare, in his beautiful sonnet 116, articulates his belief that love should be unconditional: *Love is not love / Which alters when it alteration finds, / Or bends with the remover to remove: / O no! it is an ever-fixed mark / That looks on tempests and is never shaken.* We can thus conclude that Shakespeare thinks Desdemona's unchanging love for Othello is the ideal. No matter how he behaves, she is steadfast. As in the sonnet, she refuses to be 'shaken' by the storm of Othello's jealousy. Sometimes people view Desdemona's love as a weakness, but it is Othello who is the weak one. Iago did not even attempt to make Desdemona jealous, because it simply would not have worked.

Yet it is to Iago that Emilia and Desdemona express their distress. Emilia is clearly disgusted and infuriated, and once again, she seems to articulate the very emotions the audience is feeling: *my lord hath so bewhored her, / Thrown such despite and heavy terms upon her, / As true hearts cannot bear it.* She reminds us of all that Desdemona has given up for Othello, to increase our pity for her: *Hath she forsook so many noble matches, / Her father and her country and her friends, / To be call'd whore? Would it not make one weep?* Emilia also guesses that someone has been influencing Othello negatively, but she fails to guess that Iago is the culprit. Earlier in the play, Iago refers to an alleged affair between Othello and Emilia as a reason for his revenge, but Emilia reminds Iago that this never happened: *That turn'd your wit the seamy side without, / And made you to suspect me with the Moor.*

As our opinion of Othello lessens, our admiration of Desdemona grows. Shakespeare creates eloquent dialogue for her which is wonderfully expressive and poignant. For example:

*If I do die before thee, prithee shroud me
In one of those same sheets*

– DESDEMONA (ACT IV SCENE III)

*Unkindness may do much,
And his unkindness may defeat my life,
But never taint my love.*

At the end of Scene II, Roderigo arrives to inform Iago that he is returning to Venice, and once again the audience hopes that things will stop progressing so smoothly for Iago. However, Iago has no real difficulty convincing Roderigo to stay, and even persuades him to kill Cassio – because then Othello, and Desdemona, would stay in Cyprus: *by making him uncapable of Othello's place – / knocking out his brains.*

The tone of this final scene in Act IV is a despondent one. Othello tells Desdemona to go straight to bed, and in Desdemona's conversation with Emilia, her innocence and purity are seen once more. Chillingly, Desdemona asks Emilia to wrap her in her wedding sheets for burial, if she dies first: *If I do die before thee, prithee shroud me / In one of those same sheets*. Desdemona also recalls her mother's maid, Barbary, who was left by her lover who had gone mad, and sang a haunting song called 'Willow' before she died. 'Willow' has connotations of sadness and loss, and Desdemona's sense of connection with this wronged woman is one of the few times she comes even close to criticising Othello. The song itself has a melancholy air, and, in performance, the music adds much to the atmosphere of the scene.

Desdemona also asks Emilia if there could possibly be women who would betray their husbands, reminding us of her youth and innocence: *tell me, Emilia – / That there be women do abuse their husbands / In such gross kind?* Desdemona says that she would not do such a thing for the whole world, but Emilia honestly replies that, for the whole world at least, she would: *The world's a huge thing. It is a great price for a small vice*.

Shakespeare is striking among his contemporaries for his enlightened attitude to women, and Emilia may be articulating his own views when she says: *I do think it is their husbands' faults / If wives do fall*. She explains that women have a desire for affection too, and that they can be as weak as men in not being able to resist temptation. She questions why the rules for men and women are so very different. She concludes by saying that if men want women to be good partners, they have to be good partners too: *Then let them use us well, else let them know / The ills we do, their ills instruct us so*.

At the end of Act IV, Desdemona is in bed, awaiting her husband, and the audience can't help but be reminded of what Othello intends to do to her there.

IMPORTANT THEMES IN ACT IV

• The theme of jealousy is developed even more in this act, specifically the fact that jealous people seem perversely to enjoy the torment of their emotions. Several times, Othello has the opportunity to turn the situation around, for example when he speaks with Desdemona, or when he questions Emilia, but ultimately he commits

to his desperate course of action, and seems to have lost the ability, or perhaps the desire, to control his emotions.

• The theme of love is seen in Desdemona's continued love for a man who has rejected her, humiliated her, accused her. Her exemplary character is very much a contrast to Othello's ruined one.

• The role of women is highlighted in Emilia's perceptive comments on male–female relationships, which are very enlightened considering this play was written over four centuries ago.

CHARACTER DEVELOPMENT IN ACT IV

• Othello is becoming unrecognisable to us. His language has changed, and has become a despicable corruption of the eloquence we first associated with him. He refuses to listen to Desdemona's pleas, and seems to lack any kind of self-control, probably because this is the first time in his life that he has allowed his emotions to govern him so completely.

• Desdemona is very much the heroine of this act, as well as the play on the whole. She is dignified and shows great integrity at all times. She is innocence personified, and the audience is very much on her side.

• Iago continues to baffle us with his total immersion in hatred and revenge. His nefarious schemes are sickening, and the role of coincidence and fate in assisting him adds to our sense that this antagonist is unstoppable.

• Emilia is spirited in her love for Desdemona and her disgust at Othello's behaviour. She is the link between the audience and the action of the play. Imagine the original audience's reaction to her speech about sexual equality.

QUESTIONS ON ACT 4

1. Write the text of a letter that Lodovico might send to the Venetian senate, reporting on Othello's changed character.

2. How do you think Othello feels when he hears that Cassio witnessed his 'epileptic fit'? Refer to the text in support of your answer.

3. What do you think of Cassio's attitude towards Bianca? Do you think the original audience's opinion would have been the same as yours or would it have been different? Give reasons for your answer.

4. Write an entry for Bianca's diary, in which she describes her feelings for Cassio.

5. Why, in your opinion, does Othello not believe Emilia when she assures him of Desdemona's fidelity? Support your answer with reference to the text.

6. Pick five examples of imagery from Othello's dialogue in Act IV that you think best illustrate his state of mind.

7. How does Iago convince Roderigo that he should kill Cassio? Refer to the text in support of your answer.

8. Can you think of a modern song that would fit into this scene instead of the 'Willow' song? Use quotes from the song to explain your choice. (It should have a sad tune, and it should be about lost love.)

9. 'Treat your wives better!' Write an article with this title (in tabloid or broadsheet style) for a newspaper in Shakespeare's day. You may draw from Emilia's points in your piece.

10. Pick out what you think are the ten best quotations from Act IV, explaining in each case why you have chosen that quotation. Make sure they cover a range of characters and themes.

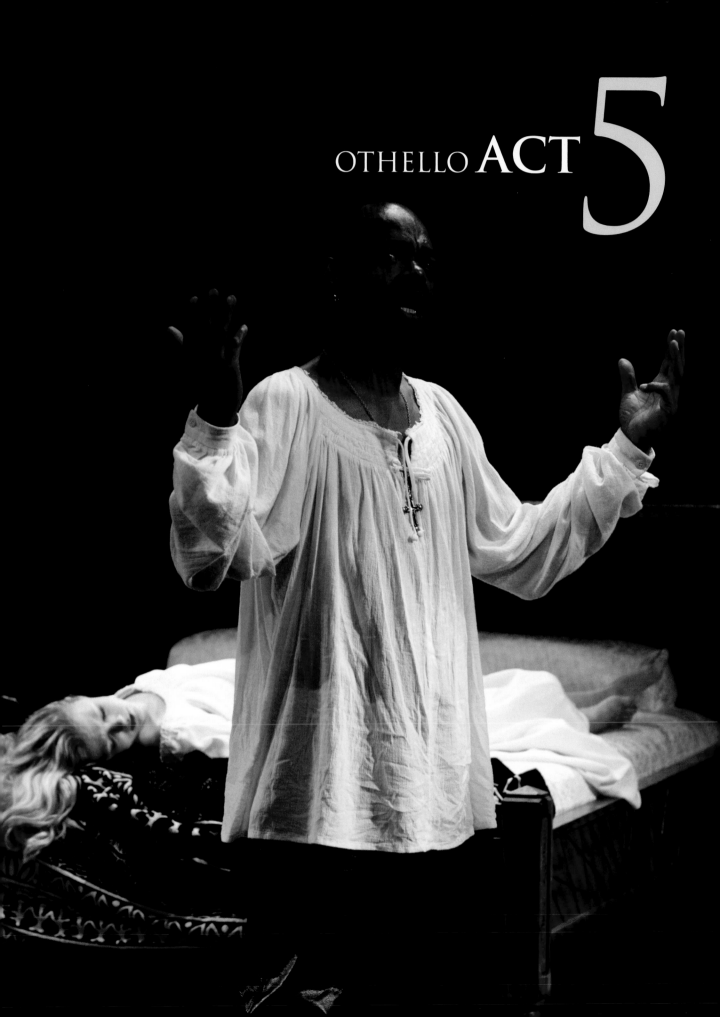

CYPRUS. A STREET

Enter Iago and Roderigo

Iago	Here, stand behind this bulk.[1] Straight will he come.
	Wear thy good rapier bare,[2] and put it home.
	Quick, quick, fear nothing. I'll be at thy elbow.
	It makes us, or it mars[3] us. Think on that,
	And fix most firm thy resolution. 5
Roderigo	Be near at hand. I may miscarry[4] in't.
Iago	Here at thy hand. Be bold, and take thy stand.

Retires

Roderigo	*[Aside]* I have no great devotion to[5] the deed,
	And yet he hath given me satisfying reasons.
	'Tis but a man gone. Forth my sword – he dies! 10
Iago	*[Aside]* I have rubb'd this young quat almost to the sense,[6]
	And he grows angry. Now, whether he kill Cassio
	Or Cassio him, or each do kill the other,
	Every way makes my gain. Live Roderigo,
	He calls me to a restitution[7] large 15
	Of gold and jewels that I bobb'd[8] from him,
	As gifts to Desdemona.
	It must not be. If Cassio do remain,
	He hath a daily beauty in his life
	That makes me ugly;[9] and besides, the Moor 20
	May unfold[10] me to him – there stand I in much peril.
	No, he must die. But so, I hear him coming.

Enter Cassio

Roderigo	I know his gait, 'tis he. Villain, thou diest!

Makes a pass at Cassio

Cassio	That thrust had been mine enemy indeed,
	But that my coat is better than thou know'st[11] 25
	I will make proof of thine.[12]

Draws, and wounds Roderigo

---

[1] Wall

[2] Unsheath his dagger

[3] Ruins

[4] Fail

[5] Enthusiasm for

[6] He has squeezed the pimple until it has almost popped

[7] Reparation

[8] Stole

[9] Iago feels inferior in comparison to Cassio

[10] Reveal

[11] Cassio has armour on under his coat

[12] He will see if Roderigo is wearing armour

	Roderigo	O, I am slain!
		Iago from behind wounds Cassio in the leg, and exits
[13] *Seriously injured*	**Cassio**	I am maim'd for ever.[13] Help, ho, murder, murder!
		Falls *Enter Othello*
	Othello	The voice of Cassio. Iago keeps his word.
	Roderigo	O, villain that I am! 30
	Othello	It is even so.
	Cassio	O, help, ho! Light, a surgeon!
	Othello	'Tis he. O brave Iago, honest and just,
		That hast such noble sense of thy friend's wrong –
[14] *Slave*		Thou teachest me. Minion,[14] your dear lies dead, 35
[15] *Terrible fate approaches*		And your unblessed fate hies.[15] Strumpet, I come.
[16] *Out*		Forth[16] of my heart those charms, thine eyes, are blotted.
		Thy bed, lust-stain'd, shall with lust's blood be spotted.
		Exit *Enter Lodovico and Gratiano*
[17] *Passers-by*	**Cassio**	What ho, no watch, no passage?[17] Murder, murder!
[18] *Misfortune* [19] *Dreadful*	**Gratiano**	'Tis some mischance.[18] The voice is very direful.[19] 40
	Cassio	O, help!
	Lodovico	Hark.
	Roderigo	O wretched villain!
	Lodovico	Two or three groan. 'Tis a heavy night.
[20] *False cries, i.e. a trap*		These may be counterfeits.[20] Let's think't unsafe 45
		To come into the cry without more help.
	Roderigo	Nobody come? Then shall I bleed to death.
	Lodovico	Hark.

Re-enter Iago, with a light

Gratiano   Here's one comes in his shirt, with light and weapons.

Iago   Who's there? Whose noise is this that cries on murder?   50

Lodovico   We do not know.

Iago   Did not you hear a cry?

Cassio   Here, here. For heaven's sake, help me.

Iago   What's the matter?

Gratiano   This is Othello's ensign, as I take it.   55

Lodovico   The same indeed; a very valiant fellow.

Iago   What are you here that cry so grievously?

Cassio   Iago – O, I am spoil'd,[21] undone by villains.
Give me some help.   [21] Injured

Iago   O me, lieutenant, what villains have done this?   60

Cassio   I think that one of them is hereabout
And cannot make away.

Iago   O treacherous villains!
What are you there? Come in and give some help.
[To Lodovico and Gratiano]

Roderigo   O, help me here!   65

Cassio   That's one of 'em.

Iago   O murderous slave! O villain!

Stabs Roderigo

Roderigo   O damn'd Iago! O inhuman dog!

Iago   Kill men i'th' dark? Where be these bloody thieves?
How silent is this town! Ho, murder, murder!   70

[To Lodovico and Gratiano]
What may you be? Are you of good or evil?

Lodovico   As you shall prove us, praise us.[22]

Iago   Signor Lodovico?

Lodovico   He, sir.

Iago   I cry you mercy. Here's Cassio hurt by villains.   75

Gratiano   Cassio?

Iago   How is't, brother!

Cassio   My leg is cut in two.

Iago   Marry, heaven forbid!
Light, gentlemen. I'll bind it with my shirt.   80

Enter Bianca

Bianca   What is the matter, ho? Who is't that cried?

Iago   Who is't that cried?

Bianca   O my dear Cassio, my sweet Cassio. O Cassio, Cassio!

[23] Notorious prostitute

Iago   O notable strumpet![23] Cassio, may you suspect
Who they should be that have thus mangled you?   85

Cassio   No.

Gratiano   I am to find you thus. I have been to seek you.

[24] Band

Iago   Lend me a garter.[24] So. O for a chair,
To bear him easily hence!

Bianca   Alas, he faints. O Cassio, Cassio, Cassio!   90

Iago   Gentlemen all, I do suspect this trash
To be a party in this injury.
Patience a while, good Cassio. Come, come,
Lend me a light. Know we this face or no?

| | Alas my friend, and my dear countryman | 95 |
| | Roderigo? No – yes, sure – O heaven, Roderigo. | |

Gratiano   What, of Venice?

Iago   Even he, sir. Did you know him?

Gratiano   Know him? Ay.

Iago   Signor Gratiano. I cry[25] you gentle pardon.   100
These bloody accidents must excuse my manners
That so neglected you.

[25] *Beg*

Gratiano   I am glad to see you.

Iago   How do you, Cassio? O, a chair, a chair!

Gratiano   Roderigo.   105

Iago   He, he 'tis he.

A chair brought in

O, that's well said, the chair!

Gratiano   Some good man bear him carefully from hence.
I'll fetch the general's surgeon.
[To Bianca] For you, mistress,   110
Save you your labour. He that lies slain here, Cassio,
Was my dear friend. What malice was between you?

Cassio   None in the world, nor do I know the man.

Iago   *[To Bianca]* What, look you pale? O, bear him out o'th' air.

Cassio and Roderigo are borne off

[To Lodovico and Gratiano] Stay you, good gentlemen.   120
[To Bianca] Look you pale, mistress?
[To Lodovico and Gratiano] Do you perceive the
    ghastness[26] of her eye?
[To Bianca] Nay, if you stare we shall hear more anon.
[To Lodovico and Gratiano] Behold her well; I pray you
    look upon her:

[26] *Fear*

Do you see, gentlemen? Nay, guiltiness   125
Will speak, though tongues were out of use.[27]

Enter Emilia

Emilia   Alas, what is the matter? What is the matter, husband?

Iago   Cassio hath here been set on in the dark
By Roderigo and fellows that are scaped.[28]
He's almost slain, and Roderigo dead.   130

Emilia   Alas, good gentleman! Alas, good Cassio!

Iago   This is the fruits of whoring.[29] Prithee, Emilia,
Go, know of Cassio where he supp'd[30] tonight.
[To Bianca] What, do you shake at that?

Bianca   He supp'd at my house, but I therefore shake not.   135

Iago   O, did he so? I charge you go with me.

Emilia   O, fie upon thee,[31] strumpet!

Bianca   I am no strumpet, but of life as honest
As you that thus abuse me.

Emilia   As I? Fough, fie upon thee!   140

Iago   Kind gentlemen, let's go see poor Cassio dress'd.[32]
Come, mistress, you must tell's another tale.
Emilia run you to the citadel
And tell my lord and lady what hath happ'd.
Will you go on afore?   145
[Aside] This is the night
That either makes me or fordoes me quite.[33]

Exit

[27] Guilt always reveals itself

[28] Have escaped

[29] Result of consorting with prostitutes
[30] Dined

[31] Damn you

[32] Cassio's wounds bandaged

[33] This night will either make him or ruin him completely

THE FIRST SCENE of the final act is as exciting as we could wish for. Roderigo attacks Cassio, attempting to kill him, as he returns from his evening with Bianca. But Roderigo only succeeds in wounding Cassio, and Iago, unseen in the shadows, seizes the opportunity to kill Roderigo.

In his lodgings, Othello hears the ruckus, and assumes Iago is carrying out his promise to kill Cassio. He is now ready to murder Desdemona, and, although we don't see him for the rest of the scene, we have that uncomfortable sense of foreboding in the back of our minds, and this adds to the tension of this visually arresting scene.

Iago also stabs Cassio in the leg, and still manages to get away with it. Fortuitously, Lodovico and Gratiano (Desdemona's uncle) arrive, and are impressed by Iago's condemnation of violence and show of concern for Cassio. Iago also cleverly insinuates that Bianca knows more than she is saying, thus implanting the idea in everyone's minds that it was criminal associates of hers who set upon Cassio. Iago also realises that he is in real danger of discovery. It is one of the few times he shows any doubt, and a good actor playing this part will show his unease through agitated body language. By the close of this scene, it seems that it is all to play for.

KEY **POINTS**

- *Cassio is attacked by Roderigo, but in the scuffle, it is Rodergio who is killed by the unseen Iago.*

- *Unseen, Iago stabs Cassio in the leg.*

- *Othello, hearing the commotion, thinks Cassio is dead.*

- *Lodovico and Gratiano are impressed by Iago's quick wit and control.*

- *Iago displays doubt for the first time in the play.*

Wear thy good rapier bare,
and put it home.
Quick, quick, fear nothing.
I'll be at thy elbow

– IAGO

ACT 5 SCENE II

A BEDCHAMBER IN THE CASTLE:

Desdemona in bed asleep; a light burning

Enter Othello

Othello	It is the cause,[1] it is the cause, my soul.
	Let me not name it to you, you chaste[2] stars.
	It is the cause. Yet I'll not shed her blood,
	Nor scar that whiter skin of hers than snow,
	And smooth as monumental alabaster.[3]
	Yet she must die, else she'll betray more men.
	Put out the light, and then put out the light.
	If I quench[4] thee, thou flaming minister,[5]
	I can again thy former light restore
	Should I repent me; but once put out thy light,
	Thou cunning'st pattern[6] of excelling nature,
	I know not where is that Promethean[7] heat
	That can thy light relume.[8] When I have pluck'd the rose
	I cannot give it vital growth again.
	It needs must wither. I'll smell thee on the tree.

[Kissing her]

	Ah balmy[9] breath, that dost almost persuade
	Justice to break her sword![10] One more, one more.
	Be thus when thou art dead, and I will kill thee
	And love thee after. One more, and that's the last.

[Kisses her]

	So sweet was ne'er so fatal. I must weep,
	But they are cruel tears. This sorrow's heavenly,
	It strikes where it doth love. She wakes.
Desdemona	Who's there? Othello?
Othello	Ay, Desdemona.
Desdemona	Will you come to bed, my lord?
Othello	Have you pray'd tonight, Desdemona?
Desdemona	Ay, my lord.
Othello	If you bethink yourself of any crime
	Unreconciled as yet to heaven and grace,
	Solicit for it straight.

Line numbers: 5, 10, 15, 20, 25, 30

Margin notes:

[1] *He has just reason for his actions*

[2] *Faithful*

[3] *A smooth stone similar to marble*

[4] *Extinguish* [5] *Candle flame*

[6] *Beautifully made*

[7] *In Greek myth, Prometheus gave fire to humans*

[8] *Relight*

[9] *Sweet*

[10] *Justice is often depicted holding a sword, signifying that satisfying justice may mean taking a life*

If she can think of any sin for which she has not asked God's forgiveness, she should ask forgiveness now

Desdemona   Alack, my lord, what do you mean by that?

Othello   Well, do it, and be brief. I will walk by.
I would not kill thy unprepared spirit.
No, heavens forfend![11] I would not kill thy soul.

Desdemona   Talk you of killing?   35

Othello   Ay, I do.

Desdemona   Then heaven
Have mercy on me.

Othello   Amen, with all my heart.

Desdemona   If you say so, I hope you will not kill me.   40

Othello   Hum!

Desdemona   And yet I fear you, for you're fatal then
When your eyes roll so. Why I should fear I know not,
Since guiltiness I know not, but yet I feel I fear.

Othello   Think on thy sins.   45

Desdemona   They are loves I bear to you.

Othello   Ay, and for that thou diest.

Desdemona   That death's unnatural that kills for loving.
Alas, why gnaw[12] you so your nether lip?
Some bloody passion shakes your very frame.   50
These are portents,[13] but yet I hope, I hope
They do not point on me.

12 Chew

13 Signs of disaster

Othello   Peace, and be still!

Desdemona   I will so. What's the matter?

Othello   That handkerchief   55
Which I so loved and gave thee, thou gav'st to Cassio.

Desdemona   No, by my life and soul. Send for the man
And ask him.

Othello Sweet soul, take heed, take heed of perjury.[14]
Thou art on thy deathbed.   60

Desdemona Ay, but not yet to die.

Othello Presently.[15]
Therefore confess thee freely of thy sin,
For to deny each article with oath
Cannot remove nor choke the strong conception   65
That I do groan withal.[16] Thou art to die.

Desdemona Then Lord have mercy on me.

Othello I say amen.

Desdemona And have you mercy too. I never did
Offend you in my life, never loved Cassio   70
But with such general warranty of heaven
As I might love.[17] I never gave him token.

Othello By heaven, I saw my handkerchief in's[18] hand.
O perjured woman! Thou dost stone my heart,[19]
And makest me call what I intend to do   75
A murder, which I thought a sacrifice.
I saw the handkerchief.

Desdemona He found it then.
I never gave it him. Send for him hither.
Let him confess a truth.   80

Othello He hath confess'd.

Desdemona What, my lord?

Othello That he hath used[20] thee.

Desdemona How, unlawfully?

Othello Ay.   85

Desdemona He will not say so.

Othello No, his mouth is stopp'd.[21]
Honest Iago hath ta'en order for't.

Desdemona   O, my fear interprets! What, is he dead?

Othello   Had all his hairs been lives, my great revenge   90
Had stomach for 'em all.

Desdemona   Alas, he is betray'd and I undone.

Othello   Out, strumpet! Weep'st thou for him to my face?

Desdemona   O, banish me, my lord, but kill me not.

Othello   Down, strumpet!   95

Desdemona   Kill me tomorrow; let me live tonight.

Othello   Nay, an you strive[22] –

[22] *Struggle*

Desdemona   But half an hour.

Othello   Being done, there is no pause.

Desdemona   But while I say one prayer.   100

Othello   It is too late.

He stifles her

Desdemona   O Lord, Lord, Lord.

Emilia   *[Within]* My lord, my lord, what, ho, my lord, my lord!

Othello   What noise is this? Not dead? Not yet quite dead?
I that am cruel am yet merciful.   105
I would not have thee linger in thy pain.
So, so.

Emilia   *[Within]* What ho, my lord, my lord!

Othello   Who's there?

Emilia   *[Within]* O, good my lord, I would speak a word with you. 115

Othello   Yes – 'tis Emilia. By and by! – She's dead.
'Tis like she comes to speak of Cassio's death.

[23] Loud

The noise was high.[23] Ha! No more moving.
Still as the grave. Shall she come in? Were't good?
I think she stirs again. No. What's best to do?   110
If she come in, she'll sure speak to my wife.
My wife, my wife! What wife? I ha' no wife.
O insupportable![24] O heavy hour!
Methinks it should be now a huge eclipse
Of sun and moon, and that th'affrighted globe   120
Should yawn at alteration.

Othello thinks there should be an eclipse of the moon and an earthquake to symbolise what has just happened

[24] Indefensible

Emilia [*Within*] I do beseech you
That I may speak with you, O, good my lord!

Othello I had forgot thee. – O, come in, Emilia. –
Soft, by and by. Let me the curtains draw.   125
Where art thou?

Unlocks the door
Enter Emilia

What's the matter with thee now?

Emilia O, my good lord, yonder's foul murders done!

Othello What, now?

Emilia But now, my lord.   130

Othello It is the very error of the moon,
She comes more nearer earth than she was wont,
And makes men mad.[25]

[25] The full moon was thought to turn some men crazy

Emilia Cassio, my lord, hath kill'd a young Venetian
Call'd Roderigo.   135

Othello Roderigo kill'd
And Cassio kill'd?

Emilia No, Cassio is not kill'd.

[26] Out of sync **Othello** Not Cassio kill'd? Then murder's out of tune,[26]
And sweet revenge grows harsh.   140

Desdemona O, falsely, falsely murder'd!

Emilia	O Lord, what cry is that?
Othello	That? What?
Emilia	Out and alas, that was my lady's voice!
	Help, help, ho, help! O lady, speak again! 145
	Sweet Desdemona, O sweet mistress, speak!
Desdemona	A guiltless death I die.
Emilia	O, who hath done this deed?
Desdemona	Nobody, I myself. Farewell.
	Commend me to my kind lord. O, farewell! 150

Dies

Othello	Why? How should she be murder'd?
Emilia	Alas, who knows?
Othello	You heard her say herself it was not I.
Emilia	She said so, I must needs report the truth.
Othello	She's like a liar gone to burning hell. 155
	'Twas I that kill'd her.
Emilia	O, the more angel she, and you the blacker devil!
Othello	She turn'd to folly,[27] and she was a whore.
Emilia	Thou dost belie[28] her, and thou art a devil.
Othello	She was false as water. 160
Emilia	Thou art rash as fire
	To say that she was false. O, she was heavenly true!
Othello	Cassio did top[29] her. Ask thy husband else.
	O, I were damn'd beneath all depth in hell
	But that I did proceed upon just grounds 165
	To this extremity. Thy husband knew it all.

[27] *Madness*

[28] *Falsely accuse*

[29] *Sleep with*

He would be damned even beyond hell, except for the fact that he was justified in killing Desdemona

Emilia	My husband?	
Othello	Thy husband.	
Emilia	That she was false to wedlock?	
Othello	Ay, with Cassio. Had she been true,	170
	If heaven would make me such another world	
	Of one entire and perfect chrysolite[30]	
	I'd not have sold her for it.	
Emilia	My husband?	
Othello	Ay, 'twas he that told me on her first.	175
	An honest man he is, and hates the slime	
	That sticks on filthy deeds.	
Emilia	My husband?	
Othello	What needs this iterance?[31] Woman, I say thy husband.	
Emilia	O mistress, villainy hath made mocks with love.	180
	My husband say she was false?	
Othello	He, woman.	
	I say thy husband. Dost understand the word?	
	My friend, thy husband, honest, honest Iago.	
Emilia	If he say so, may his pernicious[32] soul	185
	Rot half a grain a day.[33] He lies to th' heart.	
	She was too fond of her most filthy bargain.	
Othello	Ha?	
Emilia	Do thy worst.	
	This deed of thine is no more worthy heaven	190
	Than thou wast worthy her.	
Othello	Peace,[34] you were best.	
Emilia	Thou hast not half that power to do me harm	
	As I have to be hurt. O gull,[35] O dolt,[36]	
	As ignorant as dirt! Thou hast done a deed –	195
	I care not for thy sword, I'll make thee known	

30 *Jewel*

31 *Repetition*

32 *Wicked*
33 *Rot (in hell), bit by bit*

34 *Stay quiet*

35 *Fool*   **36** *Idiot*

Though I lost twenty lives. Help, help, ho! Help!
The Moor hath kill'd my mistress. Murder, murder!

Enter Montano, Gratiano, Iago, and others

Montano What is the matter? How now, general?

Emilia O, are you come, Iago? You have done well,   200
That men must lay their murders on your neck.

Gratiano What is the matter?

Emilia Disprove this villain, if thou be'est a man.
He says thou told'st him that his wife was false.
I know thou didst not. Thou'rt not such a villain: 205
Speak, for my heart is full.[37]

[37] *She is too emotional to say any more*

Iago I told him what I thought, and told no more
Than what he found himself was apt and true.

Emilia But did you ever tell him she was false?

Iago I did.   210

Emilia You told a lie, an odious,[38] damned lie,
Upon my soul a lie, a wicked lie.
She false with Cassio? Did you say with Cassio?

[38] *Repulsive*

Iago With Cassio, mistress. Go to, charm your tongue.[39]

[39] *Shut your mouth*

Emilia I will not charm my tongue; I am bound to speak.   215
My mistress here lies murder'd in her bed.

All O heavens forfend![40]

[40] *Forbid*

Emilia And your reports have set[41] the murder on.

[41] *Caused*

Othello Nay, stare not, masters. It is true indeed.

Gratiano 'Tis a strange truth.   220

Montano O monstrous act!

Emilia Villainy, villainy, villainy!

	I think upon't, I think. I smell't. O villainy!
	I thought so then. I'll kill myself for grief.
	O villainy, villainy! 225
Iago	What, are you mad? I charge you get you home.
Emilia	Good gentlemen, let me have leave to speak.
	'Tis proper I obey him, but not now.
	Perchance,[42] Iago, I will ne'er go home.
Othello	O, O, O! 230

He falls on the bed

Emilia	Nay, lay thee down and roar,
	For thou hast kill'd the sweetest innocent
	That e'er did lift up eye.
Othello	*[Rising]* O, she was foul! 235
	I scarce did know you, uncle. There lies your niece,
	Whose breath indeed these hands have newly stopp'd.[43]
	[To Gratiano] I know this act shows horrible and grim.
Gratiano	Poor Desdemona, I am glad thy father's dead.
	Thy match was mortal to him,[44] and pure grief 240
	Shore his old thread in twain.[45] Did he live now
	This sight would make him do a desperate turn,
	Yea, curse his better angel from his side,
	And fall to reprobance.[46]
Othello	'Tis pitiful. But yet Iago knows 245
	That she with Cassio hath the act of shame
	A thousand times committed. Cassio confess'd it,
	And she did gratify his amorous works[47]
	With that recognizance[48] and pledge of love
	Which I first gave her. I saw it in his hand. 250
	It was a handkerchief, an antique token
	My father gave my mother.
Emilia	O God! O heavenly God!
Iago	'Swounds, hold your peace!
Emilia	'Twill out, 'twill out. I peace? 255

Side notes:

[42] *Maybe*

[43] *He has just strangled her*

[44] *Her marriage was so hateful to him that he died*
[45] *Cut the thread of his life in two (broke his heart)*

[46] *Damnation*

[47] *Seduction*
[48] *Bond*

No, I will speak as liberal[49] as the north.[50]
Let heaven, and men, and devils, let 'em all,
All, all cry shame against me, yet I'll speak.

[49] *Freely*   [50] *North wind*

Iago   Be wise and get you home.

Emilia   I will not.   260

Iago offers to stab

Gratiano   Fie, your sword upon a woman?

Emilia   O thou dull Moor, that handkerchief thou speak'st of
I found by fortune and did give my husband,
For often, with a solemn earnestness[51] –
More than indeed belong'd to such a trifle –   265
He begg'd of me to steal it.

[51] *Intensity*

Iago   Villanous whore!

Emilia   She give it Cassio? No, alas, I found it,
And I did give't my husband.

Iago   Filth, thou liest.   270

Emilia   By heaven I do not, I do not, gentlemen.
O murderous coxcomb![52] What should such a fool
Do with so good a wife?

[52] *Fool*

Othello   Are there no stones[53] in heaven
But what serves for the thunder? Precious villain!   275

[53] *Thunderbolts*

He runs at Iago. Iago, from behind, stabs Emilia, and exits

Gratiano   The woman falls. Sure he hath kill'd his wife.

Emilia   Ay, ay. O, lay me by my mistress' side!

Gratiano   He's gone, but his wife's kill'd.

Montano   'Tis a notorious villain. Take you this weapon
Which I have here recover'd[54] from the Moor.   280
Come, guard the door without. Let him not pass,
But kill him rather. I'll after that same villain,

[54] *Taken*

For 'tis a damned slave.

Exit Montano and Gratiano

Othello   I am not valiant neither,
55 Skinny youngster

But ever puny whipster[55] gets my sword.   285
But why should honour outlive honesty?
Let it go all.

56 Mean
57 Dying swan

Emilia   What did thy song bode,[56] lady?
Hark, canst thou hear me? I will play the swan,[57]
And die in music.   290
[Singing] 'Willow, willow, willow. –
Moor, she was chaste. She loved thee, cruel Moor.
So come my soul to bliss as I speak true.
So, speaking as I think, alas, I die.

Dies

Othello   I have another weapon in this chamber.   295

58 Tempered with ice to make it extra strong

It was a sword of Spain, the ice-brook's temper.[58]
O, here it is. Uncle, I must come forth.

Gratiano   *[Within]* If thou attempt it, it will cost thee dear.

59 Inevitably

Thou hast no weapon, and perforce[59] must suffer.

Othello   Look in upon me then, and speak with me,   300

60 Unarmed

Or, naked[60] as I am, I will assault thee.

Re-enter Gratiano

Gratiano   What is the matter?

Othello   Behold, I have a weapon;
A better never did itself sustain
Upon a soldier's thigh. I have seen the day   305
That, with this little arm and this good sword,
I have made my way through more impediments

61 Power to stop

Than twenty times your stop.[61] But O, vain boast!
Who can control his fate? 'Tis not so now.
Be not afraid, though you do see me weapon'd.   310

62 End

Here is my journey's end, here is my butt[62]

63 Final destination

And very sea-mark of my utmost sail.[63]

64 Are you backing off, afraid?

Do you go back dismay'd?[64] 'Tis a lost fear.

Man but a rush against Othello's breast
And he retires. Where should Othello go? 315
Now, how dost thou look now? O ill-starr'd[65] wench,
Pale as thy smock! When we shall meet at count,[66]
This look of thine will hurl my soul from heaven,
And fiends[67] will snatch at it. Cold, cold, my girl,
Even like thy chastity. O cursed, cursed slave! 320
Whip me, ye devils,
From the possession of this heavenly sight.
Blow me about in winds, roast me in sulphur,
Wash me in steep-down[68] gulfs of liquid fire!
O Desdemona! Dead Desdemona! Dead! 325
O! O!

Enter Lodovico. Montano, Cassio, carried in a chair, and Officers with Iago, prisoner

Lodovico   Where is this rash and most unfortunate man?

Othello   That's he that was Othello. Here I am.

Lodovico   Where is that viper? Bring the villain forth.

Othello   I look down towards his feet, but that's a fable.[69] 330
For if that thou be'est a devil, I cannot kill thee.

Wounds Iago

Lodovico   Wrench his sword from him.

Iago   I bleed, sir, but not kill'd.

Othello   I am not sorry, neither. I'd have thee live,
For in my sense[70] 'tis happiness to die. 335

Lodovico   O thou Othello, thou was once so good,
Fall'n in the practice[71] of a cursed slave,
What shall be said to thee?

Othello   Why, anything;
An honourable murderer, if you will, 340
For naught I did in hate, but all in honour.

Lodovico   This wretch hath part confess'd his villainy.

[65] *Unfortunate*

[66] *On Judgement Day*

[67] *Demons*

[68] *Sheer*

[69] *The devil in human form was said to have cloven hooves*

[70] *Opinion*

[71] *Fell for the tricks of*

Did you and he consent in Cassio's death?

Othello   Ay.

Cassio   Dear general, I never gave you cause.   345

Othello   I do believe it, and I ask your pardon.

72 Half-devil   Will you, I pray, demand that demi-devil[72]

73 Trapped   Why he hath thus ensnared[73] my body and soul?

Iago   Demand me nothing. What you know, you know.

From this time forth I never will speak word.   350

Lodovico   What, not to pray?

74 Torture will force you to speak   **Gratiano**   Torments will ope your lips.[74]

Othello   Well, thou dost best.

75 Has happened   **Lodovico**   Sir, you shall understand what hath befall'n,[75]

Which as, I think, you know not. Here is a letter,   355

Found in the pocket of the slain Roderigo,

76 Orders   And here another. The one of them imports[76]

The death of Cassio, to be undertook

By Roderigo.

Othello   O villain!   360

77 Barbaric   **Cassio**   Most heathenish[77] and most gross.

78 Letter of complaint   **Lodovico**   Now here's another discontented paper[78]

Found in his pocket too, and this it seems

Roderigo meant to've sent this damned villain,

79 It is likely 80 Meantime   But that belike,[79] Iago in the interim[80]   365

Came in and satisfied him.

81 Evil villain   **Othello**   O thou pernicious caitiff![81]

How came you, Cassio, by that handkerchief

That was my wife's?

Cassio   I found it in my chamber,   370

And he himself confess'd but even now,

That there he dropp'd it for a special purpose

	Which wrought to[82] his desire.		[82] *Served*
Othello	O fool, fool, fool!		
Cassio	There is besides in Roderigo's letter	375	
	How he upbraids[83] Iago, that he made him		[83] *Scolds*
	Brave[84] me upon the watch, whereon it came		[84] *Antagonise*
	That I was cast;[85] and even but now he spake		[85] *Dismissed*
	After long seeming dead, Iago hurt him,		
	Iago set him on.	380	

Lodovico   You must forsake this room and go with us.
Your power and your command is taken off,
And Cassio rules in Cyprus. For this slave,
If there be any cunning cruelty[86]   [86] *Form of torture*
That can torment him much and hold him long,   385
It shall be his. You shall close[87] prisoner rest   [87] *Confined*
Till that the nature of your fault be known
To the Venetian state. Come, bring away.

Othello   Soft you, a word or two before you go.
I have done the state some service, and they know't.   390
No more of that. I pray you, in your letters,
When you shall these unlucky[88] deeds relate,   [88] *Unfortunate*
Speak of me as I am. Nothing extenuate,[89]   [89] *Mitigate/defend*
Nor set down aught[90] in malice. Then must you speak [90] *Write down anything*
Of one that loved not wisely but too well,   395
Of one not easily jealous but, being wrought[91]   [91] *Manipulated*
Perplex'd in the extreme; of one whose hand,   [92] *Stories were often told of Native Americans accepting meaningless trinkets in exchange for precious gems, because they were unaware of their monetary value*
Like the base Indian,[92] threw a pearl away
Richer than all his tribe; of one whose subdued[93] eyes, [93] *Sad*
Albeit unused to the melting mood,[94]   400 [94] *Although not used to crying*
Drop tears as fast as the Arabian trees
Their medicinable gum.[95] Set you down this,   [95] *Sap*
And say besides, that in Aleppo[96] once,   [96] *Alexandria*
Where a malignant and a turban'd Turk
Beat a Venetian and traduced[97] the state,   405 [97] *Insulted*
I took by the throat the circumcised dog
And smote him thus.

Stabs himself

Lodovico   O bloody period![98]   [98] *Ending*

Gratiano   All that's spoke is marr'd.[99]   [99] *Spoiled*

100 Before	**Othello**	I kiss'd thee ere[100] I kill'd thee. No way but this:
		Killing myself, to die upon a kiss.

410

Falls on the bed, and dies

Cassio This did I fear, but thought he had no weapon,
For he was great of heart.

Lodovico *[To Iago]* O Spartan dog,

More fell[101] than anguish, hunger, or the sea,   415
Look on the tragic loading of this bed.
This is thy work. The object poisons sight.
Let it be hid. Gratiano, keep the house,
And seize upon the fortunes of the Moor,
For they succeed on you. To you, lord Governor,   420

102 Sentencing Remains the censure[102] of this hellish villain.
The time, the place, the torture. O, enforce it!
Myself will straight aboard, and to the state
This heavy act with heavy heart relate.

Exit

Filth, thou liest

— IAGO

MODERN ENGLISH VERSION

A BEDROOM IN THE CASTLE:
Desdemona in bed asleep; a light burning

Enter Othello

Othello   I have good reason for what I'm about to do, very good reason. I can't bear to say it aloud, but I have good reason. But I'm not going to spill her blood, or scar her snowy white skin, as flawless as marble. But she has to die, or she'll betray more men. I had better put out the light. If I blow out this candle, it is not out for ever, I can always relight it if I regret extinguishing it. But if I kill you, beautiful, intelligent ... but unfaithful, there is no way I can bring you back to life. When I pluck a rose, I have effectively killed it. I cannot bring it to life again, it will soon wither. I will smell it before I pluck it.
[Kisses Desdemona]
Oh, your sweet breath almost persuades me not to kill you, but justice must be done. If you are still this beautiful when you are dead, I'll still love you. One more kiss, which must be the last. Such a sweet kiss, and so deadly! I can't help but cry. This just act pains me, because I have to kill what I love. She's waking up.

Desdemona   Othello, is that you?

Othello   Yes, it is.

Desdemona   Are you coming to bed, love?

Othello   Have you said your prayers, Desdemona?

Desdemona   Yes.

Othello   If you can think of anything you need to ask God's forgiveness for, now is the time to confess.

Desdemona   What ... what do you mean by that?

Othello   Just confess your sins quickly, I'll wait over here. Go on, confess. God forbid I should kill your eternal soul.

Desdemona   Did you say something about killing me?

Othello   Yes, I did.

Desdemona   Oh God help me!

Othello	Yes, God help you. I mean that from the bottom of my heart!
Desdemona	If you really mean that, then you won't hurt me.
Othello	I have to do this ...
Desdemona	I'm frightened of you, because you have that look in your eyes. I shouldn't be afraid, because I haven't done anything wrong, and I don't deserve to have anything bad happen to me. But I'm still scared.
Othello	Think of your sins.
Desdemona	My only sin is that I love you too much.
Othello	Yes, and for that you have to die.
Desdemona	I don't deserve to die for loving you. Why are you biting your lower lip like that? And your whole body is shaking with emotion. These aren't good signs ... but I still hope you are not angry at me.
Othello	Just be quiet. Let me think.
Desdemona	Okay. But what is all this about?
Othello	You gave the handkerchief, that you knew meant so very much to me, to Cassio.
Desdemona	I swear on my life I did not! Ask Cassio if you don't believe me.
Othello	Sweetheart, don't lie. You are on your deathbed.
Desdemona	But I am not dying!
Othello	You're going to die very soon. So there's no point lying to me now. You're not going to change my mind, so you might as well confess before you die.
Desdemona	God have mercy on me!
Othello	Amen to that.
Desdemona	And you have mercy on me too! I don't deserve this. I've been a good wife. I never loved Cassio, except as a friend. I never gave him a token of my love, I certainly didn't give him that handkerchief.

Othello   That's a lie. I saw my handkerchief in his hand! Your lies are turning my heart to stone, and making me feel that killing you is murder, not sacrifice. I saw the handkerchief.

Desdemona   He must have found it, then. I didn't give it to him. Call him, and ask him for yourself.

Othello   I did ask him. And he admitted it.

Desdemona   Admitted what?

Othello   That he slept with you.

Desdemona   That he slept with me?

Othello   Yes.

Desdemona   Cassio would never tell such a lie.

Othello   He won't say anything any more. Iago has taken care of that.

Desdemona   I'm almost scared to ask ... is he dead?

Othello   Yes, and I'd be more than happy to kill him again. And again and again!

Desdemona   Then someone has betrayed him, and me.

Othello   You slut! Are you crying for your boyfriend in front of your husband?

Desdemona   Send me away if you hate me! Don't kill me!

Othello   You're a slut!

Desdemona   Kill me tomorrow instead, let me live tonight!

Othello   No. Don't even try to change my mind.

Desdemona   Just let me live another half an hour!

Othello   No.

Desdemona   Let me say just one prayer!

Othello   No.

He smothers her

Emilia	*[Within]* Othello! Othello!
Othello	She's still breathing. I'm not so cruel that I would have her suffer longer than necessary. I'll put her out of her misery.
Emilia	*[Within]* Othello!
Othello	Who's there?
Emilia	*[Within]* Othello, I need to speak to you urgently!
Othello	Oh no – it's Emilia. But Desdemona is dead now. Emilia has probably come to tell me that Cassio is dead. Desdemona is as still as the grave. Or is she still partly alive? I don't know what to do. If Emilia comes in, she'll want to speak to my wife. Oh wait, I don't have a wife any more. Oh God, I can't bear this. It's unbearable. I feel that there should be a huge eclipse of the sun or the moon casting a dark shadow over the earth to signify the horror of what I have done.
Emilia	*[Within]* Please let me speak to you, Othello.
Othello	Sorry, Emilia, I forgot about you. Hang on a minute while I open the door.
	Unlocks the door *Enter Emilia*
	What's the matter with you now?
Emilia	You won't believe this, but murder has been committed tonight!
Othello	What? Just now?
Emilia	Yes!
Othello	It's this full moon. It is making people crazy.
Emilia	Cassio has killed a young Venetian called Roderigo.
Othello	Roderigo is dead! And Cassio too!
Emilia	No, just Roderigo, Cassio is alive.
Othello	Cassio is still alive? Then only one person has received their rightful comeuppance tonight.
Desdemona	I have been killed for nothing.

Emilia	Oh, what was that?
Othello	That? What?
Emilia	Oh God, that was Desdemona, what on earth has happened to her?
Desdemona	I am innocent.
Emilia	Oh my God! Who did this to you?
Desdemona	Nobody, I've killed myself. Tell Othello I love him.
	Dies
Othello	I wonder what happened to her?
Emilia	I don't know!
Othello	It wasn't me. You heard her admit that herself.
Emilia	Yes, she did. I won't deny it.
Othello	Then she's a liar, and she's going to hell! It was me who killed her.
Emilia	Well then, she is an even better person than I thought, and you are worse than I thought anyone could possibly be. She was an angel, but you're the devil.
Othello	She deserved it, after what she did. She was a whore.
Emilia	That is slander, you bastard!
Othello	She was unfaithful.
Emilia	You are so wrong. She was completely faithful to you.
Othello	Cassio slept with her. Ask your husband if you don't believe me. Let me be damned to hell if I wasn't completely justified in killing her. Go on, ask your husband.
Emilia	My husband?
Othello	Your husband.
Emilia	Iago told you Desdemona was unfaithful?

Othello	Yes, with Cassio. If she had been faithful I wouldn't have parted with her for the most precious jewel in the whole world.
Emilia	My husband!
Othello	Yes, he was the one who told me. He is so honest, he despises those who lie and cheat.
Emilia	My husband!
Othello	Stop saying 'my husband'. I already told you it was your husband.
Emilia	Oh, Desdemona, someone has deliberately destroyed your life! Did you say my husband?
Othello	For the last time, yes! Your husband! My dear friend, your husband – honest, honest Iago.
Emilia	If Iago said Desdemona was unfaithful, he deserves to rot in hell. He was lying through his teeth. She loved you too much to ever do such a thing.
Othello	Whatever.
Emilia	Do your worst. What you have done is no more worthy of heaven than you were worthy of her.
Othello	You had better be quiet now.
Emilia	You don't have half the power to hurt me as I have to be hurt! You stupid, stupid fool! You are such an idiot, you have committed murder! I don't care if you kill me! I'll accuse you if it costs me twenty lives to do so. Help! Someone! Help! The Moor has killed Desdemona! Murder!
	Enter Montano, Gratiano, Iago, and others
Montano	What is going on here? General?
Emilia	Oh, you're here, Iago? You must be proud of yourself. A man has committed murder because of you.
Gratiano	What's the matter?
Emilia	If you're a man, tell Othello he made a mistake. He says you told him that his wife was unfaithful. I can't believe you could do such a thing. You couldn't be so evil. I'm too upset to say any more.

Iago	I only gave him my opinion. I didn't tell him anything that he didn't already suspect.
Emilia	But did you ever tell him she was unfaithful?
Iago	Yes.
Emilia	Then you lied. You told one of the worst, most horrible lies imaginable. Desdemona cheated with Cassio? That is ridiculous!
Iago	Yes, with Cassio. Now shut your mouth.
Emilia	I will not stay silent. I have to speak the truth when I see my mistress lying murdered in her own bed!
All	Heaven forbid!
Emilia	And your lies were responsible, Iago.
Othello	Don't stare at me like that. It's true.
Gratiano	It's hard to believe such a thing is true.
Montano	This was a monstrous act!
Emilia	Iago is the villain – I thought it, I felt it, I feel like dying with shame that I stayed silent about my suspicions!
Iago	Have you gone crazy? Go home at once. I order you.
Emilia	Gentlemen, please listen to what I say. I know a wife should obey her husband, but this is one occasion when I simply can't. Maybe I will never go home again.
Othello	Argh!
	He falls on the bed
Emilia	Yes, it is well you might roar in pain, because you have killed the most innocent woman who ever lived.
Othello	[Rising] Oh, she deserved it! I hardly know you, Gratiano, but your niece lies dead because I have strangled her. I know this looks bad.
Gratiano	Poor Desdemona! I am glad your father didn't live to see this, when your marriage alone was enough to break his heart. If he saw you now, he would do something desperate. He

would lose his faith in God completely.

Othello   I know she looks pitiful lying there, but Iago knows that she slept with Cassio a thousand times. Cassio confessed it, and she demonstrated her love for him by giving him a token, the very handkerchief I had given her. It had great sentimental value because my father had given it to my mother, but Desdemona gave it away to Cassio.

Emilia   My God!

Iago   Be quiet. Don't say anything.

Emilia   I will speak; there isn't a man on earth who could stop me saying what I have to say.

Iago   If you're clever, you'll go home.

Emilia   No, I won't.

Iago makes as if to stab Emilia

Gratiano   What the hell? You would use your sword on a woman?

Emilia   Oh, stupid Moor! I found the handkerchief you're talking about by accident, and gave it to my husband, because he had often begged me to steal it for him. I couldn't understand why he wanted a mere handkerchief so much, but now I do.

Iago   You stupid whore!

Emilia   She didn't give it to Cassio, I gave it to my husband.

Iago   You lying piece of filth!

Emilia   I am not lying. You murdering fool! How did a fool like you end up with such a good woman?

Othello   Won't heaven strike him down? You evil bastard!

He runs at Iago. Iago stabs Emilia from behind, and exits

Gratiano   Oh my God! Iago has just killed his own wife.

Emilia   Please lie me by my mistress's side.

Gratiano   Iago's gone, and his wife is dead.

Montano   He is as evil as they come. Take the Moor's sword and guard the door. Don't let him in. If he tries to get in, kill him. I'm going after him; he's dangerous.

Exit Montano and Gratiano

Othello   I am not as strong as I thought if another man can just take my sword. But what do I care about my honour now? I have none after what I have done. I have lost everything.

Emilia   What did your song mean, my lady? Can you hear me? I'll die like a swan – they sing when they die.
[Singing] 'Willow, willow, willow,' –
She was pure and chaste, Othello, she loved you – yes, cruel you. I'm telling the truth with my dying breath.

Dies

Othello   I have another sword in this room, a Spanish sword tempered in ice. Uncle, I need to leave.

Gratiano   If you even attempt to leave, we'll make you suffer. Remember, you have no weapon now.

Othello   Come in and speak to me, then, or I'll attack you – weapon or no weapon.

Re-enter Gratiano

Gratiano   What is it?

Othello   Look, I have a weapon. No soldier has ever had better. I have fought twenty times as many men as you with this dagger. But it is pointless boasting now. Who can control his fate? Don't be afraid of my weapon. I am only going to use it on myself, for I have come to the end of my journey. Don't be afraid, there is no need. Touch me with a rush, and I'd back away. Where should I go? You're as pale as your shirt, and you're looking at me in disgust. When we meet on Judgement Day, that look will hurl me from heaven, and send me straight to hell. Desdemona, you are so cold, as cold as the chastity I doubted. Damn Iago! Let the devil whip me, or let me roast in sulphur or drown in liquid fire. Anything, so that I don't have to look at what I have done. Desdemona is dead! Oh God! Oh no!

Enter Lodovico. Montano, Cassio carried in a chair, and Officers with Iago, prisoner

Lodovico	Where is the unfortunate man who acted so recklessly?
Othello	I am here. The one who was Othello.
Lodovico	Where is that viper? Bring him here.
Othello	I know it's just a fable, but I can't help looking at your feet to see if you have cloven hooves. It's good you're not a devil, because I can kill you if you're mortal.
	Wounds Iago
Lodovico	Grab his sword!
Iago	I'm just wounded, you haven't killed me.
Othello	Good. I'd rather you try to live with what you've done.
Lodovico	Othello, you were once such a good man, and you allowed this villain to trick you. I don't know what to say to you.
Othello	Say anything: call me an honourable murderer, if you must call me a murderer, because I didn't do this out of hate. I really thought I was justified.
Lodovico	Iago has confessed everything. Is it true that you and Iago conspired to kill Cassio as well?
Othello	Yes.
Cassio	Othello, I never gave you reason to kill me!
Othello	I know that, and I ask your forgiveness. Will you ask that devil Iago why he tried to destroy me?
Iago	You can't demand anything of me. I'm not going to explain myself. I'm not going to say another word.
Lodovico	Not even to pray?
Gratiano	Torture will open your lips.
Othello	Well, do your best to get an explanation from him.
Lodovico	Sir, you should know everything that has happened. I don't think you know the full story yet. Here are the letters we found in Roderigo's pockets after he died. One of them is from Iago telling Roderigo to murder Cassio.

Othello	Oh, villain!
Cassio	This is disgusting, not to mention unfair!
Lodovico	Now here's another unopened letter we also found in his pocket. It seems Roderigo meant to send this to Iago, but Iago killed him first.
Othello	Oh, the villainous animal! How did you get hold of my wife's handkerchief anyway, Cassio?
Cassio	I just found it in my room, and Iago confessed that he planted it there to arouse your suspicions.
Othello	I am such a fool!
Cassio	Roderigo's letter also criticised Iago for telling him to get me angry while I was on duty, which led to me being demoted.
Lodovico	You must leave this room and come with us. Your power is henceforth taken away and Cassio will rule in Cyprus. Iago will be tortured in the worst ways imaginable. You will be our prisoner, until the Venetian state decides your sentence. Take him away.
Othello	Hang on a moment. Please let me say a word or two before you go. I have served Venice well, and they know it. I'm not saying any more about that, I only ask that in your letters to them you speak the truth about me. That I was someone who loved not wisely, but too well. Someone who didn't get jealous easily in the first place, but when he did, it was an overwhelming jealousy that he could not control. Someone who threw away a precious pearl, because he thought it was just a pebble. Someone who had never cried before, but who came to know sorrow that made tears drop from his eyes as sap oozes from Arabian trees. Someone who once stabbed a Turkish man for beating a Venetian citizen, just like this …
	Stabs himself
Lodovico	What a bloody end to this whole business!
Gratiano	Everything has been ruined.
Othello	I kissed you before I killed you, and now I kiss you before I kill myself.
	Falls on the bed, and dies

Cassio   I was scared he would do this, because he was a noble man when all is said and done, but I didn't think he had a weapon.

Lodovico   You bloodthirsty dog! Crueller than sadness or hunger, or the sea. Look at this tragic sight, these dead bodies on this bed! You did this. It is a horrific sight – someone cover them. Gratiano, this house and all Othello's goods are yours. Cassio, you have to decide how to punish Iago. Punish him severely. I will go to Venice and report these tragic events with a very heavy heart.

           Exit

FOCUS ON ACT 5

'Iago's total lack of conscience is so shocking that we constantly wait for some cracks to appear, and for him to feel some remorse'

IT IS hard to imagine a more catastrophic ending than the one we find in *Othello*. Scene I is a visually arresting and exciting scene, whereas Scene II is very tragic and emotional.

The first scene is full of action and tension. The fight scenes present us with a dramatic visual spectacle, which is not fully revealed to us by just reading the script. Like many scenes, it is crucial to see it in performance.

Iago's machinations have reached a crucial point. There is a sense of urgency in this scene for the audience too, as we desperately hope Iago will get his comeuppance. If he is to remain undiscovered, he needs to get rid of Roderigo, of whom he speaks in disparaging yet humorous terms, describing him as a pimple he has squeezed to bursting point: ***I have rubb'd this young quat almost to the sense, / And he grows angry. Now, whether he kill Cassio / Or Cassio him, or each do kill the other, / Every way makes my gain***. Iago's total lack of conscience is so shocking that we constantly wait for some cracks to appear, and for him to feel some remorse, but this certainly doesn't happen in this scene. When Roderigo ambushes Cassio, and tries to kill him, it is, predictably, the foolish Roderigo who is killed instead, by the unseen Iago. Slyly, Iago stabs Cassio in the leg, as that is as much as he can do without being seen. Othello hears the commotion from his lodgings, and when Cassio cries, ***I am maim'd for ever***, he assumes that Cassio's injuries are fatal, and proceeds with his own desperate plans.

Lodovico and Gratiano arrive to investigate, and once again, Iago's consummate skill as an actor is obvious. This reminds us not to judge Othello too harshly, for he certainly isn't the only one fooled by Iago's duplicity. Iago convincingly expresses shock and dismay, and even pretends to be wary of Lodovico and Gratiano. He seems to have thought of everything: ***Kill men i'th' dark? Where***

Sweet soul, take heed, take heed of perjury. Thou art on thy deathbed

– OTHELLO (ACT V SCENE II)

be these bloody thieves? / How silent is this town! Ho, murder, murder! / What may you be? Are you of good or evil?

When Bianca arrives into this chaotic scene, Iago also tries to implicate her. He tries to insinuate that Bianca, whom he calls a notorious prostitute, arranged to have Cassio set upon, and even throws in a comment designed to make Lodovico and Gratiano think less of Cassio: *This is the fruits of whoring*. However, Iago's plot is nothing if not precarious. It relies on misinformation, appearance and circumstance. No one is more aware of how flimsy it is than Iago, who mutters to himself as the scene closes: *This is the night / That either makes me or fordoes me quite*.

The final scene of the play is very upsetting. Even by bour modern standards, the premeditated strangling to death of a young girl by the man whom she loves unconditionally is heartbreaking. The scene begins with Othello gazing at the sleeping Desdemona. Even at the moment he is about to kill her, he seems more preoccupied with her physical beauty than with anything else: *Yet I'll not shed her blood, / Nor scar that whiter skin of hers than snow, / And smooth as monumental alabaster*. There is also something eerie about the way he compares her to a rose, and killing her to plucking a rose: *When I have pluck'd the rose / I cannot give it vital growth again. / It needs must wither. I'll smell thee on the tree*. What is perhaps most unsettling to a modern audience is that Othello feels quite justified in killing her, just because he believes she is guilty of adultery. He takes the high moral ground, urging her to confess her sins, believing himself to be magnanimous in this gesture: *I would not kill thy unprepared spirit. / No, heavens forfend! I would not kill thy soul*.

Desdemona tries her best, as she has since the first time

It is too late

– OTHELLO (ACT V SCENE II)

Othello accused her, to convince him he is utterly wrong: *That death's unnatural that kills for loving*. If Othello were in a logical frame of mind, he would realise that Desdemona's continued denials show her innocence, because at this time Christians believed that you could never get to heaven if you didn't confess before you died. But, no matter how powerful Desdemona's words, her pleas fall on deaf ears:

> *I never did*
> *Offend you in my life, never loved Cassio*
> *But with such general warranty of heaven*
> *As I might love. I never gave him token.*

She then begs him to kill her in the morning, or even let her live another half an hour. Her desperation to live is easy to empathise with.

When Emilia arrives, she is distraught to discover Desdemona virtually dead. The dying girl manages to declare her innocence one last time, but her final words are particularly profound, as she nobly claims suicide, and asks for Othello's blessing: *Nobody, I myself. Farewell. / Commend me to my kind lord. O, farewell!* Emilia's fury once again echoes how the audience feels towards Othello; she articulates our despair at his desperate actions.

At this point, Iago is very close to getting away with it all, and now that Desdemona is beyond rescue, the audience is tensed for his discovery. Fittingly, it is the person who – theoretically at least – knows him best who realises everything he has done: *that handkerchief thou speak'st of / I found by fortune and did give my husband, / For often, with a solemn earnestness – / More than indeed belong'd to such a trifle – / He begg'd of me to steal it*. The entire plot hangs on such a tiny, trivial thing, and, in a way, this emphasises the tragedy of it all. Iago tells Emilia to shut her mouth, but she is too disgusted by his treachery, and too devastated by Desdemona's death to stay silent. When Iago tries to send her home, Emilia says that she won't go, and may never go home again. Iago stabs Emilia after her revelation (the only crime he commits that is witnessed). The fact that Iago can kill his wife so casually is truly shocking, but it also tells everyone that she could reveal terrible things about him. This is the only moment Iago loses control, and he seals his own fate by doing so. Emilia has become a character we truly care about. She seemed strong and streetwise in comparison with Desdemona, but she was no more able to defend herself against the very person who was supposed to love her most than Desdemona was. Emilia dies beside her mistress, singing the 'Willow' song, which now has the same significance for her that it had for Desdemona.

Once the sickening realisation of his terrible mistake has sunk in, Othello tries to kill Iago but only wounds him. He begs to know Iago's motives: **Will you, I pray, demand that demi-devil / Why he hath thus ensnared my body and soul?** At this point, it would indeed be fascinating to know something of Iago's motivation, but he has the last laugh, choosing to deny Othello any satisfaction, even now: **Demand me nothing. What you know, you know. / From this time forth I never will speak word.**

Once Cassio and Othello have made their peace, Othello does the only thing he can at this stage: he kills himself, but not before returning to the eloquence that was notable in the first two acts of the play; an eloquence that manages to do the unthinkable, and make the audience feel some pity for him:

> Speak of me as I am. Nothing extenuate,
> Nor set down aught in malice. Then must you speak
> Of one that loved not wisely but too well,
> Of one not easily jealous but, being wrought

> Perplex'd in the extreme; of one whose hand,
> Like the base Indian, threw a pearl away
> Richer than all his tribe ...

Cassio, Lodovico and Gratiano are left stunned by the events. Desdemona, Emilia and Othello lie dead upon the marital bed. Cassio shows his unending loyalty when he describes Othello as **great of heart**. The fact that, as the play ends, Iago is still alive may seem initially frustrating, but not when you consider that he is about to experience the most agonising torture imaginable. Shakespeare's audience members would have known all the horrific methods that could be used on a man such as Iago: the rack, for example, or being hanged, drawn and quartered. They would have seen Iago's survival as worse punishment than a modern audience might.

Lodovico speaks the final lines of the play and we can only imagine the Venetian response to the horrific events in Cyprus: **O, enforce it! / Myself will straight aboard, and to the state / This heavy act with heavy heart relate.**

IMPORTANT THEMES IN ACT V

• The theme of jealousy is seen in Othello's tragic actions. Jealousy has been alluded to throughout the play as a monster and a poison, and the death of Desdemona makes an undeniable point about its insidious nature.

• The theme of revenge is also seen in Othello's actions. The fact that he feels justified in taking Desdemona's life is deeply disturbing.

• The theme of evil is seen in Iago's character. The pang of conscience or shred of remorse we have been waiting for never arrives. Iago is truly evil – a sociopath who sees other human beings as disposable pawns in his games.

Then must you speak
Of one that loved not wisely but too well

– OTHELLO (ACT V SCENE II)

Demand me nothing. What you know, you know. From this time forth I never will speak word

— IAGO (ACT V SCENE II)

He even denies Othello the comfort of an explanation; his silence is his final evil act.

• The theme of love is seen in Desdemona's claim that she has killed herself. Her very last act is to protect the husband who has betrayed her so terribly.

• The theme of appearance versus reality is seen in the shocked reaction of every other character to 'honest' Iago's treachery.

CHARACTER DEVELOPMENT IN ACT V

• Othello seems calmer in this act than he was in Act IV, but this is only because he has decided on his course of action, and will not sway from it, no matter how vehemently Desdemona denies his allegations. Othello's stubborn refusal shows a certain strength of mind, which has served him well in a turbulent life, but now he has channelled it in entirely the wrong direction. Othello ruins his own life, and, despite what he has done, it is impossible not to feel some measure of pity for him.

• Iago shows no remorse. We hope he will answer Othello's question, because the audience needs to know more about his underlying motivation too, but this never happens. Iago is a study in pure evil.

• Desdemona, Cassio and Emilia remain the admirable characters they have always been. The tragedy of the final scene is largely due to the pity the audience feels for the angelic Desdemona. Cassio forgives Othello without hesitation, demonstrating his good heart. Emilia stands up to Othello, and reveals her husband's evil plot, even though it costs her her life.

QUESTIONS ON ACT 5

1. Describe how you would stage Scene I if you were directing a new version of **Othello**. Refer to props, lighting, costume and sound effects in your answer.

2. Did you feel any pity for Othello? Refer to the text in support of your answer.

3. Write out the text of a report Lodovico might write to the Venetian senate on the events described in Scene I.

4. To which flower does Othello compare Desdemona in Scene II? Why, in your opinion, does he pick this particular flower?

5. Do you think there was anything Desdemona could have said to stop Othello from killing her? Give reasons for your answer.

6. Why, in your view, did Emilia not realise the significance of the handkerchief until this point? Refer to the text in support of your answer.

7. We learn that Roderigo died with several incriminating letters on him. Write out the text of one of these letters.

8. Do you admire Emilia as a character, a woman, a friend and a wife? Refer to the text in support of your answer.

9. Write a newspaper article for **The Cyprus Post** entitled 'Three Dead in Othello's House'.

10. Pick out what you think are the ten best quotations from Act V, explaining in each case why you have chosen that quotation. Make sure they cover a range of characters and themes.

OTHELLO

KEY WORDS TO DESCRIBE HIM

brave
valiant
leader
eloquent
insecure
mistrustful
outsider
paranoid
vulnerable
jealous
enraged
ferocious
loner
barbaric
stubborn
egotistical
remorseful
penitent

NONE OF Shakespeare's tragic heroes could be termed straightforward, boring or perfect. A tragic hero is always flawed. Yet, in Othello, Shakespeare may have attempted his most audacious tragic hero: he expects us to have sympathy for a man who kills his innocent wife. Othello is a curious choice in many ways. Even physically, he would not have been the hero that the audience expected to see. Othello is black, at a time when England was almost uniformly white and monocultural. Yet it is soon clear to us that Othello has many excellent characteristics, and the audience eventually stops seeing him as different. Othello is clearly an eloquent, captivating speaker (something even the Duke comments on). He is an acclaimed military expert (shown by the fact that the Venetian state has entrusted the highest military office to a foreigner). He is very loving and respectful towards his wife (initially), and he is also a model of restraint and etiquette (when he imposes a curfew on the celebrations in Cyprus).

Was Shakespeare a racist? Like many questions about Shakespeare, we have no clear idea. His choice of a black man as the protagonist may seem to prove that he is not racist, but then Othello ends up killing his innocent wife, on the most circumstantial and insubstantial proof. Shakespeare seems to be depicting a character who has learned to fit in, and even excel, in this society, but with also a dark, even savage, side to his character that, once

If it were now to die,
'Twere now to be most happy

– OTHELLO (ACT II SCENE I)

I would not kill thy unprepared spirit.
No, heavens forfend! I would not kill thy soul

– OTHELLO (ACT V SCENE II)

unleashed, cannot be controlled. Then again, Iago is white, and he is the villain. Add to this the theory that Shakespeare himself may have been in love with a black woman, and the question becomes even more difficult to answer. Like *The Merchant of Venice* (which seems straightforwardly anti-Semitic, until you realise that Shakespeare was actually criticising the views of his society, and showing that Jews and Christians are fundamentally the same), *Othello* is a provocative text which forces us to question our own views.

Othello's role in society is complicated. We see this in his relationship with the high-ranking Brabantio, who, Othello reveals, ***loved me, oft invited me***; but Brabantio's love stops far short of approving of Othello marrying his precious daughter. This was clearly why Othello married Desdemona in secret. Brabantio is confident that Othello will be punished, but Othello is immensely valuable to the Venetian state, and although the Duke concedes that Othello's tales of adventure would have won his daughter too, there is a real sense that Othello can marry whom he likes, and do as he likes, as long as he continues to protect the Venetian state's valuable interests oversees. Othello thinks he is valued for his character: ***My parts, my title***

and my perfect soul / Shall manifest me rightly. But this is only part of the story. Othello is a stranger in a strange land, and as soon as he oversteps the boundaries of etiquette, which are not always visible to him, his position becomes precarious. Even when people, such as the Duke, are complimenting him, they are saying he is a good man despite his racial differences. We might be shocked by Iago calling Othello ***thick-lips***, but the Duke's attempts to comfort Brabantio are, arguably, just as insulting: ***If virtue no delighted beauty lack, / Your son-in-law is far more fair than black***.

The change in location to Cyprus (an exotic place at that time) seems to affect Othello's character too. It is hard to believe that the brilliant military strategist we hear so much about in Act I is the gullible, credulous puppet of the succeeding acts. It seems far too easy for Iago to insinuate his poison into Othello's mind. However, if we consider that Othello is, deep down, an insecure person, the ease with which Iago manipulates Othello becomes far more credible. Othello has married a woman he is deeply in love with, but also deeply in awe of. He cannot believe that such a wonderful creature loves him back, and is so stunned by his good luck that he seems to be

OTHELLO

waiting for someone to tell him that there is a catch. Once again, Shakespeare's psychological acuity is far ahead of his time: many relationships do flounder or even fail, not because of a lack of love, but because of low self-esteem. If people don't truly love themselves, they can't really believe that others could love them. This explanation may sound trite, but is there any other?

Othello's descent into jealousy is rapid. By Act III he has already resolved to kill Cassio and punish Desdemona severely. Once unleashed, his feelings cannot be contained. The entire action of this play takes place over just a few days. Othello acts rashly and hastily. He does not take the time to get real proof, but, then again, this is a crime of passion. Iago and Othello's interactions seem incredible. As we, the audience, are always aware of Iago's plots and schemes, it seems unbelievable that Othello cannot see what he is up to. But it is not just Othello – everyone believes Iago: Cassio, Desdemona, Montano; even Emilia only belatedly discovers her own husband's treachery.

In Act IV, a real lack of control is apparent in Othello's character. As a soldier, Othello has been trained to respond with violence. When he thinks that Desdemona has been unfaithful, all that strength and passion (which ensured his rapid military and social ascent) has no outlet but through violence. Othello trusts in the wrong person.

It is in the final act of the play that Shakespeare really takes a risk with the character of Othello. Othello's words upon gazing at the sleeping Desdemona are chilling to say the least: ***When I have pluck'd the rose / I cannot give it vital growth again. / It needs must wither. I'll smell thee on the tree***. And his final conversation with her, when she pleads for her life, is deeply upsetting: ***Kill me tomorrow; let me live tonight***.

Yet somehow Shakespeare succeeds in making us feel some degree of pity for Othello. For a start, this was a time when death was considered a suitable punishment for many crimes, and Othello certainly thinks the punishment fits the crime in this case. When Emilia reveals the truth to him, he is horrified and remorseful. He tries, and fails, to kill Iago, but does succeed in killing himself. It is a pathetic and shameful end to a heroic life, and no one is more aware of that fact than Othello himself: ***one whose hand, / Like the base Indian, threw a pearl away / Richer than all his tribe***.

CHARACTER
FOCUS

IAGO

KEY WORDS TO DESCRIBE HIM

conniving
sly
cunning

sinister
sneaky
deceitful
duplicitous
clever
insecure
intuitive
perceptive
sociopath
nefarious
malicious
Machiavellian
evil
villainous
malevolent

I follow but myself.
Heaven is my judge, not I for love and duty,
But seeming so for my peculiar end.
For when my outward action doth demonstrate
The native act and figure of my heart
In compliment extern, 'tis not long after
But I will wear my heart upon my sleeve
For daws to peck at. I am not what I am.

THE DEFINITION of a villain is 'a person guilty or capable of a crime or wickedness', but this hardly seems an adequate description of Iago. Shakespeare created many great villains throughout his literary career: in *Hamlet*, Claudius murdered his own brother so that he could marry his widow and gain the throne; the titular character in *Macbeth* also murders the king to take his throne. But even these two heinous villains suffer from pangs of conscience. Iago has absolutely no conscience. He also has no convincing motivation for what he does. Neither is Iago evil out of ignorance or a lack of intelligence; he is incredibly astute and perceptive. He can read people like an expert psychologist, and he knows exactly what to say and do to manipulate their entire personalities. He is the puppet-master who makes everyone do exactly what he wants them to do. Not one person in this entire play suspects Iago at any point. It is only in the final scene that he is discovered, and it takes his own wife to realise that

With as little a web as this will I ensnare as great a fly as Cassio

– IAGO (ACT II SCENE I)

THERE IS A SAMPLE ESSAY ON IAGO ON PAGE 279

*This is the night
That either makes me or fordoes me quite*

– IAGO (ACT V SCENE I)

he is the one who has ruined so many lives.

One of Iago's greatest skills is his rhetoric. He has a gift for language which is unsurpassed in the play. His language is not always eloquent, but it is always effective. In the very first scene of the play, we see him using this gift to control Roderigo and antagonise Brabantio. Brabantio was never going to be pleased that his daughter had run away with Othello, but there is no doubt that he is doubly incensed by Iago's offensive, racist and sexualised descriptions: *an old black ram / Is tupping your white ewe* and *you'll have your daughter covered with a Barbary horse, you'll have your nephews neigh to you, you'll have coursers for cousins and gennets for germans* and *your daughter and the Moor are now making the beast with two backs*.

Iago repeatedly uses the metaphor of poison to describe the powerful effect that well-chosen words can have – *The Moor already changes with my poison* – and he also realises that words may not have a dramatic effect initially, but their cumulative effect can be devastating: *Dangerous conceits are in their natures poisons. / Which at the first are scarce found to distaste, / But with a little act upon the blood, / Burn like the mines of Sulphur*.

It is interesting that Iago's weapon of choice, so to speak, is the metaphorical poison of jealousy, because when he justifies his decision to destroy Othello, his rationale is:

*For that I do suspect the lusty Moor
Hath leap'd into my seat, the thought whereof
Doth, like a poisonous mineral, gnaw my inwards;
And nothing can or shall content my soul
Till I am even'd with him, wife for wife –
Or failing so, yet that I put the Moor
At least into a jealousy so strong
That judgement cannot cure ...*

Because Iago is a jealous person himself, he recognises the power of jealousy. He is jealous of Cassio, and it is easier for Iago to destroy what he is jealous of than to dwell upon the painful reasons for the emotions.

Iago uses the hapless Roderigo's unrequited infatuation for Desdemona as the bait to lure him into his game. Iago only tolerates Roderigo because he is rich – *Thus do I ever make my fool my purse*. Roderigo is such an objectionable character, it is hard to feel much sympathy for him. Iago seems quite fond of Desdemona, judging by

IAGO

their light-hearted banter as they await Othello's arrival in Cyprus. Desdemona thinks Iago is being deliberately sexist to make everyone laugh, but it is clear that Iago has a deep-rooted hatred of women when he jokes, *You are pictures out of doors, / Bells in your parlours, wildcats in your kitchens, / Saints in your injuries, devils being offended, / Players in your housewifery, and hussies in your beds*. One of the most chilling moments in the entire play is when Iago tells Othello how he should kill Desdemona: *Do it not with poison. Strangle her in her bed, even the bed she hath contaminated*. For it is at this moment that we realise Iago is not just manipulative, embittered, jealous and cruel, he is actually a sociopath, coldly advising the murder of a completely innocent woman.

Iago's relationship with Emilia raises more questions than it answers. Emilia is clearly besotted with her husband, and the fact that she is so eager to give him the handkerchief proves this. Iago seems quite indifferent to his wife beyond throwing the odd insulting comment her way. Killing her is the only time he shows any feelings towards her one way or the other.

The role of Iago is a demanding one to play. A lot of the acting is quite physical, for Iago is always darting in and out of the shadows, from the very first scene onwards. The penultimate scene in the play is a great example of this. Iago sets Roderigo up as his hitman, and then loiters unseen in the shadows. He stabs Cassio in the leg, then runs off, only to arrive back in his nightgown to bandage Cassio up and express his dismay at what has transpired.

Iago is called honest a total of eighteen times throughout the play, not just by Othello, but by Cassio and Desdemona too. His greatest achievement is that his Machiavellian plots remain completely unsuspected until the very last moments. They are only discovered by chance by Emilia. We never get the satisfaction of Iago's remorse, or even his confession, and his final words in the play deny us any explanation: *Demand me nothing. What you know, you know. / From this time forth I never will speak word*.

Shakespeare is quite unequivocal in how he presents Iago. There are no grey areas or mitigating factors. He presents Iago to the audience as a study in pure evil, and it has the same discomfiting effect as it does in real life when we learn of an evil act that we cannot rationalise or explain.

DESDEMONA

irreproachable

innocent

faultless

guiltless

honourable

truthful

exemplary

noble

steadfast

loyal

unwavering

dignified

moral

admirable

kind

tolerant

self-aware

AS THE daughter of a Venetian senator, Desdemona would have lived a sheltered, privileged life. She is often accused of being too passive, but close study of the text proves this view erroneous. Roderigo is one example of a man she refused, but as Emilia reveals later in the play, there were many suitors, none of whom Desdemona would accept: **she forsook so many noble matches**. This, in itself, shows a strong and independent spirit.

Desdemona was also an active participant in her courtship; indeed, she seems to have been quite brazen (for the times). She was clearly smitten with the exotic visitor to her father's house, and didn't hesitate to let him know of her feelings once she was sure of them:

... she wish'd
That heaven had made her such a man. She
thanked me,
And bade me, if I had a friend that loved her,
I should but teach him how to tell my story.
And that would woo her. Upon this hint I spake.
She loved me for the dangers I had pass'd,
And I loved her that she did pity them.

One of the most difficult decisions Desdemona could ever have made in her young life was to marry Othello without permission. Her elopement shows a daring spirit. It was clearly not a decision she took lightly, but she went through with it because (knowing her father) it was the only way she could be with Othello. When her father

Unkindness may do much,
And his unkindness may defeat my life,
But never taint my love

– DESDEMONA (ACT IV SCENE II)

THERE IS A SAMPLE ESSAY ON
DESDEMONA ON PAGE 276

*Why I should fear I know not,
Since guiltiness I know not,
but yet I feel I fear*

– DESDEMONA (ACT V SCENE II)

accuses Othello of witchcraft, Desdemona stands up to him with firmness, but also kindness. She gently tells him that her husband is now her priority: ***My noble father, / I do perceive here a divided duty***. In Shakespeare's day, women were looked on as possessions; they belonged to their fathers until they married. But Brabantio would never have allowed Desdemona to marry Othello, hence her actions. His bitter words to Othello have repercussions he could never have imagined: ***Look to her, Moor, if thou hast eyes to see. / She has deceived her father, and may thee***. Othello does come to believe that Desdemona's choosing her own fate was a kind of betrayal, and if she could do it once, she could do it again. Therefore, Desdemona's grand gesture ultimately works against her, but it clearly shows a brave, resourceful and independent young woman, and it also reveals a girl deeply in love. She even asks to go to Cyprus with her husband. As far as she knows she could be going straight into a war zone, so this too shows great backbone.

Desdemona's quick wit is referred to by Othello and Cassio, but best seen when she deftly handles Iago's sexist comments: ***O heavy ignorance! Thou praisest the worst best. But what praise couldst thou bestow on a deserving woman indeed – one that, in the authority***

DESDEMONA

of her merit, did justly put on the vouch of very malice itself? She also has a sense of humour, and seems every bit as wonderful as Cassio describes her: *One that excels the quirks of blazoning pens ...*

Desdemona's principles are seen in her staunch defence of her friend Cassio. She tells him that when she makes a promise, she keeps it, and this reminds us of the promise she made to Othello when she married him: *If I do vow a friendship I'll perform it / To the last article*. Ironically, her promise to Cassio costs her dearly. Her constant references to him are positively incendiary to Othello, but make her more admirable to the audience.

Desdemona's reaction to Othello's sudden change in attitude is very realistic. She is bewildered and saddened. She tries at every opportunity to make things better, and her heartbreak is painful to witness. When Othello strikes her in front of everyone, he humiliates her, but Desdemona responds with a quiet dignity, and a simple, yet utterly true statement: *I have not deserved this*. The simple truth of this statement contrasts with the complicated lies Iago tells at every turn. Even when Emilia blurts out that she wishes Desdemona had never met Othello, Desdemona replies that she still loves him. It is clear that the love Desdemona has for Othello is

unconditional, and this, in itself reminds us how very conditional his love turned out to be.

The final scene of the play is a very distressing one. The slow, methodical way in which Othello carries out the murder is deeply disturbing. Desdemona's pleas are all in vain; no matter how strongly she protests her innocence, Othello has made up his mind. She is a young girl, just a few days married, and he is an older man, a soldier of great strength and ability. Desdemona doesn't stand a chance. Her last words to Emilia – *Commend me to my kind lord* – are in defence of Othello and she even claims that she committed suicide in order to protect the man she still loves: *Nobody, I myself*.

Cassio refers to Desdemona as 'divine' and this doesn't just mean that she is beautiful or has a wonderful personality; it also means that she is god-like, and she certainly does emulate God in her incredible capacity to forgive.

Desdemona is not just an interesting character, she is also a way for Shakespeare to express his views on male–female relationships and the imbalance of power in marriages at the time. Desdemona does nothing wrong, but dies because the man she loves is insecure and jealous.

EMILIA

KEY WORDS TO DESCRIBE HER

pragmatic

sensible

practical

grounded

rational

honest

level-headed

devoted

loyal

steadfast

brave

realistic

strong

feisty

gutsy

EMILIA IS a lively, outspoken, realistic woman whose earthiness is far easier to relate to than Desdemona's perfection. Because she is Iago's wife, we are initially wary of her, but it quickly becomes apparent that she is not in her husband's confidence. This was another feature of Shakespeare's times. We know that many royal marriages were arranged for dynastic reasons, but many ordinary marriages were also more like business transactions than romantic unions, and this might explain why Emilia seems to have no idea what her husband is up to.

Shakespeare's views of women, as a man living four centuries ago, are always fascinating to consider. In *Othello* we have three female characters, and all are archetypes of different kinds of woman. Emilia is a lady-in-waiting. She has not led the sheltered life that Desdemona has, and she is realistic and pragmatic about the world around her. She is also fiercely loyal to her mistress: ***Alas, Iago, my lord hath so bewhored her, / Thrown such despite and heavy terms upon her, / As true hearts cannot bear it***. Emilia is quick-witted and outspoken and not only are her lines entertaining for the audience, but she also tends to articulate what we, the audience, are thinking. For example: ***Hath she forsook so many noble matches, / Her father and her country and her friends, / To be call'd whore? Would it not make one weep?***

Emilia certainly makes a crucial mistake in giving Iago

I durst, my lord, to wager she is honest,
Lay down my soul at stake

— EMILIA (ACT IV SCENE II)

Do thy worst.
This deed of thine is no more worthy heaven
Than thou wast worthy her

– EMILIA (ACT V SCENE II)

the handkerchief, but it is a bad decision (made in the hope of pleasing her husband) rather than an intentionally malicious act. She doesn't even steal it, she just finds it on the ground. She knows Desdemona will miss it badly, but can't seem to resist the opportunity to please her husband:

> *I am glad I have found this napkin.*
> *This was her first remembrance from the Moor.*
> *My wayward husband hath a hundred times*
> *Woo'd me to steal it, but she so loves the token –*
> *For he conjured her she should ever keep it –*
> *That she reserves it evermore about her*
> *To kiss and talk to. I'll ha' the work ta'en out,*
> *And give't Iago. What he will do with it*
> *Heaven knows, not I.*
> *I nothing but to please his fantasy.*

The conversation Emilia and Desdemona have just a few hours before both women die at the hands of their husbands is one of the most important and revelatory dialogues of the play. Desdemona is so innocent that she cannot even conceive of an unfaithful wife, let alone be one herself: ***Dost thou in conscience think – tell me,***

Emilia – / That there be women do abuse their husbands / In such gross kind? Emilia's response is, like everything she says, practical and realistic: ***There be some such, no question***. When Desdemona asks if Emilia could commit such a deed for the whole world, Emilia also answers honestly rather than diplomatically: ***The world's a huge thing. It is a great price for a small vice***. Many more women could identify with Emilia than Desdemona at this point. She brings a degree of perspective that Othello has completely lost. Emilia goes on to explain that she believes women are just like men, and, if that is true, then both sexes are capable of being weak and of making the wrong decisions:

> *But I do think it is their husbands' faults*
> *If wives do fall. Say that they slack their duties,*
> *And pour our treasures into foreign laps,*
> *Or else break out in peevish jealousies,*
> *Throwing restraint upon us; or say they strike us,*
> *Or scant our former having in despite;*
> *Why, we have galls; and though we have some grace,*
> *Yet have we some revenge. Let husbands know*
> *Their wives have sense like them. They see, and smell,*

EMILIA

And have their palates both for sweet and sour,
As husbands have. What is it that they do
When they change us for others? Is it sport?
I think it is. And doth affection breed it?
I think it doth. Is't frailty that thus errs?
It is so, too. And have not we affections,
Desires for sport, and frailty, as men have?
Then let them use us well, else let them know
The ills we do, their ills instruct us so.

This is quite an audacious speech for a woman to make at this time, when women were expected to be pure and chaste. They were expected to be virgins when they married and to remain completely faithful. There were completely different rules for men, and one can only imagine the reaction in the Globe Theatre to this controversial view. The female members would certainly have applauded loudly. Yet Emilia is quite dismissive and insulting to Bianca, showing that it is not only men who are guilty of double standards.

It is in Emilia's verbal attacks upon Othello at the close of the play that we see her real potential as character. Emilia is, after all, dealing with a man capable of killing his wife, so she is in very real danger, but, admirably, she holds nothing back: *If he say so, may his pernicious soul / Rot half a grain a day. He lies to th' heart. / She was too fond of her most filthy bargain*. Emilia's loyalty and unswerving devotion to Desdemona, whom she is still willing to die for, forms an unappealing contrast with Othello's disloyalty: *Thou hast not half that power to do me harm / As I have to be hurt. O gull, O dolt, / As ignorant as dirt! Thou hast done a deed – / I care not for thy sword, I'll make thee known / Though I lost twenty lives*.

Emilia is sickened by the unwitting role she played in assisting Iago's nefarious schemes and tells him she is finished with him: *Perchance, Iago, I will ne'er go home*. When Iago stabs her, Emilia realises that Barbary's song 'The Willow', which Desdemona sang before her death, is her song too. It is a song about a woman's vulnerability to the whims and desires of her lover. Emilia and Desdemona are two very different woman, but they are both ultimately victims: *What did thy song bode, lady? / Hark, canst thou hear me? I will play the swan, / And die in music*.

CASSIO

gallant
noble
gentlemanly
brave

gracious
chivalrous
eloquent
obliging
devoted
honourable
trusting
earnest
loyal
sincere

HE HATH a daily beauty in his life are astute words from Iago that sum up Cassio's appealing character and his dramatic function in this play. Cassio is a handsome, charming, titled, charismatic young man. He is one of those people who have a certain something about them that incites jealousy in others. He has the quality the French might term a 'je ne sais quoi', meaning that there is an elusive attractive quality about him that makes others feel lacking in comparison.

Cassio is an Italian gentleman through and through. Although he is from Verona, he has been schooled in the complex Venetian etiquette, and he is also full of spirit and life. Iago is jealous of Cassio for all these reasons, and he also guesses that Cassio, being so opposite to Othello, would be the perfect person to accuse Desdemona of having an affair with. Ironically, Cassio is one of the few characters in the play who really love Othello, regardless of his racial and cultural differences. Even Desdemona was attracted to Othello for his exotic roots, so Cassio's complete indifference to Othello's foreign background is truly exceptional in the play.

His devotion to his general is apparent as he awaits Othello's safe arrival on Cypriot shores, and his genuine good wishes for the newly married couple are also clear:

Great Jove, Othello guard,
And swell his sail with thine own powerful breath,
That he may bless this bay with his tall ship,

*He hath achieved a maid
That paragons description and wild fame*

– CASSIO (ACT II SCENE I)

I will rather sue to be despised than to deceive so good a commander with so slight, so drunken, and so indiscreet an officer

– CASSIO (ACT II SCENE III)

Make love's quick pants in Desdemona's arms ...
It is clear that Cassio has an open and frank admiration for Desdemona, but he has absolutely no agenda, and that is why he feels he can compliment her so effusively. Also, his excellent manners are a Venetian custom, and the envious Iago jealously comments on Cassio's attentions to Desdemona in a visually evocative aside:

> **Ay, smile upon her, do. I will gyve thee in thine own courtship. You say true, 'tis so, indeed. If such tricks as these strip you out of your lieutenantry, it had been better you had not kissed your three fingers so oft, which now again you are most apt to play the sir in. Very good, well kissed, an excellent curtsy 'tis so indeed; yet again your fingers to your lips? Would they were clyster-pipes for your sake.**

Cassio seems too good to be true, but it turns out that Cassio has two weaknesses that Iago can exploit for his own ends. First, he cannot handle his drink and becomes aggressive when he is drunk. Second, he has an attachment to a courtesan, Bianca. These two vices, unacceptable in a woman, would have been considered

CASSIO

perfectly fine in a man. Men were expected and allowed to sow their wild oats, but had to do so with some measure of discretion. Iago gets Cassio drunk and has Roderigo ready to antagonise him. It is a simple plan, but it works. Cassio gets into a drunken brawl and Othello is, understandably, disgusted at his second-in-command, not least because his target is Montano, a well-connected nobleman.

Cassio is distraught at losing his position, and wastes no time in trying to reconcile with Othello. This conveniently plays into Iago's scheme, when he convincingly suggests to Cassio that Desdemona is the one to approach:

> *Confess yourself freely to her. Importune her help to put you in your place again. She is of so free, so kind, so apt, so blessed a disposition, she holds it a vice in her goodness not to do more than she is requested. This broken joint between you and her husband entreat her to splinter, and, my fortunes against any lay worth naming, this crack of your love shall grow stronger than it was before*.

All Cassio can see is a good friend trying to help. He has no reason to question Iago's motives, or to think that Othello might grow jealous: after all, he was the go-between for the couple during their courtship.

Othello's orders to kill Cassio create great suspense. It is only through the good fortune of wearing armour that Cassio escapes being killed by Roderigo: *That thrust had been mine enemy indeed, / But that my coat is better than thou know'st / I will make proof of thine*.

It must also be noted that Cassio makes no attempt to defend Bianca, of whom he had seemed so fond – a sad reflection of the accepted treatment of women at the time.

While Cassio is certainly not perfect, he is always very likeable, because he has a big heart. He shows this when he is generous enough to speak highly of Othello even after learning that his general wanted him dead. If ever there was a time to abandon your loyalty to a comrade, this would seem to be it, but Cassio does not do so, and his final words in the play show the good man that he (almost) consistently is: *This did I fear, but thought he had no weapon, / For he was great of heart*.

RODERIGO

rich
gullible
credulous
naive
obsessive
foolish
deluded
weak
impotent
inept
ineffectual
exploitable
jealous

I T IS very hard to have any sympathy for, much less empathy with, Roderigo. He is infatuated with Desdemona, a woman who has already refused him, and he allows Iago to treat him as a lucrative pawn in his unscrupulous game. He has more money than sense, and he is often played for laughs, and usually gets booed by the audience.

Roderigo is also spineless, the perfect sidekick for Iago. He antagonises Cassio to get him fired, and even tries – entirely unjustifiably – to kill him. His obsession with Desdemona is creepy. Following a woman who has rejected you on her honeymoon, and waiting for her to be done with her husband (and then with Cassio, according to Iago) makes Roderigo a stalker rather than a suitor. Iago's vivid metaphor, describing Roderigo as a pimple he has squeezed until it is fit to burst is insultingly apt: *I have rubb'd this young quat almost to the sense, / And he grows angry*. Roderigo's dramatic function is to help drive the plot onwards, and his death succeeds in bringing everything to a head. As Roderigo is the character with whom Iago was probably most genuine, we might expect Iago to feel some measure of guilt over his death, but Iago simply sees one less problem to deal with. Roderigo's role is to propel the plot, and provide some humour.

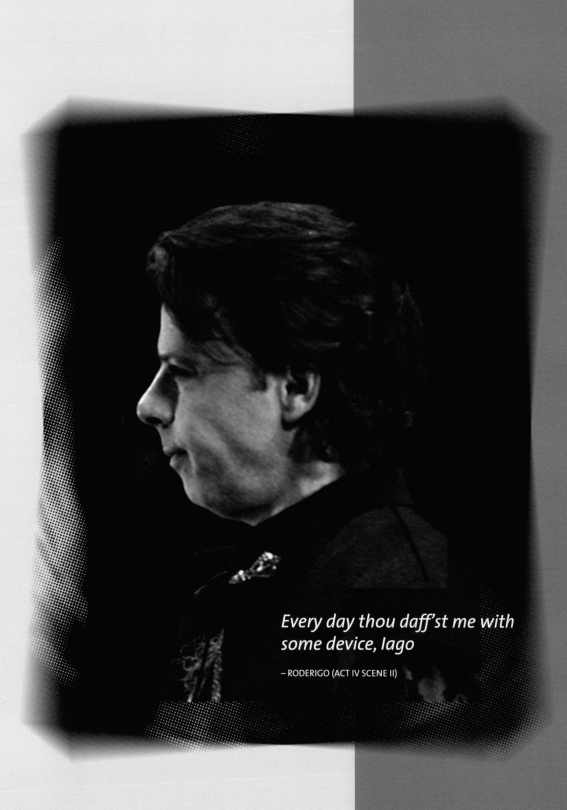

Every day thou daff'st me with some device, Iago

– RODERIGO (ACT IV SCENE II)

BIANCA

play-thing
vulnerable
mistreated
lovelorn

WHILE BIANCA does not have a very large role in the play, as one of just three female characters, she is still significant: *A hussy that by selling her desires / Buys herself bread and clothes: it is a creature / That dotes on Cassio – as 'tis the strumpet's plague / To beguile many and be beguiled by one. / He, when he hears of her, cannot refrain / From the excess of laughter*. Bianca is clearly a vulnerable woman. She sells her body for food and clothing, not for wealth or luxuries. She loves Cassio, but he just thinks of her as a pleasant distraction: someone who loves him, but whom he just laughs about.

Iago recognises Bianca's vulnerability when he insinuates that she had something to do with the attack on Cassio and Roderigo, and there is something deeply sad about the humiliated Bianca's appeal to Emilia: *I am no strumpet, but of life as honest / As you that thus abuse me*. Women in this play are depicted as being very much at the mercy of men. Bianca seems the most obvious candidate to be vulnerable in this way, but are Desdemona and Emilia really in a better position?

I am no strumpet; but of life as honest
As you that thus abuse me

— BIANCA (ACT V SCENE I)

BRABANTIO

KEY WORDS TO DESCRIBE HIM

rich
nobleman

politician
heart-broken

B RABANTIO PLAYS a relatively small role in the play, as his speaking role is limited to Act I, but in a way his character helps show how Othello is viewed by society in general. We know Brabantio loved Othello, and frequently invited him to his home so that he could hear tales of his exciting adventures. But while Brabantio saw Othello as an exotic entertainment, he certainly didn't want him to marry his only daughter. We might wonder why, in that case, he invited Othello to his house, and why he didn't take steps to prevent the pair from ever meeting. However, Brabantio clearly thought that such a union was out of the question; it obviously never entered his mind that his daughter could fall in love with and marry such a man. Brabantio is quite convinced that Desdemona was wooed by witchcraft, and he is confident enough to accuse Othello of this before the entire senate.

What point is Shakespeare making with Brabantio's reaction to Desdemona's marriage? Initially it seems he is condemning Brabantio, but given what actually transpires, is he in fact suggesting that Brabantio was correct in assuming Othello's manners were superficial, and that a barbaric savage lay underneath?

We learn in the final scene that Brabantio died, a broken man, soon after the loss of his daughter. It seems almost a hasty afterthought by Shakespeare, and he may well have forgotten about Brabantio, as his dramatic purpose is satisfied in Act I.

*I never yet did hear
That the bruised heart was
pierced through the ear*

– BRABANTIO (ACT I SCENE III)

IMAGERY IN OTHELLO

POISON

... poison his delight ...

Doth, like a poisonous mineral, gnaw my inwards ...

The Moor already changes with my poison..

— IAGO

ANIMALS

*I took by the throat the circumcised dog
And smote him thus*

— OTHELLO

Where is that viper? Bring the villain forth

— LODOVICO

... you'll have your daughter covered with a Barbary horse

*... an old black ram
Is tupping your white ewe*

Ere I would say I would drown myself for the love of a guinea-hen, I would change my humanity with a baboon

— IAGO

*I will play the swan,
And die in music*

— EMILIA

BLACK/WHITE

If virtue no delighted beauty lack,
Your son-in-law is far more fair
than black

— DUKE

If she be black, and thereto
have a wit,
She'll find a white that shall
her blackness fit

— IAGO

Her name, that was as fresh
As Dian's visage, is now
begrimed and black
As mine own face

Yet I'll not shed her blood,
Nor scar that whiter skin of hers
than snow,
And smooth as monumental
alabaster

— OTHELLO

O, the more angel she, and you
the blacker devil!

— EMILIA

BLOOD/VIOLENCE/DEATH

Even so my bloody thoughts, with
violent pace ...

Thy bed, lust-stain'd, shall with
lust's blood be spotted

I will withdraw
To furnish me with some swift
means of death
For the fair devil

The worms were hallow'd that
did breed the silk,
And it was dyed in mummy
which the skilful
Conserved of maidens' hearts

— OTHELLO

Alas, why gnaw you so your
nether lip?
Some bloody passion shakes
your very frame

— DESDEMONA

THE HANKERCHIEF

The worms were hallow'd that
did breed the silk,
And it was dyed in mummy
which the skilful
Conserved of maidens' hearts

— OTHELLO

Have you not sometimes seen a
handkerchief
Spotted with strawberries in your
wife's hand?

— IAGO

HOW TO WRITE ESSAYS
ON OTHELLO

In the Leaving Certificate exam, you will always have the choice of two essays on *Othello*. The essay is worth 60 marks, which is 15 per cent of your total marks for English.

Throughout your essay, you must answer the question. Remember, you only get marks for relevant points. You must quote as much as possible, and you can also refer to the text. Two quotations per paragraph would be ideal, but it is quality, not quantity, that counts. Pick quotations that are versatile and can be used in lots of different essays. For example, ***jealousy ... is the green-eyed monster which doth mock / The meat it feeds on*** can be used for a question on imagery, a question on the theme of jealousy, a character essay, an essay on the relevance of the play, etc.

There are four possible styles of question for any Shakespearean text:

1. On a theme
2. On a character
3. On imagery or style or on a specific scene
4. An opinion question, for example 'Is *Othello* still relevant to a modern audience?'

The character who comes up most often in a question on his own is Othello, and next is Iago. Desdemona is also a major character, followed by Cassio and Emilia. Any of the main themes, particularly jealousy, can come up. A stylistic question on imagery, which occurs from time to time, may seem quite difficult, but the main thing is to know relevant quotations.

When answering a question on *Othello:*

• Do not summarise the play. The examiner will assume you have a thorough knowledge of it and is looking for your ability to analyse, not summarise.

• If the question takes the form of a statement with which

you are asked to agree or disagree, as a general rule it is better to agree. Of course there are exceptions, but mostly it is easier to argue for the statement than against it.

• Shape the question to your individual needs. Make it work for you. For example, if you are asked whether *Othello* is still interesting to a modern audience, you could say it is, because of the fascinating characters, and you could then pick the character you know best to discuss. You could also bring in the theme you know best, the scene you know best, and so on.

• Plan your answer carefully. A plan should consist of six to ten points that you can develop throughout the essay. This will ensure that you do not:

1. run out of ideas after a page or two,
2. become irrelevant,
3. spend too much time exploring just one or two issues, or spend too much time on just one character,
4. run out of time,
5. forget any quotations that pop into your mind; you can simply jot them on your plan and slip them in where appropriate.

When you are preparing for your Leaving Certificate, have pen and paper in hand and plan, plan, plan! Whether it is a bubble plan, a spider plan or bullet points, once you get used to planning, it is easy to do well in this question.

A STEP-BY-STEP APPROACH TO WRITING AN ESSAY ON *OTHELLO*

There are 60 marks for the single text question. The table on the right illustrates how the marks are broken down, and what you need to do to get marks in each section.

18 **Clarity of Purpose**
To get high marks for clarity, you need to read the question properly, show a clear understanding of it, and sustain your response throughout the entire essay. **Relevance** is a key word here.

18 **Coherence of Delivery**
To ensure your answer is coherent, it needs to be well planned and organised into sensible paragraphs, and your sentences should be concise and well formed, rather than long and convoluted.

18 **Language Efficiency**
You use language efficiently when you show a range in your vocabulary, use quotation and punctuation appropriately and don't go off the point or waffle.

6 **Accuracy and Mechanics**
This refers to spelling and grammar. Use online grammar exercises to work on this area if necessary: they are an excellent resource.

STEP 1

Read the essay title carefully, underline the key words, and decide how you are going to approach it. For example, this question from the 2008 exam:

'Othello's foolishness rather than Iago's cleverness leads to the tragedy of Shakespeare's Othello.'

Discuss this statement, supporting your answer with the aid of suitable reference to the play.

(LEAVING CERTIFICATE HIGHER LEVEL, 2008)

Thoroughly examine what the question is asking you. This question is essentially saying that Othello's foolishness is more to blame for the tragic events than Iago's clever plotting. Think about the question for a few moments, and decide whether you agree or disagree with the statement. You can partly agree and partly disagree, too. Make sure you are 100 per cent clear on what the question is really asking before you move on to the next step.

STEP 2

Brainstorm alternatives for the key words in the question to gain marks for language efficiency. Use a thesaurus if necessary. For example:

Foolishness	*Cleverness*
Stupidity	*Intelligence*
Gullibility	*Cunning*
Naivety	*Shrewdness*
Innocence	*Perceptiveness*

STEP 3

Start your plan. A plan is crucial for both clarity and coherence. You can interpret the question in any way you like as long as it is relevant, and you can support your points with reference to the play. In the plan on the right, the student is both agreeing and disagreeing with the statement.

	AGREE	DISAGREE
1	Othello seems to have an impeccable character initially and we assume that as he is a general, he must be extremely intelligent.	
2		Iago is an evil genius. Othello is not being fooled by just anyone. Many other characters are manipulated by Iago – e.g. Roderigo, Cassio – yet it initially seems unlikely that he will be able to dupe Othello.
3		Iago is unbelievably shrewd. He can spot vulnerabilities no one else can and knows exactly how to exploit them.
4	Othello's jealousy is much more to blame than Iago's intelligence.	Iago is astute enough to see Othello's capacity for jealousy: who else but Iago would have realised that Othello had this fatal flaw?
5	Othello *is* a fool to believe that Desdemona could be unfaithful – she shows her loyalty to him in many ways. Even if Othello is certain that Desdemona has betrayed him, he doesn't have to kill her. This is a very foolish, reckless act.	Iago is a sociopath. He lies brilliantly because he doesn't have to hide his emotions – he has none. His many soliloquies demonstrate his lack of conscience.
6	Othello is silly to put his faith in such flimsy and circumstantial evidence. Fate and coincidence favour Iago rather than Othello, but Othello cannot be blamed for this.	Iago's success is not just down to his brains; luck is also on his side in the play.

STEP 4

Write your introduction. Simply repeat the wording of the question, clearly stating whether you will be agreeing, disagreeing or both, and, using your plan, mention the main areas you plan to discuss through the course of your essay.

STEP 5

Have your relevant quotations prepared to slot in. If possible, learn them before you start writing. For this essay, you need quotations showing that Othello is foolish and quotations showing that Iago is clever. Two quotations per paragraph would be ideal, but you can also refer closely to the play, and even paraphrase.

STEP 6

Start writing the main body of your essay, focusing on one paragraph at a time. Also, try to write the essay in an hour or less, as this is all the time you'll have in the exam. At the end of each paragraph check that what you are writing is completely relevant to the question, and if you have gone off the point, make sure to get back on track in the next paragraph. Also refer to performances of the play (stage and film) you have seen in support of your answer, be sure to mention the original audience, and give lots of personal opinion.

STEP 7

Write your conclusion. Refer to the question once again, tie up any loose ends, restate your main points and, most importantly, give your personal opinion.

Introduction: I both agree and disagree with the statement that it is 'Othello's foolishness rather than Iago's cleverness which leads to the tragedy of Shakespeare's *Othello*.' I agree that Othello can be naive and gullible, and he can even be downright stupid at times. But I also think that Iago is an

Repeat the wording of the question, and briefly discuss which areas you will be exploring throughout the essay

extremely powerful and ultimately unbeatable adversary. 'Cleverness' is a bit of an understatement: in fact, Iago is an evil genius and an arch manipulator. If it was just Othello whom he fooled, I would completely agree with the statement. However, Iago misleads every character in this play, and even his own wife remains duped for a very long time. In my essay, I will discuss how foolish Othello is at times, but also how clever Iago is, while exploring which factor ultimately leads to tragedy.

Paragraph 1: At the start of the play, I really admired Othello. He seems like such a romantic figure, a man who has survived slavery and all sorts of trials, to end up as a general in the Venetian army: '... the story of my life / From year to year, the battles, sieges, fortunes, / That I have

*The first paragraph discusses how at first Othello does **not** appear foolish*

passed.' He and Desdemona clearly have a deep love for one another – 'O my soul's joy!' – and their elopement seems daring and passionate. I also thought that Othello was a true gentleman, with a lovely, eloquent way of speaking: 'So justly to your grave ears I'll present / How I did thrive in this fair lady's love, / And she in mine'; and, like Desdemona, I found his exoticism very attractive. The last word I would have used to describe him, initially, is 'foolish'!

Paragraph 2: Unlike my view of Othello, my opinion of Iago changed little throughout the play. His villainy and intelligence are obvious right from the start. He uses Roderigo for his money – 'put money in thy purse' – and upsets and riles Brabantio, a harmless old man, while remaining cunningly hidden in the shadows:

The second paragraph contrasts Iago's intelligence with Othello's cleverness

'an old black ram / Is tupping your white ewe'. I also found his racist comments disgusting and offensive. But, while Iago clearly stated his desire to ruin Othello's life – 'I follow him to serve my turn upon him' – I didn't really believe he would succeed. To be a general you would have to possess intelligence and insight, and be brave and strong: 'the flinty and steel couch of war / My thrice-driven bed of down.' I thought about Othello's escapades and how many times he must have escaped danger by relying on his own intuition, and it just seemed unlikely that these attributes would suddenly betray him.

Paragraph 3: However, as the play progresses, it becomes apparent that Othello has a formidable adversary in Iago. While Roderigo is a silly man, Cassio is not, yet Iago has no trouble manipulating him either. I also saw that Iago has a great talent for guessing at a person's vulnerabilities and exploiting

Next, Iago's ability to 'read' people and exploit their vulnerability is discussed

them. For example, Cassio's chivalry is used against him when Iago gets him to drink more than he is comfortable with, on the pretext that it would seem rude if he didn't: 'O, they are our friends! But one cup.' To me, Othello didn't seem to have any vulnerabilities to exploit, but Iago shrewdly deduces that Othello feels

like an outsider deep down, and he is clever enough to exploit this, for example when he suggests that Othello doesn't have a clue what Venetian women (i.e. Desdemona) are really like: 'I know our country disposition well. / In Venice they do let heaven see the pranks / They dare not show their husbands.'

Paragraph 4: Aside from Othello's foolishness and Iago's cleverness, there is another factor that brings about the catastrophic ending of the play: Othello's jealousy, 'the green-eyed monster'. But again, it is Iago who is clever enough to see

Iago cleverly spots Othello's jealousy

Othello's fatal flaw. This was obviously well hidden, as even Desdemona claimed that her husband was incapable of jealousy: 'Who, he? I think the sun where he was born / Drew all such humours from him.' Iago understands jealousy, because he is just as jealous a person as Othello. Iago chooses Cassio as a target because he is jealous of him: 'He hath a daily beauty in his life / That makes me ugly.' Then Iago provokes and exacerbates Othello's envy with cruel expertise. There are very few people who could act in such a relentlessly duplicitous way. However, Iago is a sociopath. He doesn't need to hide his guilt, for he doesn't feel any. Iago contributes to Othello's tragic downfall with crafty malevolence. He truly disgusted me when he said such things as: 'Do it not with poison. Strangle her in her bed, even the bed she hath contaminated' – but in spite of myself I also had a grudging admiration for his nefarious talents.

Paragraph 5: However, I do think that Othello was foolish to believe that Desdemona could ever be unfaithful. Desdemona gave up everything for him, and he knows this. She even chose him over her father – 'My noble father, / I do perceive here a divided duty' – and she also insisted on accompanying him to Cyprus: 'Let me go with him.' She is consistently affectionate and loving, even when Othello starts to mistreat her: 'My love doth so approve him / That even his stubbornness, his checks, his frowns ... have grace and favour in them.' But the astute Iago perceives that Othello loves his wife so much that he does not feel worthy of her. He uses Othello's own insecurity as a powerful weapon against him. I found the final scene of the play utterly heart-breaking. Othello could have divorced Desdemona or exiled her, but to kill her with so little proof was reckless and imprudent: 'That death's unnatural that kills for loving.'

Show how Othello was a fool to mistrust Desdemona

Paragraph 6: No matter how clever Iago is (and his many soliloquies and asides show his brilliance), it is clear that coincidence and fate favour him far more than Othello. Is Othello all that foolish to suspect something is amiss when he sees Cassio scurrying from his wife's company?

Coincidence and fate are significant factors in the play

'I cannot think it, / That he would steal away so guilty-like / Seeing your coming.' The serendipitous way Iago comes by the handkerchief certainly aids the plot too. It isn't just any old rag, but the very first gift Othello gave Desdemona, and a family heirloom: 'I am glad I have found this napkin. / This was her first remembrance from the Moor. / My wayward husband hath a hundred times / Woo'd me to steal it.' Even the fact that Iago gets Cassio to have a disparaging conversation about Bianca without ever once mentioning her name is just

pure luck: 'She was here even now. She haunts me in every place.' So Iago is lucky: everything falls into place for him; and this contributes significantly to the tragic nature of the play. By the same token, Othello is really unlucky, for his ensign is an evil genius with a grudge against him! Watching the 1995 film version of the play really made me feel sorry for Othello, as Laurence Fishburne played him with such emotional depth, his voice breaking when he asked: 'Will you, I pray, demand that demi-devil / Why he hath thus ensnared my body and soul?'

Conclusion: In conclusion, as I have shown throughout my essay, while Othello is undoubtedly a fool for believing Iago over Desdemona, and much more than a fool for killing his innocent wife, having considered this statement throughout my essay, I do think the tragedy was mostly due to the diabolical machinations of the devious Iago. Everyone is fooled by 'honest'

Conclude your essay clearly. Refer to the question once again, and give your personal opinion

Iago not just Othello – 'O, that's an honest fellow' – and this in itself is proof of what an unbeatable adversary he is. Othello's inner demon, his jealousy, is also a major contributing factor, and so too is chance and coincidence, but I believe Emilia (also fooled to the last) put it best when she unequivocally blamed Iago's clever scheming for the tragic events: 'You have done well, / That men must lay their murders on your neck.'

SAMPLE PLANS
ON OTHELLO

Below are examples of some of the most common questions on *Othello* and advice on how to tackle the essay titles. Before you start any essay, however, forget about having the text open in front of you as you write. Learn off your quotations, read through your notes, then shut your books and do the question in 50 to 60 minutes. This may sound tough, but you must recreate exam conditions as closely as possible in order to get the best possible mark.

SAMPLE PLAN 1

Discuss the importance of the character Cassio in the play *Othello* as a whole. Support your answer with quotation from or reference to the play.

Note: For a character essay, remember to discuss the character's characteristics, dramatic function, language and interaction with others. Refer to a particular actor's interpretation of the role too, for example, Laurence Fishburne as Othello in the 1995 film.

Introduction: Cassio is one of the only characters never to express any feelings of jealousy. This is very significant as the play is essentially about jealousy; so, primarily, Cassio's character forms a contrast with the others.

Paragraph 1: Cassio is the best male character, and Desdemona the best female. However, showing the double standards of the time (and ours!), Cassio has flaws (drink, Bianca) and this is completely acceptable.

Paragraph 2: Cassio is also one of those people who has it all and thus incites jealousy in others. Not everyone could have inspired the type of jealousy in Othello that Cassio does. Iago picked him because he is also very jealous of him.

Paragraph 3: Cassio unwittingly propels the plot forward by his friendship with Desdemona; his drunken brawl and his subsequent entreaties to her for help; talking about Bianca to Iago; and using the handkerchief.

Paragraph 4: Cassio's loyalty to Othello forms a sharp contrast to Othello and Iago. It reminds us that Othello should have given him the benefit of the doubt. Cassio is loyal to Othello right to the very end.

Paragraph 5: Finally, Cassio is the only major character to survive the events of the play. Even Iago is to be tortured and killed. This is because Cassio was not jealous, nor did he seek revenge, and in a way, this is the moral of the whole play.

SAMPLE PLAN 2

'In his play **Othello***, Shakespeare provides us with many compelling scenes.'*
Choose a scene you found compelling and explain your choice, supporting your answer by reference to the play.

Notes:

1. While it is always a good idea to refer to a performance of the play in any essay, it is absolutely crucial for a question like this. It is a good idea to look at several performances, a stage version (if possible) and as many film versions as you can find, and analyse them under the headings of costume, props, soundtrack, acting, physical movement and lighting. YouTube is a great resource to research this type of question.

2. The key word in this question is **compelling***, so to gain extra marks for language, try to vary your vocabulary and use alternatives such as interesting, intriguing, fascinating, riveting, gripping, mesmerising, spellbinding, enthralling, engrossing and absorbing.*

Act V Scene II

- It is the climax of the whole play.

- We watch Othello's uncontrollable anger with appalled fascination.

- The suspense is unbearable as we earnestly hope that he will draw back from the brink.

- Desdemona's innocence and bewilderment is heart-breaking to witness.

- Othello's madness and Desdemona's ultimate loyalty are astonishing.

- Othello's quick remorse is sickening to witness.

- Iago never redeems himself, or even explains himself, defeating our expectations.

- Emilia comes into her own as a character.

- Iago's murder of his wife shows he is not just a Machiavellian manipulator, but is truly evil to the core.

- The devastation in the final scene is visually arresting (refer to a performance or performances).

- Othello being told of the deception is suspenseful and tense.

- Othello's suicide is the final tragic act.

SAMPLE PLAN 3

'In Shakespeare's play Othello*, we meet characters who show us the best and worst in human nature.'*
Discuss this statement, supporting your answer with quotation from or reference to the play.

Best

- **Desdemona:** her love of Othello seen in her defying her father, and loving unconditionally

- **Emilia:** her loyalty to Desdemona and her brave attack on Othello and on Iago in Act V Scene II

- **Cassio:** aside from his drunkenness and his dalliance with Bianca he is an honourable character who is loyal, fair and forgiving.

Best and worst

- **Othello:** he is the best in that he is brave, clever, talented, eloquent, heroic and loving; but he is also the worst in that he is jealous and gullible, and allows himself to be manipulated. He is also rash and has a terrible temper, and is a very harsh judge of others.

Worst

- **Roderigo:** a character the audience loves to hate – is greedy, grasping and weak.

- **Iago:** a psychopath with no redeeming characteristics whatsoever. He is greedy, arrogant, offensive, manipulative, cruel, scheming and utterly evil.

SAMPLE PLAN 4

'Despite his flaws, Othello deserves the sympathy of the audience.'
Discuss this statement, supporting the points you make with quotation from or reference to the play.

AGREE	DISAGREE
Othello is always an outsider.	Desdemona does nothing to arouse his suspicion.
No one could see through Iago; he is an evil genius.	He is insecure and too ready to believe the worst.
His jealousy springs from his deep love.	He allows jealousy to destroy him.
Fate and coincidence conspire against him.	He is a harsh judge of others (Cassio, Desdemona), so why should we not judge him?
Desdemona should have stood up for herself more forcefully.	He does not have to kill Desdemona, even if she had been unfaithful.
Everyone wants a piece of Othello.	
He is insecure in this alien environment.	
He is truly remorseful and commits suicide.	

SAMPLE PLAN 5

'The destructive power of jealousy is the dominant theme of Shakespeare's Othello*.'*
Write a response to this statement supporting your answer by reference to the text.

1. **Iago:** Iago's jealousy of Othello's role in society and the military, along with his jealousy of Cassio's

promotion, is the catalyst for everything that happens.

2. **Roderigo:** Roderigo allows himself to be used as a pawn, because he loves Desdemona and is jealous of Othello.

3. **Bianca:** even this minor character's jealousy is used to taunt Othello.

4. **Othello:** nowhere is the expression '[jealousy is] the green-eyed monster which doth mock / The meat it feeds on' more true than in the case of Othello.

- He truly loves Desdemona, but never really feels as if he truly deserves her. So insecurity leads to jealousy.

- Iago manipulates this insecurity. Shakespeare may be suggesting that Othello sees white men, such as Cassio, as being fundamentally superior.

- Othello works hard to fit into this alien society, but never truly feels that he does; his deep-rooted anxiety is fertile soil in which jealousy can trive.

- In a way, Othello humanises jealousy, as his successful life is completely destroyed by it. His is a cautionary tale on the destructive power of jealousy.

SAMPLE PLAN 6

In your view, does Emilia play an important role in Shakespeare's Othello?
Support your answer with quotation from or reference to the play.

1. Emilia is Iago's wife, the person closest to him in the whole play. Through their exchanges, we get to know him better. We see his misogyny, but also his jealousy, wit and humour.

2. Emilia is neither an 'angel nor a whore' [see note below], but a realistic portrayal of a woman – *a very modern woman.* She has a lot to do with why modern audiences like the play, and she also voices the audience's sentiments.

3. She unwittingly contributes to Iago's heinous plot when she takes the handkerchief.

4. Emilia is very witty and shrewd. She is reminiscent of Portia (in *The Merchant of Venice*) and Kate (in *The Taming of the Shrew*).

5. She also *contrasts with Othello*: she is Desdemona's lady-in-waiting yet she displays far more loyalty to Desdemona than Othello does.

6. Emilia is very much the *heroine* of the last act. She stands up to Othello and, most importantly, she reveals the entire plot.

7. Emilia's bravery and death in Act V Scene II are in marked contrast to the conduct of both Othello and Iago. Neither she nor Desdemona deserved their awful fate. Her death makes the ending more catastrophic, but it also shows that there is nothing Iago won't do to protect himself. Singing the 'Willow' song shows that, for all her mettle, Emilia is just as vulnerable as Desdemona and Bianca, the other female characters in the play.

Note: The expression 'angel or whore' is often used to explain how female characters were polarised in Renaissance literature and art. They were either perfect angels or fallen women. Shakespeare was one of the first artists to depict female characters with both good and bad attributes.

SAMPLE ESSAYS ON OTHELLO

SAMPLE ESSAY 1

'In the play Othello, Desdemona is not a credible character, but a weak woman, at best an unrealistic saint, who does nothing to try and prevent her fate.' **Discuss this statement with the aid of suitable reference to the play.**

'[A] most exquisite lady ...
That paragons description and wild fame.'
I wholeheartedly disagree with this statement. Desdemona is a credible character, and she is a real woman, not a saint, and she is certainly not weak. She does everything in her power to prevent her fate. She cannot by judged by the standards of a modern audience, for she was not written for us, but for an audience who lived more than four centuries ago. Women had a different role and far fewer rights in those days. They were considered possessions, and were secondary to men. Even the female parts in Shakespeare's plays were played by men, as a woman would never have been allowed to do such a thing as act. A woman's reputation was everything. She had to behave perfectly, according to the demanding etiquette of the time, or she would be cast out from genteel society. So Desdemona may not slap Othello back, as a modern heroine like Bridget Jones probably would, but inasmuch as she can defend herself, she does. In assessing the character of Desdemona, I believe it is vital to consider the cultural context of the play. Marriages in those days were not the conclusion of a long and thorough courtship as they mostly are these days. Marriage marked the very beginning of a relationship. Couples would rarely have been intimate prior to marriage; indeed, they may never even have

been alone together. A man got to decide who he would marry, but a woman had no say in the matter unless her father permitted her the kind of choice Brabantio seems to have permitted Desdemona. She rejected suitors such as Roderigo, so we know she stood up for herself. And she took a very active part in the courtship: '... she wish'd / That heaven had made her such a man. She thanked me, / And bade me, if I had a friend that loved her, / I should but teach him how to tell my story. / And that would woo her. Upon this hint I spake.'

Desdemona as good as asked Othello out, and even nowadays, a woman asking a man out is still a little unusual! But when Othello starts to treat Desdemona badly, she has no point of comparison. She has no idea what is normal or acceptable in marriage. She is confused, bewildered and upset, but she is not unbelievable. I find her reaction completely normal: I think I would react just the same; but I hope I would have Desdemona's dignity and strength too.

Also, in Shakespeare's time, women were not considered as individuals in their own right. They were possessions – first their father's, and then their husband's. That is why Desdemona's expression of her love for Othello in marrying him without the permission of her father is an incredibly brave act of defiance, and certainly not the action of a weak person! 'I am hitherto your daughter. But here's my husband.' Desdemona disobeyed her father for the best of all possible motives – love. We can see by Brabantio's reaction that he would never have agreed to the marriage. But, in his heart, Othello fears that this means Desdemona is capable of betrayal, and this tiny seed of distrust is the beginning of the end for Desdemona. Brabantio's angry words are never forgotten: 'Look to her, Moor, if thou hast eyes to see. / She has deceived her father, and may thee.' (Indeed, Iago throws these same words back in Othello's face to convince him that she is unfaithful.) Desdemona chose her own husband, so she certainly does choose her fate. To see Desdemona as weak and submissive is to ignore the bravery it must have taken to elope: 'My noble father, / I do perceive here a divided duty.' Here Desdemona is clearly telling her father that he might not like it, but Othello is her husband now.

Desdemona also asks to go to war with her Othello: '... if I be left behind ... / The rites for which I love him are bereft me ...'; certainly not the actions of an unrealistic saint, but of a confident woman who knows her own mind. This is a brave act, too, for Desdemona was not to know that there would be no war. Even when it is feared that Othello's ship is lost at sea, she controls her emotions and cuts a dignified figure: 'I am not merry, but I do beguile / The thing that I am by seeming otherwise.' Also, she has many lively conversations with Cassio and Iago, and clearly has a bright, alert mind. When Iago jests chauvinistically about women, making comments, such as 'She never yet was foolish that was fair; / For even her folly help'd her to an heir', Desdemona boldly responds: 'These are old fond paradoxes to make fools laugh i'th' alehouse.' This verbal jousting shows her to be the conversational equal of even Iago. Few women would have dared venture an opinion, so she shows great mettle in doing so.

Desdemona is also brave and believable in her friendships. Cassio is a friend of hers, and Desdemona sees no reason to be coy about this friendship as she has nothing to hide. It is not her fault that Iago manipulates the situation to his own advantage, nor is it her fault that Othello allows himself to be manipulated. Desdemona can only be responsible for her own conduct. When she promises Cassio, 'Be thou assured, good Cassio, I will do / All my abilities in thy behalf', she is trying to help Othello too, as she knows that he needs Cassio. And when asking her husband to reconsider, Desdemona does not pander and flatter, she is open and honest: 'I wonder in my soul, / What you would ask me that I should deny ...?' As Cassio was the go-between for the pair prior to their marriage, I do not see why Desdemona should suddenly feel as if she has to cut Cassio out of her life. To her credit, Desdemona really thinks that the husband she loves so dearly is incapable of such a miserable emotion as jealousy: 'my noble Moor / Is true of mind, and made of no such baseness / As jealous creatures are ...' This doesn't make her innocent, naive or saintly, just a good wife. In Shakespeare's day, those who thought well of others, and gave them the benefit of the doubt, were not considered gullible or gluttons for punishment, just good people. I think we should revert to this view, instead of blaming victims for what criminals do. For example, I have read articles in which Desdemona is blamed for losing her handkerchief! She dropped it because she was so concerned about her husband's headache, and put him first: 'I am most unhappy in the loss of it.'

Desdemona loves Othello unconditionally, no matter what he does. She excuses Othello, not because she is weak, but because she is strong. She is strong enough to keep loving him, and never stops believing in him: 'Something sure of state ... / Hath puddled his clear spirit.'

One of the key moments in the play that is often cited to prove Desdemona's supposed passivity is in the first scene of Act IV, when Othello strikes her. Iago has manipulated Othello into emotional turbulence, and it is his innocent wife who bears the brunt of this when, in front of the assembled company, he hits her. Desdemona simply says 'I have not deserved this.' I think this is an incredibly brave and arresting statement. These are the dignified words of a woman who has been badly hurt, but does not accept undeserved blame. No other words are needed. The truth suffices.

Also, Desdemona is desperately in love. She is struggling to comprehend how this relationship could have changed in this way. She is very young, and very confused. Just because she does not react with anger does not make her a weak character. In a way it makes her strong. She has been married just three days. Her life has changed dramatically, she is in a vulnerable position, and then her beloved hits her, and calls her vile names such as 'strumpet', and 'cunning whore'. Poor Desdemona is probably in state of shock for the latter half of the play. But she is always strong and believable in my view.

Desdemona asks Emilia to put her wedding sheets on the bed, and asks her to bury her in one of those sheets should she die first: 'If I do die before thee, prithee shroud me / In one of those same sheets.' I don't think that this means she is offering herself up as some sort of sacrificial lamb, but instead I think she is trying to control the small details that she has power over. The last time we see Desdemona before Othello kills her, she sings a song she learned from her mother's maid: 'She was in love, and he she loved proved mad / And did forsake her. She had a song of willow. ... And she died singing it. That song tonight / Will not go from my mind.' I think that Shakespeare (a man ahead of his time regarding women, in my view) has Desdemona identify herself with other victims of male cruelty in an attempt to show how badly women were treated at this time. So many women (then and now) were abused, beaten, even killed, because of their husband/partner's jealousy.

I found the moment when Othello strangles Desdemona deeply upsetting: 'guiltiness I know not, but yet I feel I fear.' I cannot even begin to imagine the horror of this violent death for Desdemona, and yet she loves Othello so much that she continues to make excuses for him: 'Alas, he is betray'd and I undone'; 'A guiltless death I die', and then, amazingly, she tries to take the blame for her own death: 'Nobody, I myself. Farewell.' I thought this was a bit too saintly, but I also think it is consistent with Desdemona's character throughout the play, as perfect as the Virgin Mary. This is a most generous act of forgiveness, but no matter how badly Othello behaves, Desdemona is always true to herself, and their love: 'Commend me to my kind lord. O, farewell!'

In conclusion, as I have demonstrated throughout my essay, Desdemona is very believable as a woman, especially when you consider the time in which the play is set. She is also brave and real. I was fascinated by Desdemona, and by the role of women at this time in history. As Emilia wryly notes: 'They are all but stomachs, and we all but food. / To eat us hungrily, and when they are full, / They belch us.' I think Shakespeare presents us with a character who turns the other cheek, who does what she thinks is right, and who never compromises herself, but always behaves with great integrity. Ironically, is her husband who finally realises her worth: 'a pearl ... richer than all his tribe.'

SAMPLE ESSAY 2

'In the play Othello, what intrigues us the most is the villain Iago who plots and manoeuvres to bring those around him to doom and destruction.'
Write a response to the above statement. Support your answer with the aid of suitable reference to the text.

'I am not what I am'
I wholeheartedly agree with the above statement that Iago is, indeed, the most intriguing character in this play. What is universally fascinating about the amoral Iago is that he operates entirely without conscience. He appears incapable of guilt, and this makes him incredibly dangerous. Iago can orchestrate the downfall of others because he is intelligent and shrewd. He is able to sum people up in a moment, and can then prey on their weaknesses. Each character in the play has a flaw which Iago is aware of. Othello is insecure, Roderigo is smitten, and Desdemona is gullible. Iago becomes everybody's best friend, because he says what people want to hear. Through sheer intuition, he does indeed plot and manoeuvre those around him to doom and destruction. And he steals the show while doing so!

Iago treats Roderigo with utter contempt, while seeming to be the best friend who is striving to give him his heart's desire, Desdemona. Roderigo means one thing only to Iago – money: 'Thus do I ever make my fool my purse.' Not only does Iago spend all Roderigo's money, he also tries to use him as a hit-man to get rid of Cassio: 'whether he kill Cassio / Or Cassio him, or each do kill the other, / Every way makes my gain.' While Roderigo is himself an unattractive character, and therefore I didn't really care about him, Iago's callous manipulation and then calculated killing of him is nothing less than deplorable. He stabs him under cover of darkness and then has the audacity to ask 'Kill men i'th' dark? Where be these bloody thieves?' Iago describes his treatment of Roderigo as merely picking at a pimple: 'I have rubb'd this young quat almost to the sense ...'

Iago and Emilia have a tempestuous relationship. It is clear that she loves him, and wants to please him, but I found his attitude to her far more complex. Presumably Emilia is beautiful, as Iago is only interested in people for what he can get from them. He speaks disrespectfully to her from the start of the play; however, he veils his misogyny with humour: 'You rise to play and go to bed to work.' He uses Emilia's loyalty to secure the handkerchief, even though this causes Emilia great distress when she realises what he has done: 'O God! O heavenly God!' It horrifies her to know that she has unwittingly contributed to the downfall of her beloved mistress. Iago kills his wife easily, proving that no one matters to him, and that he has no attachments to anyone: 'The woman falls. Sure he hath kill'd his wife.' Emilia meant no more to Iago than did anyone else. She too is a mere pawn in his complex game. I thought their relationship was brilliantly performed in Kenneth Branagh's version of *Othello*.

Iago's expert manipulation is most obvious in his treatment of Othello. Many of his other victims, such as Desdemona and Emilia, are incidental to his destruction of Othello. Yet his reasons for destroying Othello seem unconvincing and flimsy. He is angry at Cassio's promotion, and he also improbably claims, 'it is thought abroad that 'twixt my sheets / He has done my office'. Iago has a history of trustworthiness; the adjective used most frequently to describe him is, ironically, 'honest'. He quickly sees the insecurity in Othello, and it is this that he uses to destroy his life: 'I put the Moor / At least into a jealousy so strong / That judgement cannot cure.'

He starts by insinuating that Desdemona may be too fond of Cassio, sets Cassio up to be demoted and then gets Desdemona to plead his case. Meanwhile, he works on Othello's deep insecurity about being a stranger in a strange land: 'In Venice they do let heaven see the pranks / They dare not show their husbands.' Iago knows that Othello was deeply shaken by Brabantio's reaction to his marriage – 'She has deceived her father, and may thee' – after all, Othello and Brabantio were good friends, or so he thought. So Othello has never been more aware of his different colour: 'I may fear / Her will, recoiling to her better judgement, / May fall to match you with her country forms'. Iago's brilliance is in hiding his own racism ('black ram', 'Barbary horse') and appearing concerned for his friend.

Coincidence and fate also help Iago. For example, Cassio has a long conversation with him about Bianca without ever once mentioning her name, so that Othello is quite sure that Cassio is talking about his own wife: 'I marry! What, a customer? ... Ha, ha, ha!' and there is also the fact that Desdemona drops her handkerchief. Yet Emilia would simply have returned this to her mistress if Iago hadn't already realised it's significance: 'I am glad I have found this napkin ... / My wayward husband hath a hundred times / Woo'd me to steal it.' Iago's systematic battering down of Othello's defences is shrewd and intelligent. He even appeals to the hero in Othello, suggesting that Othello's revenge would not just be for himself, but for other cuckolded husbands: 'be a man. / Think every bearded fellow that's but yoked / May draw with you. There's millions now alive / That nightly lie in those unproper beds.' Othello is often criticised for failing to guess what Iago was up to, but no one suspects Iago, and this is why he is so intriguing, despite his malevolence. Even Othello's suicide is completely due to Iago's evil brilliance.

I think the statement that Iago plots and manoeuvres to destroy those around him is particularly true in the case of Desdemona. She is a complete innocent, and at times he seems very fond of her, but she is destroyed first emotionally and then physically because of his machinations. I think Iago's casual involvement of Desdemona in the plot is also down to the fact that he knows he cannot have her, and so he will destroy her: 'Now I do love her too, / Not out of absolute lust, though peradventure / I stand accountant for as great a sin – / But partly led to diet my revenge ...' As Desdemona is an exemplary character, and I grew to really care for her and pity her vulnerability, it was her destruction that affected me most. This young bride, so in love, suffers awful torment and a hideous death. Iago even suggests that Desdemona should be strangled rather than poisoned. 'Do it not with poison. Strangle her in her bed, even the bed she hath contaminated.' He has no pity for her, no heart at all. Her murder is simply a means to an end. Because Desdemona is such an angelic character, his treatment of her is the worst of all, in my view. No wonder Iago calls on the 'divinity of hell' and compares himself to the devil!

'With as little a web as this I will ensnare as great a fly as Cassio.' Cassio is everything Iago wishes he was, and for this Iago feels he should die: 'He hath a daily beauty in his life / That makes me ugly.' Like Othello, Cassio trusts Iago, and Iago rewards this trust by trying to ruin Cassio's life and using him as a pawn in his revenge against Othello. Cassio is charming and kind. His only flaw is his inability to hold his drink, and this small thing is what Iago abuses. Ironically, it is to Iago

that Cassio confesses this weakness: 'I have very poor and unhappy brains for drinking.' In observing the interaction between these two very different men, I realised that Iago's best weapon is in appearing to be everyone's best friend. I think there are lots of Iagos around – people who appear to care only for others, while really they are furthering their own ends. Cassio's likeability means that the audience takes his side against the malignant Iago. Cassio is guileless and honest, but Iago manages to use Cassio's great, but platonic, love for Desdemona ('He hath achieved a maid / That paragons description and wild fame ') and his dalliance with Bianca to twist the plot to his own desires. Cassio is one of the few characters to emerge unscathed, a reward for his personality, which is the polar opposite to Iago's. Unlike the others, he is not destroyed or doomed.

In conclusion, as I have demonstrated throughout my essay, Iago is the ultimate puppet-master, plotting and manoeuvring everyone, and causing much devastation and tragedy in the process. He never feels even a momentary pang of conscience, and this, coupled with a fierce intelligence, makes him powerful. He confides in no one. His many Machiavellian soliloquies enlighten, intrigue and astound the audience. He is the catalyst for the plot, and he drives it relentlessly forward to its brutal end. The original audience would have appreciated the dramatic irony of this play, as no one guesses what Iago is up to until the final scene, and even then it is Emilia who realises what he has done. Iago could so easily have got away with it all: he is the great deceiver, the great strategist, and even when his plans are foiled, he defeats our expectations again, by refusing to speak or explain: 'Demand me nothing. What you know you know. / From this time forth I never will speak word.' The perfect last words from the perfect anti-hero, Iago.

SAMPLE ESSAY 3

'In the play Othello, Shakespeare powerfully portrays a world dominated by jealousy and revenge.'
To what extent would you agree with this view of the play? Support the points you make with the aid of suitable reference to the text.

Jealousy is the 'monster which doth mock /
The meat it feeds on.'

I wholeheartedly agree with the statement that Shakespeare portrays a world that is completely dominated by the destructive emotion of jealousy and the insatiable desire for revenge displayed by some of the characters. The four characters who experience jealousy are Iago, Roderigo, Bianca and, of course, Othello. Both Iago and Othello are swift and brutal in their revenge. *Othello* is a fascinating play. It is full of intrigue and suspense, but it is also a very moral play. Shakespeare is warning us of the dangers of jealousy and the futility of revenge, so, as well as being a compelling work of utter brilliance, the play is also a didactic play which teaches us so much.

Roderigo's unrequited love for Desdemona and subsequent manipulation by Iago make him extremely jealous of Othello. As Roderigo is rich, and therefore useful to Iago, his jealousy is a useful tool in getting him to do Iago's bidding. This is most notable towards the end of the play, when Iago tries to use Roderigo as a hitman to get rid of Cassio: '... by making him uncapable of Othello's place – knocking out his brains'. Roderigo has no reason to kill Cassio, yet, blinded by envy, he acquiesces to Iago's outrageous demands, and tries to take his clumsy, ill-thought-out revenge. However, Cassio is the stronger of the two men, and even though

Roderigo attempts to murder him, he succeeds only in wounding him. Iago, Roderigo's supposed friend and confidante, then kills him. Roderigo realises too late that his jealousy of Othello has led to a terrible end for himself: 'O damn'd Iago! O inhuman dog!'

Another minor character who experiences the excruciating feeling of jealousy is Bianca, a prostitute with whom Cassio consorts. Bianca has fallen for the handsome, charming Cassio, but typically for that time, she can never be taken seriously as a love interest. Bianca knows this deep down, yet cannot help feeling jealous of Cassio's ability to attract other women. Bianca's jealousy is used by Iago to orchestrate a fake scenario in which he and Iago appear to the hidden Othello to be talking about Desdemona, when they are really talking about Bianca: 'This is the monkey's own giving out. She is persuaded I will marry her out of her own love and flattery, not out of my promise.'

Iago may provoke and fan the flames of Othello's jealousy, but he himself is also a jealous character. His reasons for wanting revenge stem from jealousy, which he describes as a 'poisonous mineral' that 'gnaws' at his soul. He is jealous of Cassio's promotion: 'Preferment goes by letter and affection, / And not by old gradation, where each second / Stood heir to th' first'; and he also accuses Cassio and Othello of having sexual relations with his wife: 'I hate the Moor / And it is thought abroad, that 'twixt my sheets / He has done my office'; 'I fear Cassio with my nightcap, too.'

But more than this, Iago is jealous of Cassio and Othello not only for tangible reasons, but also for more abstract reasons. Both men possess qualities that Iago will never have. He knows that if he leaves Othello alone, Othello will be happy, something he will never experience: 'The Moor – howbe't that I endure him not

– / Is of a constant, loving, noble nature, / And I dare think he'll prove to Desdemona / A most dear husband.' And as for Cassio, Iago picks him as the catalyst for Othello's jealousy because he is so jealous of him: 'He hath a daily beauty in his life / That makes me ugly.' It is because of Iago's own close relationship with jealousy that he decides to use it as a weapon in his revenge, for he knows its power: '… nothing can or shall content my soul / Till I am even'd with him, wife for wife – / Or failing so, yet that I put the Moor / At least into a jealousy so strong / That judgement cannot cure.' Iago's jealousy leads to a desire for revenge so strong that no one can stand in his way. Even his wife Emilia is used, and her loyalty to Desdemona abused, just so that Iago can get hold of Desdemona's handkerchief.

Othello occupies a high rank in the military and is well thought of by the Duke of Venice. At the start of the play he seems to be in a secure position in Venetian society. Yet Othello is always an outsider, never completely accepted, and deep down he knows this. If Iago's being a Florentine is frequently mentioned, then what hope has Othello, a black African, of being truly accepted? Othello's latent insecurity, exacerbated by Brabantio's outraged reaction to his marriage to Desdemona, provides fertile ground for jealousy to grow. Deep down, Othello does not feel worthy of Desdemona, and the shrewd Iago knows this and exploits it. He uses Othello's alien status to suggest that he has no idea of what Venetian women really get up to: 'In Venice they do let heaven see the pranks / They dare not show their husbands.' He uses Othello's subconscious shame of his colour to suggest that Desdemona will soon reject him: 'I may fear / Her will, recoiling to her better judgement, / May fall to match you with her country forms.' As mentioned earlier, he

uses Bianca's pathetic jealousy to make it seem that Cassio is not only sleeping with Desdemona, but that he also considers her a mere prostitute: 'I marry! What, a customer? … Ha, ha, ha!' This is a further blow to Othello's ego, as is Cassio's apparent possession of the treasured handkerchief. Othello, like Iago, uses torture references to describe the agony of being jealous: 'Thou hast set me on the rack.'

Like Iago, Othello's jealousy quickly leads to a desire for a terrible revenge: 'Within these three days let me hear thee say / That Cassio's not alive.' He loses his dignity, and his post, he mumbles incoherently, and his speech becomes ever more brutal: 'I will chop her into messes.' Othello is a skilled soldier, and in Shakespeare's day your profession was really considered to be an integral part of who you were as a person. A soldier, perceiving danger, will react with violence. Othello sees no other option than to kill Cassio and Desdemona. I found his decision to kill Desdemona quite distressing, especially Iago's 'helpful' advice: 'Do it not with poison. Strangle her in her bed, even the bed she hath contaminated.' Little does Othello realise that Iago wants him to strangle Desdemona because he fears that poison might not be attributed to Othello. Othello thinks there is justice in this suggestion, because he wants to rid himself of the agony of jealousy – it is literally driving him crazy. We see this when he strikes his wife, much to the shock of the assembled noblemen, one of whom asks, 'Are his wits safe? Is he not light of brain?' He calls this angelic woman horrible names such as 'whore' and 'strumpet', and, most terrible of all, he kills her: 'Thy bed, lust-stain'd, shall with lust's blood be spotted.'

The ending of the play is truly catastrophic. Roderigo is killed by Iago, as is Emilia. Othello learns, too late, of Desdemona's innocence. In his final speech, his eloquence and sanity restored, he tries to explain his actions: 'Speak of me as I am ... Of one not easily jealous but, being wrought / Perplex'd in the extreme'. Othello never considered himself to be a jealous person, but that was because he had never been in love. Once he loves Desdemona, he has the potential to be jealous, because every human being has that potential. Most of us are lucky enough to have people around us to reassure us and counsel us when we feel a touch of the 'green-eyed monster'. Instead, Iago is constantly on hand to expertly provoke and exacerbate Othello's jealous instincts. As a tragic hero, Othello feels every emotion to an exaggerated pitch, so his jealousy is, once activated, unendurable, and this is why he kills Desdemona, but it is also why we can still feel a degree of pity for him.

In conclusion, as I have demonstrated throughout my essay, the play *Othello* does indeed powerfully portray a world which is completely consumed with jealousy and revenge. Jealousy is an awful emotion to experience, and every single one of us knows what it is like to feel jealous or envious. However, we need not lash out in our pain, we do not have to take revenge, because, as Shakespeare shows, this solves absolutely nothing. Everyone in this play sees revenge as acceptable – even Desdemona and Emilia agree that a cheating husband should be punished by revenge – but Shakespeare is warning us of the damage we can do when we let our most base emotions control our decisions. I think he was criticising his society, in which many political actions were governed by a desire for revenge. I found *Othello* a wholly compelling play, and much of this was due to the fascinating central themes of jealousy and revenge.

SAMPLE ESSAY 4

'Othello *still has a broad appeal to a modern audience.'*
Do you agree with this statement? Support your answer with suitable quotation from or reference to the play.

I wholeheartedly agree with the statement that *Othello* does indeed have much appeal for a modern audience. Despite the fact that the play is over four centuries old, the universal truths, great storylines, provocative themes, characterisation and historical interest mean that it is still a fascinating and compelling work of great genius. As a young person myself, I found this play very appealing and very enjoyable. In this essay I will discuss the reasons why I think *Othello* still has a broad appeal.

First, *Othello* is quite simply a great story. It contains all the elements necessary to hold any audience's attention; intrigue, suspense and drama. *Othello* holds our attention right from the very beginning (and held the original audience's attention, too, so that they wouldn't leave and get their money back!). Desdemona, a nobleman's daughter, has eloped with Othello. We quickly learn that Othello is black, and these were not enlightened times, so the reaction to this development is mixed. Brabantio accuses Othello of witchcraft, while the Duke defends him because of his military prowess. But we sense that Othello is on shakier ground than he realises. The complication is simple, yet brilliant. The disgruntled Iago resolves to 'pour poison' in Othello's ear, and to destroy him and Cassio, another man he is jealous of. This devious plan marks the beginning of an engaging story. It also made me think of the role of gossip, rumour and innuendo in everyday life.

Second, the central theme of jealousy is still incredibly relevant. Every comment made about jealousy is not just eloquent, but also psychologically astute. For example, Iago's ironic advice: 'O, beware, my lord, of jealousy. / It is the green-eyed monster which doth mock / The meat it feeds on'; and Emilia's description of jealousy as 'a monster / Begot upon itself, born on itself'. Shakespeare is saying that jealousy is something we grow within ourselves, and then it destroys us from the inside out. I found this to be profoundly true and it also made me feel as if Shakespeare himself had experienced jealousy as he writes so knowledgably about it. Sadly, the killing of a partner because of jealousy is not a fanciful dramatic device but a sad reality that we see all the time, and this shows how the play continues to be fascinating.

Third, I think *Othello* has a broad appeal to modern audiences because of Shakespeare's superb characterisation. Many characters depicted in film and TV today are two-dimensional stereotypes, but in *Othello* we find realistic and complex characters. All are true individuals and they don't stay static: each person changes and grows as the plot develops. For example, Othello speaks to Desdemona in very different ways according to the progress of his jealousy. Before Iago's meddling he says beautiful things, such as 'I cannot speak enough of this content. / It stops me here, it is too much of joy.' However, later on in the play he abuses Desdemona in the crudest and most vulgar of terms: 'Impudent strumpet!'; and 'I took you for that cunning whore of Venice / That married with Othello.' The changes in his speech patterns show his declining mental state.

Fourth, Shakespeare uses dramatic irony to captivate us. The original audience loved this, and would have been quite vocal in their warnings to Desdemona and Cassio. I think modern audiences enjoy this just as much, though. Why else would all the soaps, dramas and films we watch base their plotlines on this device? I thought it was ingenious to show Iago's plan from the very beginning, so that we would root for the good characters and love to hate the villain.

I really enjoyed learning about the role of women through studying *Othello*. It seems to me that women were mostly polarised into angels or whores in the literature of Shakespeare's time, and whereas Desdemona and Bianca do fall into those categories, Shakespeare also presents us with a strong, realistic, honest character like Emilia. I found Desdemona's character fascinating because she is an exemplary heroine of her time. Not only does she love Othello unconditionally, despite his appalling treatment of her, she even takes the blame for her own death: 'Nobody, I myself. Farewell. / Commend me to my kind lord.' I don't think such a heroine would be acceptable to a modern audience, but it is certainly interesting to observe the incredibly high standards expected of women at that time. I also felt sorry for Bianca. It was accepted practice in those days for men to have mistresses, yet no one considers Bianca's feelings or the economic circumstances that forced her into what was a common way of life for many women at the time: 'A hussy that by selling her desires / Buys herself bread and clothes.' I also felt sorry for her unrequited passion for Cassio: 'it is a creature / That dotes on Cassio – as 'tis the strumpet's plague / To beguile many and be beguiled by one.' However, my favourite female character was Emilia. She was so feisty and brave. I loved her outbursts which were so honest, and she usually voiced what I was thinking myself: 'Hath she forsook so many noble matches, / Her father and her country and her friends, / To be call'd whore? Would it not make one weep?'

Much of *Othello's* appeal is due to one of the most heinous, evil, unrepentant but also intriguing, charismatic and surprising of villains – Iago. Iago is a sociopath. He cares only for himself and seems entirely incapable of feeling remorse. Just when I thought I had seen the worst of Iago, he shocked me afresh. For example, having destroyed Othello and Desdemona's peace of mind, he proceeds to make a bad situation truly horrific when he advises Othello, 'Do it not with poison. Strangle her in her bed, even the bed she hath contaminated.' However, I must admit that I was expecting Iago to eventually show some remorse. I also expected him to die at the end – having first confessed and explained, of course. But although Othello tries to kill him and to get an explanation – 'Will you, I pray, demand that demi-devil / Why he hath thus ensnared my body and soul?' – Iago foils everyone by opting to (of all things!) remain silent. 'Demand me nothing. What you know you know. / From this time forth I never will speak word.' I was initially frustrated by Iago's silence, but then I realised the brilliance of it, and how completely true it is to this malevolent villain. It also keeps you thinking about the play, long after the final curtain.

Othello's broad appeal is also due to the devastating ending of the play. Shakespeare followed the conventions of tragedy so well in creating such a heart-wrenching and profoundly shocking conclusion. Even modern versions of *Othello* such as *O* and *Stage Beauty* (which also provide proof of the enduring appeal of the play) rely on the ending for the *pièce de résistance*. From Desdemona's desperate pleading for her young life, 'O, banish me, my lord, but kill me not' to Emilia's spirited defence, 'You told a lie, an odious, damned lie', the ending of this play is totally absorbing. Shakespeare even manages to make us feel Othello's pain when he utters his final, tragic and utterly beautiful lines: 'Of one that loved not wisely but too well, / Of one not easily jealous but, being wrought / Perplex'd in the extreme; of one whose hand, / Like the base Indian, threw a pearl away / Richer than all his tribe ...'

In conclusion, as I have demonstrated throughout my essay, *Othello* certainly does have an amazingly broad appeal to a modern audience. We lead very different lives from Shakespeare's original audience members – from our clothes and houses to our daily concerns. However the themes in this play – love, hate, jealousy and death – are universal, timeless and always relevant and interesting. *Othello* is a brilliant story, and brilliant stories will always appeal to us.

CLASSROOM ACTIVITIES

1. Divide the class in two. One side of the class should find images in the play of light, white, God and goodness, while the other side should find images of darkness, black, the devil and evil. Then discuss Shakespeare's purpose in using these contrasting images.

2. Divide the class into groups, allocating each group a different key character. Each group has to design a Facebook page for their character. Show who the character is friends with, their likes and status updates, etc. The aim is to reveal as much about the character as possible.

3. In pairs or small groups, write an alternative Act V Scene II. Try to be as imaginative and inventive as possible, and change the actual fates of Othello, Desdemona, Emilia and Iago.

4. *The Hotseating Game.* Write the name of the main characters – Othello, Desdemona, Iago, Cassio, Emilia, Roderigo – on slips of paper. Let students take one name from a hat, and then they must become that character, and answer questions as that character. For example, if a student picks Iago, they have to answer questions in his character. The other students in the class can ask about motivation, background, etc.

The author and publisher wish to thank the Utah Shakespeare Festival, Cedar City, Utah, USA, for permission to reproduce photographs of their productions of *Othello* in this book

Photographer: Karl Hugh, © Utah Shakespeare Festival

Cast:

Othello   PAGE 20   Jonathan Earl Peck (2008)
                   PAGE 123   David Toney (2002)

Iago   PAGE 102   James Newcomb (2008)
                   PAGE 147   Martin Kildare (2002)

Desdemona   PAGE 97   Lindsey Wochley (2008)
                   PAGE 123   Susan Shunk (2002)

Cassio   PAGE 164   Justin Matthew Gordon (2008)

Emilia   PAGE 102   Lindsey Wochley (2008)
                   PAGE 147   Carrie Baker (2002)

Roderigo   PAGE 56   Danny Camiel (2008)

Brabantio   PAGE 56   Will Zahrn (2008)

Lodovico   PAGE 236   Drew Shirley (2008)

Bianca   PAGE 164   Marcella Rose Sciotto (2008)

Duke of Venice   PAGE 55   Sam Stewart (2002)

Actors featured in illustrations:

PAGE 135   Laurence Fishburne, Kenneth Branagh – *Othello (Warner Bros.,1995)*
PAGE 175   John Maness, Ian Merrill Peakes – *Pennsylvania Shakespeare Festival (2006)*
PAGE 232   Heather Poulson – *Paradise Theatre School (2010)*